T0086440

REFLECTIONS ON THE LOSS
OF THE
FREEBORN AMERICAN NATION

REFLECTIONS ON THE LOSS

OF THE

FREEBORN AMERICAN NATION

BANKSTERS AGAINST PEOPLE

H. L. Dowless

Algora Publishing
New York

Library of Congress Cataloging-in-Publication Data —

Names: Dowless, H. L.
Title: Reflections on the loss of the free-born American nation / by H.L.
  Dowless.
Description: New York : Algora Publishing, [2016] | Includes bibliographical
  references and index.
Identifiers: LCCN 2016018813 (print) | LCCN 2016019390 (ebook) | ISBN
  9781628942071 (soft cover : alkaline paper) | ISBN 9781628942088 (hard
  cover : alkaline paper) | ISBN 9781628942095 (pdf)
Subjects: LCSH: Slavery—Economic aspects—United States—History. |
  Agriculture—Economic aspects—United States—History. |
  Plantations—Economic aspects—United States—History. | Banks and
  banking—Political aspects—United States—History. |
  Corporations—Political aspects—United States—History. | Free
  enterprise—Political aspects—United States—History. | United
  States—History—Civil War, 1861-1865—Causes. | United
  States—History—Civil War, 1861-1865—Economic aspects. | United
  States—Economic conditions—To 1865.
Classification: LCC E441 .D735 2016 (print) | LCC E441 (ebook) | DDC
  306.3/620973—dc23
LC record available at https://lccn.loc.gov/2016018813

Printed in the United States

Dedicated to the memory of the late Dr. D.K.E., who possessed the fortitude to light a guiding candle, illuminating the murky darkness and tangled webs inside that cold, neglected seaside Bastille where everyone else feared to tread, revealing the ghastly verification that we, among the cult of liberated intellectualism, had already analytically deduced as being the unsettling truth...

ACKNOWLEDGMENTS

I would like to begin by saying thank you to the supreme deity who created the universe and all of us, blessing us with a large number of gifts, one of mine being the ability to analyze information and put it all together in a logical form to enable one to see the larger picture. The gift of patience and persistence comes with it as well, and many others way too numerous to make mention of here.

I thank my parents who gave me not only an education but their support during my many days of trial and tribulation over the years. Without that initial support, it is very doubtful that this work or any of the others could have ever been realized.

My dear wife, Glenda, never gave up on me during my many late night typing sessions and numerous setbacks over the years. I am grateful for her belief that somehow I would wind up a real success; although I am well aware that there were times it appeared doubtful to her, she never uttered a single word to that effect.

I would like to thank my publishers, who saw promise in my work and allowed me the opportunity to make a name with them. In truth, without the laborious assistance of publishers, we authors can only produce unfinished works in a world that demands our product in its best form.

In the end, an author has nothing without a readership. I would like to thank all of my readers who are familiar with my past works and await those yet to come, and all of my potential readers as well.

I would like to conclude my acknowledgments by thanking all those —too many to enumerate—who have influenced my education, development and writing, one way or another.

When our last day on earth arrives as authors and individuals, all that we really have left of us is our children and our written words; thank you again, dear God in heaven above for them both. May the word, the name and the cherished endowment live forever more.

"I believe that banking institutions are more dangerous to our liberties than standing armies... If the American people ever allow private banks to control the issue of their currency, first by inflation, then by deflation, the banks and corporations that will grow up around [the banks]... will deprive the people of all property until their children wake-up homeless on the continent their fathers conquered... The issuing power should be taken from the banks and restored to the people, to whom it properly belongs."

—Thomas Jefferson
"The Debate Over the Recharter of the Bank Bill" (1809)

Table of Contents

Introduction

Slavery was not viewed as a moral horror in 1776, when the US Constitution was created, and slavery is not what caused the US Civil War. This book aims to show that the banking interests, corporations, and very wealthy individuals used and distorted the issue of slavery in order to promote their control over the land, its resources and its people, in the absolute, from the very first day of European landing in North America.

The issue of slavery versus states' rights and individual property owners' rights as determined by the Constitution serves as a model for how other issues, whether major questions or minor ones, can be used and are used to divide and conquer the American citizenry.

This trend did not end when the colonies joined to form the United States; it was baked into the essence of the new nation as certain factions continued to grow and seek absolute authority. By the time the charter for the First Bank of the United States was signed, the US House of Representatives was already divided with one bloc adamantly demanding checks on the value of the currency and the government in general, to protect the interests of US citizens, and the other bloc adamantly opposing any such limitations to their free-wheeling power plays.

What commenced was a literal war in the halls of US Congress that later on manifested on the ground among the citizens. In the end, the de facto central bank and the corporations won the fight to expunge the representatives who supported the Constitutional rights of the citizen body.

In this book, I aim to show that the entire enterprise of settlement and development of the American colonies and eventually the United States was a collusive effort between the corporate, banking and government powers, and the wealthy families that literally owned them. Their interests were then, and still are, directly opposed to the interests of the general public.

The same forces came to dominate the US political/economic system, with no countervailing representative forces standing up for the rights of the individual and the small enterprise. It is evident that when political/economic differences are turned into moralistic and emotional arguments over such inflammatory accusations as that of racism, what we are dealing with is an appeal to emotion designed to conceal the true intent. The urge to dominate in the absolute is still at work in the United States, with personal liberties being reduced every day—while voters are encouraged to be thankful for pat-down searches that provide increased "security" and other invasions of our privacy and personal security.

A constant program of propaganda has been churned out over the last 200 years to deflect attention from the real issues, to cloud the minds of the electorate, and to conceal the real power struggle from future generations and most certainly the generation of today.

The hypocrisy and abuses discussed in the following pages are outrageous, and I will allow myself to emphasize in bold print some of the most dismaying points as we go along.

CHAPTER 1. HOW DID WE GET HERE?

Quite often I have heard people ask in dismay, "How can the government do that, when the will of the people is against it?"

This work is intended to inform average people about where this country is going and where it all started. The historical facts and the arguments presented may also be of interest to scholars who do not always tie together the evidence to create a full picture of reality.

If positive change in the system ever comes, it will be because the people who represent the large, not very vocal, middle range of society have taken the initiative to take a solid stand to oppose the extortion being forced upon them.

To that end, I have struggled to write a factual, structured document in simple, direct, easy to follow language. My wish is never to offend or arouse against that which is legitimate, but to inform in a way that no other author appears to be doing.

The US populace needs to understand that they are being manipulated in small ways that work together toward a greater end, and that is the total subjugation and domination of all privately-owned resources.

The forces intending this harm will move forward even to the point of forcing huge segments of the entire population into concentrated conscript labor behind electrified razor wire fences and unspeakable torture, as well as mass execution for those who refuse to submit.

As this author shall proceed to demonstrate, virtually all of US history supports this conclusion, although in the usual telling of American history the full, hard truth has been intentionally twisted to conceal the truth.

In most circles, intentional distortion of history in order to deceive would be labeled political *propaganda*, and while we attach much opprobrium when we see this done by other countries, the shock is actually greater when we see it from our own trusted government. Most Americans refuse to believe that the US government would engage in such activity, but irrefutable evidence tells us otherwise.

Most other works dealing with this matter only mention isolated segments of the information contained herein, failing to identify the obvious links—either intentionally, due to lack of fortitude, or simply due to the lack of insight on the part of the authors. What I intend to do is show the links, explain specifically how it is that these details tie up to form a forthcoming conclusion, and why.

Make no mistake about it, the average walking American is a living straw man stuffed with idealistic imaginations resulting from this well-designed propaganda. His own presumed history and ways of thinking are testimony to its success. Most Americans feel that their government is a great liberator, a knight in shining armor who surges forward to rescue the meek from poverty and repression; and maybe there have been times, sporadically, during the economic lag time between the first and second step on the stairway to tyranny, when some national leaders did hold to such ideals, acting accordingly on the world scene and at home.

But these ideals have not always been embraced by the leadership, and most certainly not in our present age. There exists a very dark, sinister intent on part of the US government in unison with both national and multinational corporations, and the average person is none the wiser—although it is we who will be paying the price.

What average Americans steadfastly thought that they possessed and cherished so closely has been stolen right out from under their noses, continuously now, for 150 years.

Mandates Violating the People's Will

When it became mandatory to purchase car insurance, many people were upset.

This author saw it as a harbinger of many more mandatory expenditures to be imposed in the future. When the law obliging us to buy healthcare insurance was passed, more people were dismayed. Then the homosexual "marriage" mandate was passed, literally forced upon the people, even though it went completely against their majority vote in all fifty states. Even the people of California voted against it, to my surprise—rank and file

Californians truly are conservative, family-oriented people, contrary to the popularized image.

"How could the government do that? We have a Constitution that protects the will of the people!" "What happened to the people's freedom to choose for themselves, since unsuppressed liberty of the individual is the cherished, time-honored American way?"

When we examine the not so distant past, we see that the same questions have been asked many times over. In the early 1970s, counties around my home area began to draw up new school district boundaries, claiming broadly that the intent was to promote "racial integration and equality among citizens." The counties then began forcing students to attend schools so far away that there was no practical logic in doing so; but the imposed political mandate remained, all logistical concerns be damned. What most astounded me was that even as the price of gas rose, over the years, so that driving across the county to a different school became a real cost issue, rendering the political objective outrageously impractical, still the political mandate remained, even to the point of forcing people to prove their place of residence with utility receipts and affidavits! Elected leaders of the counties in question simply voted behind closed doors to raise the property taxes in order to cover the costs of an impractical and illogical mandate designed to fulfill political objectives.

These questions are very valid. Most people simply sit down and allow public officials to impose mandates and invalid fees and taxes. Yet if all would pull together, action could be taken to neutralize these ridiculous demands, breathtaking expenditures and compulsory mandates that are only designed to hand over hard-working citizens as victims to the rude, imperial extortion of corporations and their conspiring, collusive government authorities[1].

There are real reasons why and how government officials have forced such rulings upon us even when they go against the electorate's choice and even go against the Constitution itself.

My prediction is that in the near future, many more specific and direct mandates that flagrantly violate our cherished Constitutional rights and Constitutional law will be forced upon the free-born citizens of the United States. As a matter of fact I will step out on a limb here and predict that we *will very soon* see a complete suspension of the Constitution as a whole, maybe inside of twelve years from the time of this writing. I make that prediction based simply on US history for the last sixty years. I anticipate that an attempt will be made to dismantle it in piecemeal fashion at first,

---

1 http://www.usatoday.com/story/money/personalfinance/2015/08/23/credit-dotcom-student-loan-crisis/32015421/

judging from present day appearances, while intending simultaneously to arouse dissenting groups among the population as a whole.

I expect that the Second Amendment will be the first amendment to go. Of all the Amendments, this is the one that every American thoroughly understands, since it is so simple and straightforward in its wording.

> "A well regulated militia being necessary to the security of a free state, the right of the people to keep and bear arms shall not be infringed."

This amendment is also the very last check that prevents outright suspension of the Constitution and any calculated move of government against the people at large. Once it is gone, all of the other amendments will be a piece of cake to contest, with theatrical debates between opposing sides in mocking masquerade before the face of blank-minded, wide-eyed, trustful citizens, and finally remove.

Few Millennials understand just how critical this amendment is in its entirety. If you lose the Second Amendment or have it essentially rendered ineffective, US citizen, you are at the complete mercy of the tyrant. Keep in mind that the "devil" always prefers we believe that he is the good guy, bearing all of the presumed good collective intentions. All questions in regard to issues of preserving the Constitution really amount to that: only the Second Amendment gives the rest its real biting teeth.

Anyone who still thinks that their US government officials wear the white hat and would never stand as a threat to the rank and file, law-abiding American citizen, had better pay attention to his history, past and present, with a much more critical eye. The national situation is so critical that we have no choice but to stay wide awake at the wheel. As the superlative visionary Thomas Jefferson explained, *we, the individual people*, bear that responsibility for ourselves, our children, our nation and the survival of our liberties eternally secured inside our precious Constitution.

Not only are we being psychologically manipulated, but we have been outright lied too with a sinister intent, and for quite a long time now. This work is not designed to divide the public or take sides in any manner. I am sure I will receive criticism for what I say in these pages, but the harshest critics will be those who have been played the hardest, by the magisterial authority that pretends to favor them while all the time moving toward their total and compete subjugation, right along with the rest of us.

Like Paul Revere, I bring a warning: but this time the alien enemy is right here, among us, lording over our unique system and licking his lips at the fruits of all our hard earned wealth and private resources, in total disregard for his own reckless spending and incompetent management policies that destroy more than construct. *We, the people*, have entrusted these government and business leaders with the responsibility of managing the national finances and enterprise of our nation, but they have failed us miserably with the exception of a pitiful few.

The intellectual Thomas Jefferson warned us to make a forceful stand against attacks on our individual liberties and Constitutional values, whether from Federal authorities, State or local. The time he envisioned is not in some vague, distant future but right now. As the great visionary once wrote:

When, in the course of human events, it becomes necessary for one people to dissolve the political bands which have connected them with another, and to assume among the powers of the earth the separate and equal station to which the laws of nature and of nature's God entitle them, a decent respect to the opinions of mankind requires that they should declare the causes which impel them to the separation. We hold these truths to be self-evident; that all men are created equal; that they are endowed by their creator with certain unalienable rights; that among these are life, liberty, and the pursuit of happiness; that to secure these rights, governments are instituted among men, deriving their just powers from the consent of the governed; that whenever any form of government becomes destructive to these ends, it is the right of the people to alter or to abolish it, and to institute new government, laying its foundation on such principles, and organizing its powers in such form, as to them shall seem most likely to effect their safety and happiness.

The Native Experience: A Warning and an Example

Take a look at the American Indian and his national experience. The easiest place to begin might be with the Cherokee. The Cherokee Nation once covered a vast territory, including most of western North Carolina and dipping into East Tennessee and Northern Georgia. But the Cherokee Nation had not officially surveyed the parameters of their territory according to European procedures. Of course, all of the officially recognized "Five Civilized Tribes," which included the Cherokee, had the same problem.

The Cherokee, being no fools, very adaptable and quick to catch on, recognized that they needed to get to work. They paid tutors from the surrounding settlements to initiate the education process, and they sent a number of their brightest children to the college of William and Mary in Virginia and some other colleges, where they obtained law diplomas in property claim ownership, set up office in the nearest settlements and commenced to hire surveyors to mark their boundaries. This would make their claim to the land *official* with the colonist authorities who had, essentially, invaded.

However, the property claims had to be filed in the nearest courthouse land deed office. As soon as these deeds began to pour in, they attracted the notice of a number of local lawyers who worked for wealthy clients and national land companies. Soon the federal land companies got in on the act, and they began hiring their own surveyors to mark the unofficial boundaries of all five "civilized tribes" for themselves. The Federal government and these land companies beat the Indian Nations to the punch,[1] and their documents prevailed. This should be a lesson unto all of us.

In North Carolina the boundary marked by the Indian lawyers and their surveyors were eventually called the *Qualla Boundary*. In Georgia a similar sort of boundary was drawn, as well as one in Tennessee, as far as I can gather. But these "legal" boundaries were *far* from the original boundaries. Once the land companies, managed by very wealthy individuals via sponsoring states, with corrupt officials working in collusion with the Federal Government for its tainted handouts, marked their surveyed claim to the unofficial tribal holdings via land deed holding, they paid off Federal and State government legislators to initiate removal by military force.[2]

When the natives were rounded up and sent packing at a moment's notice, on what amounted to a death march into the badlands of Oklahoma, the land companies via states with corrupt officials receiving stipends from the Federal Government, began selling 40- to 160-acre tracts to illiterate, westward moving farmers at bargain prices. The land of the Five Civilized Tribes began to fill up with strangers, alien people who now felt that they were the new owners and, from a legal—though not from a moral—perspective, they in fact were. Many of the original settlers have descendants that still own to this very day the original 40-plus acre tracts that were once part of the old Cherokee Nation.

What does this very basic account have to tell those of us who are living now in this day and age, one may ask? Much, I feel. What happened to these freedom loving, rugged individualists was a harbinger of a future yet to come, a far worse one. High school textbooks give the "official" account, claiming that greedy Anglo settlers rushed in and simply robbed the Cherokee and the other tribes of their land, while their self directed military rounded the natives up to force them out, on a pilgrimage during which a third of the tribe perished. What about the land companies who paid the state legislators?

Horrible things were indeed done to the natives, as is nearly always the case when people are reduced into a state of completely helpless vulnerability

1 http://cherokee.wildsouth.org/content/lesson-11-nc-land-speculators-and-intruders-1790-1820

2 *Encyclopedia Britannica*; "The Five Civilized Tribes, history." Under the Indian Removal Act of 1830 the U.S. government claimed the lands of the five tribes in Kentucky, Tennessee, North Carolina, South Carolina, Georgia, Florida, Alabama, and Mississippi.

and placed under the unchecked authority of someone else. That someone else, even if his own background is humble, soon takes on the psychology of a lording elite. But in the case we are discussing this was done not by the ignorant, illiterate, average Anglo settler, who more than likely did not even know that he was on land that had been owned by anyone else—since most of the American Indians[1] had already been rounded up and removed by the time the main body of settlers had arrived. All he knew was that he needed land, affordable land... and here it was, all for the taking! Read very carefully and one will discover accounts where many of the initial settlers attempted to give the Indians blankets and food while they were on the death march, somberly trudging past, but they were forced away at gunpoint by, merciless government soldiers[2] who all too eagerly placed them under threat of death themselves.

It is easy to deduce, even from the official accounts, the role played by paid-off legislators and their loyal minions, the State militias, for the greedy land companies and the military in general! The forces of the corporation, Federal government and the State[3],[4],[5] were the ones who were responsible for all of the public rape, perverse child molestations before the faces of helpless parents looking on, starvation, wanton murder, theft and deprivations that we are so familiar with in regard to this deplorable time in US history; the impoverished, even near famished, Anglo settler and his ragtag barefooted family were instruments of a policy set in motion from above.

These facts are rarely presented to the public, even in the form of college level historical texts. Those who win write the history, and they always whitewash their own role.

Columbus and the Spanish: The First Corporate Government

From the very beginning, America was designated as a corporate enclave, with boundaries designed to be exploited by corporations from the very first day of recorded colonial landing. The adventures of Christopher Columbus make an excellent place to begin.

1 In recent years there has been more debate over the preferred term. While "Native American" still seems to predominate, some of the people in question have stated they prefer "American Indian." Either way, the author means no disrespect. *The Native Sun News*, "Native American vs. American Indian: Political correctness dishonors traditional chiefs of old." Accessed May 12, 2016.
2 http://www.learnnc.org/lp/editions/nchist-newnation/4532
3 http://digitalcommons.law.utulsa.edu/cgi/viewcontent.cgi?article=1862&context=tlr, Allotment Of Tribal Lands plus pgs 3&4
4 Perdue, Theda; Michael D. Green (2004). *The Cherokee Removal: A Brief History with Documents*. States stripped away the land rights in lieu of the federal passage of the Indian Removal Act.
5 http://www.blacklistednews.com/Government_Sells_Sacred_Native_Land_To_Foreign_Mining_Company/45281/0/38/38/Y/M.html

Columbus made an earnest appeal to Queen Isabella for *investor assistance*, in order to finance his initial adventure, being an exploratory effort to search out a much shorter shipping passage into the fabled spice lands of the Far East. He got his funding, but all he found was a paradise island with its native population off the coast of what is now Venezuela. The women wore rawhide strings with clear, polished, cut red and green stones on their unclothed bodies which were smeared with sandy paste of a golden hue.

This discovery prompted another appeal for investment capital from the Spanish Crown. In return, Columbus promised a hefty return, presumably in the form of gold and prodigious amounts of gems that could never be found elsewhere. For whatever reason, whether admiration or raw greed or ambition, the good queen fell for it. Christopher Columbus was well on his way into both fame and infamy, but very little in the way of fortune.

Where did the Crown find the investors? Among wealthy individuals, business co-operation owners and high end agents of the Crown. These business co-operations were the precursors to the huge conglomerate corporations that we know today. As a matter of fact, such company co-operations have been around, rising to become fairly large, since the time of the Romans and classical Greece,[1] and they were astonishingly well organized and modern in appearance.

Columbus had promised these people a profitable return, had assured them that they indeed would find that return with him. The pressure on him and his adventure company was intense, especially after his initial failure to produce the quick route to the Spice Islands. Recently discovered files in Spain confirm what we already know—very little gold or gems were discovered in North America, and specifically, the land that would later become the United States. For that reason, Columbus and his minions had no other option but to turn on the free natives of the land. He was under obligation to finance a return on the investment! If he failed, then he would have been thrown into prison or even charged with high treason, which bore a certain chilling penalty of death.[2]

Columbus studied what the natives were producing. He and his men tried to buy from them very inexpensively at first, but when the natives tired of poor quality trade items that many times even failed to perform, they eventually refused to sell. Soon they were compelled to supply him and his men with food and general supplies with no compensation at all. Once Columbus and his men saw that they had no means to resist, the tribes were

---

1 "Depersonalization of business in ancient Rome," by Barbara Abatino, Amsterdam Center For Law, paper # 2009-14
2 https://en.wikipedia.org/wiki/Francisco_Hernandez_de_Cordoba_(founder_of_ Nicaragua)

forced to comply with any and all demands.[1] This overt abuse degenerated into raping the women and children, wantonly murdering others on impulse and subjecting them to some of the worst tortures imaginable in search of valuables.[2]

As time went on, settlements were erected, such a La Navidad and Santo Domingo on the island of Hispaniola. The rage of Columbus and his abuse of authority were directed not only toward the natives but also directed upon his own people, as we can clearly see from the old accounts.[3] Matter of fact, the settlers in Santo Domingo appealed to the King of Spain in a letter detailing the abuse delivered upon them by Columbus and his officials in an effort to extort funds. Columbus was eventually arrested, bound in chains and delivered back to Spain.

The Spanish officials never learned; it appears that Columbus had set a trend, unfortunately. After further attempts in North America, the Spanish turned most of their attention to Central and South America where real riches were easier to come by. North America mainly had riches in the form of abundant agricultural products, apparently, whereas the Spanish were looking for fast profit, mainly in the form of high value metals and vast amounts of raw gems.

The French Were Next

When the Spanish gradually moved away, the French moved in. They too were interested in gold and gems, if they could be located, but domination of the international fur market was also a worthy objective, as at that time it was far reaching and very profitable. To a much lesser degree, the French were also interested in establishing small colonies for the purpose of establishing trade with ocean going vessels by providing goods that cater to the needs of sailors.

The positive feature of the French venture was that generally speaking, they did not abuse the natives or their own people for the purpose of extorting wealth and resources. This statement includes the issue of stealing land from the natives. The French fought few battles with the Indians, as history shows. Their few land acquisitions, as far as I can tell, were legal, purchases regarded as reasonably fair by both parties.

What the French did do was to dominate the fur market, including deer hides, which were used as money in the US colonies. These hides could be collected from the landscape by professional hunters and trappers, since

1 https://en.wikipedia.org/wiki/La_Isabela
2 http://blogs.telegraph.co.uk/news/dominicselwood/100283798/columbus-greed-slavery-and-genocide-what-really-happened-to-the-american-indians/
3 https://en.wikipedia.org/wiki/Christopher_Columbus, accusations of tyranny

deer existed in vast number back in those days[1]. They could also be acquired from the natives in exchange for necessary or desirable goods such as salt, gems, and even more so, goods that could only be purchased from European companies, goods that the Indians now felt were absolutely necessary and that they had no method of producing. Metal implements, cloth in many cases, sometimes glass, from European market depots such as those in Petersburg, Virginia, could be traded for hides on highly advantageous terms, for example.

The natives had been entirely self-sufficient. By the time of this narrative, they had become dependent on goods produced *outside* of their nation that they themselves were unable to produce.

If we, of this generation are not more watchful, the same horror will soon be visited upon all of us, for many of the same reasons.

In a relatively short course of time, not only had the natives forgotten many of their traditional skills of production, but professional hunters (with guns) and trappers had also severely depleted the most valuable food resources, with deer and beaver being two of the primary ones. Bear were also a resource held in value, since the hide was used for rugs and blankets, and the flesh was a rich source of easy-to-process meat. In many ways the bear was used and processed in the same manner as the pig would later be. These animal populations did not begin to recover until the 1950s, in many cases. This fact illustrates the thoroughness of the devastation brought by the fur and hide trade, although the French were not the only ones to ruthlessly exploit this trade, as we shall see later on.

It was during this time period of the French settlement that the natives first began to suffer broadly, but still had plenty of territory to retreat back into for the purpose of escaping the situation of poverty that they found themselves thrust into and forced to exist in. The corporate interests who were later to arrive on American shores, were the ones who extorted far more from the people of the land, than any of those who had already arrived. These people, of course, were the English.

Third on the Land

From Day One, with the establishment of Sir Walter Raleigh's colony on Roanoke Island, the English established themselves as a corporate venture. Queen Elizabeth I knew well that the Spanish held vast land holdings in North America, but most of it had yet to be surveyed and chartered, thus Spain was in the same position the Five Civilized Tribes would later find themselves in. And England was at war with Spain. The English also knew

1 John Lawson, *History of North Carolina*, the animals of Carolina

well that the Spanish had already found wealth in South America and were losing interest in the lands to the north. In addition, they were well aware of the French not truly interested in establishing a long-term national enclave. More than likely, the English deduced that the French were mainly interested in the hide trade, as long as it held out. As better quality hides were found northward, where the climate was much cooler and the furs thicker, a majority would migrate into Canada over time.

The Queen and her advisors decided to rush in to survey and charter the best lands for English interests, as well as to establish a base for the purpose of launching raids on the Spanish galleons which were being reported as passing by Roanoke Island and eastern shores.

Another product that had already been reported on the island in abundance and greatly valued was sassafras. The leaves were used as seasoning, and the roots and root bark were used as medicine in Europe already.

Salt was also reported in the area, inside bends of the river banks and in old, long since dried creek beds, where they served as naturally occurring animal licks; and this commodity could be nearly be as valuable as gold, since it was needed as a meat preservative and, to a secondary extent, as a medicine as well as for many other obvious and less obvious uses.

Just like his predecessor Christopher Columbus, no doubt Raleigh played up the accounts of the natural resources 'to his backers, especially the Queen, hoping to secure her appeal to investors, co-ops, wealthy individuals and people in high government, who would later finance his venture. Raleigh we must presume, made a strong sales presentation. What happened when his promises proved hard to fulfill?

Anytime a government promises high financial returns to the corporate/national lenders and they cannot meet the numbers, the government entity (with the backing of the military) turns on the people of the land, to extract those resources by extortion. Thus they not only make good on their own investment, they save face before wealthy lenders and reap the reward at the expense of the "lower orders," what we today call citizens—not "subjects." When it comes to this, the Power will tap all the target nation's privately-owned resource base, including their land.

Raleigh's ill-fated colony had "problems" with the natives almost from the beginning. Most of the colonists were upper-class gentry who possessed no skills relevant to living off the land, and those who did have the skills had no interest in making the effort for the benefit of the snobs. As they saw it, the natives, the people of the land, had plenty of food to offer. At first, the

---

1 http://docsouth.unc.edu/southlit/smith/menu.html, "General History Of Virginia, John Smith."

natives kindly accommodated the colonists, offering anything that they had on hand to give nourishment, but as time went on and the colonists failed to produce their own—even after being properly instructed—the Natives understandably stopped giving their gifts. Not only that, the Natives refused to accept worthless little brass bells and cheap red cloth in exchange for now scarce food. This is not selfishness: it has been verified that a harsh, seven-year drought had set upon the entire[1] Southeast, and they really did not have any extra resources to spare.

As a direct result, the small corporate-invested government, with their military backing, searched for any excuse to justify turning on the local people. They, the freeborn citizens of that land, had committed the "terrible sin" of withholding their hard earned resources from an imposed magisterial exploitation. The excuse was found in the form of an all night drinking party, in which the Native Americans were encouraged to indulge deeply, right along with the corporate-sponsored military colony and its well-armed soldiers; and amid the heavy haze of hangover the following morning, the unverified claim arose that a valuable silver goblet had been stolen.[2] The American Indians were sucked in by drink in hopes of acquiring even more resources from them for little or nothing in exchange. Failing to achieve this goal, the British put forth a false claim to justify a harsh response—an all-out massacre.

According to my research, men, women and children were slaughtered. This planted the seeds of a seething hatred and initiated a 400-year war that some might say continues even to this day.[3] As we study along, however, pay careful attention to the method that the overbearing authorities use to misdirect public hatred, posing as liberating saviors, moving against those who would one day stand to oppose their yet greater corporate efforts of exploitation, the average Anglo-American; although this effort of twisting the truth to conceal their own crimes, with the future corporate-sponsored government using the individual enterprising Anglo-American as a scapegoat, would come only much later.

The Primary Theme

In short,

The US has been the subject of corporate investment interest throughout its entire history. When the government entity, no matter how large or small, backed by its own military, goes into debt to these speculative cooperatives

1 http://www.serc.si.edu/education/resources/watershed/stories/roanoke.aspx
2   Blacker, Irwin (1965). *Hakluyt's Voyages: The Principle Navigations Voyages Traffiques & Discoveries of the English Nation.* New York: The Viking Press. p. 522
3 Bernardo Parrella (July 25, 2008). rights". Global. Retrieved 2010-09-26

(which usually support a national government), it does so with the promise of a profitable return to its lender. If that return fails to be delivered, then the government entity turns on the people of the land in an effort to seize their resource base and force conscripted labor from the people, even to the point of using torture and mass execution.

As we entered into the so called "Modern Age" following World War II, this mindset of the corporations and the government in disregard for any individual rights, including total domination of privately-held resources, did not change, but in fact, it has grown.

It is now so blatant that it stands on the verge of crossing the line of acceptability with the population, presently well armed, who still believes that it is free, and that its freedom is secured by Constitution.

Chapter 2. What Americans Need To Know Now

Americans have been deceived and played, one group off against the other, for generations. Most live life as though tomorrow will always come and go, in the same shape that they have always known. When we turn on the television or the computer, we see advertisements and programming that depict only the good life and bear the subliminal suggestion that we should all aspire to it, and expect it is coming; it sits just beyond our reach and is readily available to those who are industrious and intelligent.

Truth is, today's average American fits into a distorted version of Aesop's fables. We are like the poor old fox, only we are neck deep in a river of debt. Our minds are filled with visions of juicy grapes just beyond our reach: even while we are in danger of drowning, we think it might be possible to grab hold of the golden utopia of wealth and success sitting in plain sight. We live our entire lives without realizing that the propaganda and the systemic and systematic manipulation converge to convince us that financial success is still possible, so we willingly put up with all sorts of distress for thirty or forty (or more) years, our best, healthiest, strongest and brightest years, in the belief that—in some way we can't quite piece together—our participation in the "system" and the Corporate Nation will pay off in the long run.

I cannot count the number of times that I have heard people say, *"When I retire.....I am going to* ... begin to live life" or "do something that I want to do." The sad part is that nearly a third of those live to retirement will be making do in outright poverty. Those who follow the mainstream way of life probably have no alternative but to enslave themselves to the Corporate Nation. Because it mysteriously feels patriotic, productive and right to do so, mainstream people *still persist* in following the model that has been laid out, which can only lead to destitution as we are consuming more resources than we produce. And for those who end up homeless, things are beginning to get uglier than anything we ever imagined.[1],[2].

Americans need to stand strong, shoulder to shoulder, and face the corporate aristocracy and callous and even sinister National and State leadership that serve corporate interests—not ours. We, the people, did not change the laws that allowed the production base to relocate offshore so that corporations could subvert the US wage base. We did not open the borders to allow a huge flood of unmanageable illegals (and even non-productive consuming legals) to overwhelm the US resource base, to the point that the welfare and economic systems of entire states, such as California and Arizona[3], have been bankrupted or nearly bankrupted.[4]

Furthermore, when the plan of off-shoring the production base proved itself to be a devastating blow to the health of the nation and its citizens, it was not we, the people who gave permission for US leadership to borrow millions (later billions), serving only to defer the debts farther and farther back into the laps of succeeding [5]generations.

We, the people did not give the US government authority to go into debt to the tune of $14 trillion plus to China. This money finds its way into the hands of a huge US corporate aristocracy, where many individuals cycle between seats on corporate "director boards" and seats in the state and national [6]congresses. None of this money goes back into the hands of the US working population. Those who created this problem did so because it serves *their* interests!

Corporatism (Fascism) Can't Work For Long

A system of extortion might grow and go unnoticed, if the individuals managing it could control their impulsive greed and still allow for the expansion of a real opportunity base, with the people still having the freedom to engage in productive individual enterprise and hold on to 90% of what they produce. The problem is that situations almost never work that way for long. Greed simply knows no end, and the more that is funneled into the hands of the corporate owners, the less incentive workers have to keep the system functioning. The leadership eventually recognizes that it can force

1 http://www.huffingtonpost.com/2013/08/22/columbia-south-carolina-criminalizes-homelessness_n_3795397.html
2 http://humansarefree.com/2013/10/fema-camp-round-up-has-begun-homeless_7.html
3 See the next chapter; illegals cost California $10+ billion.
4 https://en.wikipedia.org/wiki/Prison%E2%80%93industrial_complex
5 The next chapter talks more about the national debt.
6 http://www.cbsnews.com/news/why-is-congress-a-millionaires-club/

people to go on producing, in complete absence of any personal profit or even basic incentive, with only those at the top receiving the benefits. This reality lies at the very heart of any corporate-managed or Fascist system. It bears a strong resemblance to outright *slavery*![1],[2],[3] Any person who questions my claim that we in America are gradually being stripped of individual liberty may simply examine the decade of the late fifties and nineteen sixties. This generation was called the "counter culture generation." These young people, the baby boom generation, were the first generation at large who questioned all aspects of American life. The Vietnam War spurred on this cultural revolt. The young people, who were sick of seeing family and friends dying or returning home maimed, rightfully questioned every area that led to the call for war in the first place.

The first huge question was about capitalism itself, since that generation correctly surmised that the war effort served only the interests of a corporate war machine and the oil conglomerates, operating outside of any reasonable checks or constraints—although the principle of checks and balances is said to underlie the very heart of the American system. The war was viewed as being initiated to further the interests of corporations, yet, in the end, restrictions were only levied upon small businesses and individual enterprise. By the middle years of the Reagan administration, the corporations had more liberty while the interests of individual enterprise and individual people at large were subjected to more regulations than ever before.

Most loyal citizens, if questioned, may have somehow dismissed the signs that are all around us, wishing to believe what they're told, that everything is "for your own good," but just ask any tax preparer if taxes have improved over the years, or ask a 35-year veteran, self employed business person about repressive regulations for proof otherwise.[4],[5] The details of how capitalism is implemented, and where the banks, corporations and Treasury officials must be restrained and regulated to ensure that national interests are served—not only those of the moneyed elite—that is the first problem. And where to draw the line on Government over-reach, imposing rules, regulations, fees and obligations on citizens for the benefit of those corporate and banking giants—that is equally important and is indivisible from the first problem.

---

1 http://ww2.cfo.com/health-benefits/2015/09/rise-health-plan-costs-continue-2016/

2 http://money.cnn.com/2015/08/14/news/economy/us-government-taxes-record/

3 http://hamptonroads.com/2008/09/mother-fined-1764-lying-get-child-different-school

4 http://consciouslifenews.com/verified-warnings-presidents-about-invisible-government-running-allegiance-people/1136001/

5 Any amount over 12% in total

Lords of Individual Enterprise

In my life time, American was still characterized by farming communities who not only produced cash crops and vegetable crops but also engaged in ventures of individual enterprise on the side. My great aunt's husband was a big time tobacco farmer. In her own home she operated a locally renowned beauty parlor. She even had a few relatively famous people drop by to have their hair done. If I recall rightly, in the passage of so many years, one was an instrumentalist in the Marshall Tucker Band, another was a guitarist in the B.J. Thomas band, and some of them actually grew up not all that far away.

Another lady in the very heart of my community had a husband who farmed 500 acres of tobacco while she ran a side business selling peas and butter beans, as well as raising pigs and cows. He and his wife owned a fenced-in pool and an adjacent snack shed. Any person who dropped by could purchase a year supply of food stored in freezer packs of vegetables and freshly cut, home processed meat. Meat was also salt cured, hung and smoke cured for a final preservation. When combined with a local salt marinade, the end result was a luscious, hickory or peach smoked local delicacy of renown among the neighbors. Also during the week in the spring and summer, people could drop off their children at the pool for two dollars a day. With three more dollars they could go to the shed and purchase potato chips, hamburgers iron cooked from freshly ground, pastured grass fed meat, and a fountain soda, with spoon homemade ice cream in nine tree-harvested, fruity flavors! The lady's sixteen-year-old granddaughters helped her manage and supervise the kids in the pool area. Needless to say, nearly every mother dropped off her kids at the local pool during the swimming season.

In my local community people farmed, but they were also backyard mechanics. Tradesmen, such as carpenters and plumbers, owned backyard welding shops. There were heat and air people, concrete workers, wood cutters, owner operators of secondhand backyard general stores and the list goes on and on. Many of these people had held these side ventures as family occupations for a hundred years or even more. General stores were once commonplace in my community during my own lifetime, but now they seem to have faded away due to the loss of liberty to operate. This precious liberty to manage one's own resources is what made America great and the individual property-owning people prosperous. . . . Then, the year 1986 arrived, and a legislative change took it all away.

The Year the Repression Began

I will never forget that year, since I had already moved from home and was living in another state at the time. I dropped back into my home area for a casual visit, around the month of May. An enterprising great aunt along with a number of cousins met me to inform me of the shocking changes. Both the local and state governments had sent undercover zoning and health department officials snooping around, speaking with people, even greasing their palms I was informed, to help locate or identify all of the independent business enterprises. Most arrived at least twice to the same scene, except on the second time the local police accompanied them, though dressed in plain clothes with the badge located on the belt and out of easy view.

The orders rendered from the zoning and health officials were inflexible and firm. Unnecessary, expensive upgrades were required, and local, state and federal permits purchased. One could either spend thousands of dollars fixing what didn't need fixing or suffer a long list of charges, up to and including tax evasion, right along with running an illegal business enterprise; the charges were always labeled with huge broad dysphemism that made the crass accusations sound like these honest, hard working business people were demon possessed, Mafioso monsters.

This order appeared to be right off the desk of a caricature of corporate-sponsored bureaucracy. A number of my neighbors were fined for running a bed and breakfast or cutting finger and toenails, as their families had done for well over fifty years. The lady with the pool business, Mrs. Hester, was fined over $2000 without prior warning for running a business operation that her family had owned and operated legally since the 1930s. The sin that she had committed was simply not knowing that regulatory laws had abruptly been changed.

The officials are not required to alert the public to such legal changes. Their favorite statement to hide behind is that "ignorance of legal changes is not an excuse for non-compliance." I can only guess that this is so because some of the largest law firms have perverted the system to their own benefit at the expense of law abiding people, in a practical sense.

My own Grandfather also suffered. He was a big time tobacco farmer, as was his father before him (who was also a land speculator, among other things). He owned a thousand acres of his own tobacco and farmed hundreds more for other people. He also owned a small roadside general store, with a service station dispensing gas and a small deli bar in the center of the store serving the local favorites: butter beans, peas, fried chicken, corn bread, hamburgers, French fries, and hot dogs topped with succulent homemade chili, slaw and crushed potato chips. All of this fine food was washed down with the best in iced tea, soda fountain soda, fresh hand-squeezed lemonade, or coffee.

In the back of the general store, he owned and operated a fertilizer distribution center that combined as a farm equipment parts delivery, that also did on-site repairs in the field; the only one of its kind in the area, as far as I can recall. He had owned and operated this affair for 60 years or more, borrowing the idea from his enterprising father.

Other services that he offered were to lend money to those who possessed real estate or jewelry, on which he allowed a one third debt ratio to two thirds value in collateral, no questions ever asked. Everyone knew him to be hard working, fair and very understanding, claiming himself that he only had to take his collateral three times in forty years. He also allowed people to place their for-sale vehicles by the roadside in front of his business for $10 a day and a 10% addition to the asking price and everything was all done up front. There again, everyone concerned was happy with the arrangements.

Back in 1986, the year that true unsuppressed individual enterprise legally died in America, as I vividly recall my grandfather telling my father, two strangers arrived in his store during the time when other business people were being heavily fined. The lady running the deli was under careful instructions *not* to serve strangers, but she did so mistakenly, and Grandfather was definitely not happy about the matter. According to his telling, the second time that strangers arrived, they were recognized but they were accompanied by four more strangers, cavalierly walking up to the cashier counter and requesting a shot of local moonshine, since according to their telling, rumor was that they could get some really fine drink there. When the clerk sternly informed them that none was served in this establishment, they casually walked over to the deli and requested the day's special dish, since the food deli was very obviously up and running. The special was fried chicken, freshly harvested squash and rice cooked in new chicken stock, served with generous rounds of sweet tea.

The six men sat quietly on the local bar stools before the deli counter, patiently waiting for the dish to be prepared. After enjoying the meal, one of them approached the lady running the deli, complimenting the food and asking her if he could speak with the manager. The family member who oversaw the establishment arrived on the scene, and the remaining five men approached her, carefully showing her their badges and giving her their ultimatum: either close the deli and the money-lending operation down within the week or suffer a long list of charges that would have basically bankrupted them, as well as subjecting the store property to outright authoritarian confiscation. This is repression of private enterprise and interference with the exercise of one's own property rights, the kind of abuse we never associate with "American liberties."

My grandfather called the local zoning board, negotiated his best, and only got a cut throat deal in which he was forced to spend more than $10,000 .... and then he could serve food, but could not continue lending money or allowing people to place their automobiles out front for sale, for a small fee. His frustrated response was to huff brazenly about it, then simply close down the deli, choosing to serve prepackaged foods in the store instead, to the understandable disappointment of his customer base. Later on his brother purchased the deli, spent the demanded loads of money unnecessarily upgrading the food preparation equipment to the imposed standard, and purchased the overpriced permits, then begrudgingly paid the extortionist fees; he proceeded to run the business until the day he died, always complaining that purchasing the deli may not have been worth the effort it in the long run, since the profit incentive had basically been removed.

The point is that Grandfather's deli equipment was working just fine, and was safe as well as sanitary. The real problem that the authorities had with it was that *all of it had been paid off* years before, and that *Grandfather had generated thousands of dollars in hard cash off the books.* The authorities felt they were entitled to at least one half of what Grandfather took in, but then, where was the incentive to engage in the business at all?

As many readers may recall, this crass persecution of independent individual enterprise came about at the same time Ronald Reagan did away with the law that had been put into place at the close of[1],[2] World War II, that forced large corporations to remain *inside* of US borders with the largest part of their business enterprise, since outsourcing the employment base had already been determined to have been a major cause of the Great Depression of 1929. This same law also outlawed corporate importation of foreign labor to subvert the US wage base.[3]

Personally, I thought at the time that if US corporate business was to be sent offshore, regulations would ease up on individual enterprise, since people need to work somewhere; but I was terribly wrong. Regulations only increased *dramatically*, going beyond obligatory upgrading the standard of quality (as the authorities always euphemistically claim), to out-right persecution with the intent of stamping out all individual enterprise—to accommodate the corporations who chose to remain within US borders.

This is just what Soviet Russia and China did back in the 1950s and 1960s. This has no place in the America we all were raised to believe in.

The Great Scam

Those corporations that remained stateside, and their institutional investors, began complaining to the government, declaring that they could

1 https://en.wikipedia.org/wiki/Employment_Act_of_1946
2 http://www.citizen.org/documents/ProsperityUnderminedFINAL.pdf
3 This law replacing the original citizen directed post WW2 law was called *"Fast Track"* to intentionally facilitate outsourcing opportunity.

not compete with those companies relocating offshore. The latter had no need to pay US-style wages, as workers living in the Third World had less expectation of a comfortable standard of living. They were exploiting what amounted to outright slave labor in many cases (or conditions barely above that line[1]). They would say that they would either be forced to dramatically cut pay to below minimum wage level, eliminate all benefits or lay off in drastic numbers, up to and including closing down the enterprise altogether, rather than reduce the company profit margin.

At the same time, US colleges who depended on young Americans going into increasing amounts of debt, especially via government loans, began complaining that outsourcing all of the top-paying corporate opportunities took away their job prospects. College enrollment had already plummeted just in the first stage of the new era. "How would such a reduction in university income [and, increasingly, profits—as many "institutions of learning" were opened on a for-profit basis] going to be offset?" they all cried to the powers that be. We either have compensation or we, too, will downsize, bust wages and lay off in heavy numbers, they whined.

The Federal government declared via Reagan's national address [2]that they alone held the perfect solution to every problem. All sorts of businesses began requiring that candidates hold a four-year degree; forget about apprenticeship schools,[3] on-the-job training, company-paid college courses and the like. Especially corporations getting a government subsidy of any sort [4]refused to discuss employment with any person who did not already possess the degree. Then the credentials of the schools should be examined and cross examined again, to ensure that the facilities issuing the degrees were accredited by the Federal Education Authority—in essence, the same people who had created this requirement in the first place!

I base this claim on the observation fact that virtually all of corporate enterprise was relaying this message at that time, nationwide, according to people from all areas of the nation that this author has spoken with. In this manner young people, and even older people, were forced to enter into an already expensive college system or be denied opportunity of employment. But back in the early 1980s, the great, damning secret intent was still unclear—that is, with the exception of the steel mills in the Northern States who had already demonstrated the future corporate intent, that the plants

---

1 https://en.wikipedia.org/wiki/Laogai
2 1983, he was going to place a "special emphasis on education."
3 Which could be owned and operated by individual tradesmen, if he possessed the freedom to do so
4 Statistics say the eighty percent of US business does receive subsidy

would soon close down anyway and never really intended to do any hiring in the first place.[1]

As I was to witness later on, the primary reason for demanding a four-year degree was that the job base had already contracted dramatically as a result of the off-shoring. For all practical purposes, they were over-saturated with job seekers. There simply were no more opportunities.

Opportunity was being off-shored faster than it could be replaced at home, if it was in fact ever being replaced at all. Those who endeavored to start their own business enterprise were met with new, extensive, rigid permit and qualification standards, to discourage individuals from competing with corporations. To secure employment at the few remaining stateside corporate or government enterprises, one must first obtain a four-year degree, even though it had nothing to do with the job itself in a majority of cases. Dreadfully expensive as college already was, the cost soon commenced to escalate as the requirement became obvious to the public. The university system was guaranteed a steady flow of money via the system, and with no accountability, no way of requiring university faculty to guarantee anything afterward to the student[2]; the corporations were guaranteed a highly-skilled work force, into which they were not required to make any contribution, with the only loser being the individual in search of a job opportunity when in 80% of the cases,[3] none even existed.

Obviously, individuals would have been better served to have gone to school on the side and worked a job by day, learning and testing to increase their productive skill level, but such programs were eliminated to benefit the college system and the corporations, at the expense of the young people.

This new requirement of often irrelevant "credentials" achieved at least two primary objectives and maybe a dozen or more secondary ones. First and foremost, it locked young people out of the job market completely, as well as many older people who still needed to work, no matter what their experience or skill level. The young generation was the group most likely to complain first about lack of opportunity and very low starting wages. The psychological propaganda manipulation was that *blame for unemployment would be forced upon the individual* who did not possess the degree, rather than on the act of off-shoring by the company and by the government sanctioning it. The demands of acquiring this certification would also distract attention from the reality that government, banking and the corporations were

---

1 http://www.forbes.com/sites/susanadams/2013/05/28/half-of-college-grads-are-working-jobs-that-dont-require-a-degree/

2 The students instead are made accountable, guaranteeing the university or tech establishment that the indenture (*euphemism: loan*) will be paid back in full. Thus the banks and the lending companies profit immensely.

3 http://newsfeed.time.com/2011/05/10/survey-85-of-new-college-grads-moving-back-in-with-mom-and-dad/

working against the American public, endeavoring to extort their most productive years from them and even the very product of their laborious efforts.[1]

Secondly, the individual was deeply indebted to the *bank/system* before even starting out in life and owning anything; so in that manner, he was *forced* to labor at *something* offered only by the corporations who held all the cards. The labor pool was expanded to a level far greater than opportunity available. The corporations could then drop wages and anyone wishing to feed himself was increasingly forced to *give away* their most fruitful labor.

Thirdly, the individual in search of opportunity was coerced into proving to the corporation that he possessed the ability of giving certified journeyman-quality work; whereupon the corporation, by legal sanction, retained the right to hire him in at green helper pay level, and to specify when, and even *if*, they would ever give raises at all. Quality of work had nothing to do with future raises, since the worker was already functioning at a high level when he was hired; what took precedence was the supervisor's personal opinion conditioned by whatever was the corporate intent—whether to give raises or allow employee benefits.

Most corporate entities simply just chose to give a small raise or two over a period of years, then *fire* the individual after five years or a bit more to knock him out of his unemployment check, since they could just hire another in fresh from the schools at rock bottom pay and with very few, if any benefits, while knowing well that the State supported tech schools or private college system had educated the deceived individual so that he could give the purloining entity his very best efforts, and the rapacious corporation would be saved from the responsibility and expense of training him or paying him what his labor was truly worth.

Inexpensive highly-educated, skilled labor and loads of state and federal subsidy, courtesy of tax payer money, was the corporation's magisterial reward for remaining inside national borders—only to fool the population into believing that all would be well. Meanwhile their production base was increasingly being outsourced and employment in-sourced, by bringing in skilled foreign professionals to do the highest paying work for a mere fraction of the standard salary.

The corporations demanded all of this proof in skills up front, pretended to hire for a while, then simply just relocated somewhere offshore, anyway. Often workers had little warning, as corporations prepared to relocate operations; and in innumerable instances, they robbed the workers of their entire retirement fund and stock option funds. Inaction by government, on

---

1http://www.marketwatch.com/story/tax-rates-are-far-higher-than-we-realize-2015-06-08

both state and federal levels, to rectify this obtrusive theft of resources from the poor employees demonstrates the corporate–government collusion.

The Great Deceptions Continue

The DuPont corporation ran a large advertisement in my local paper a number of times throughout the 1980s and early 1990s. Other corporations did as well, such as Goodyear Tire, for example, and basically the same rule here applies. This advertisement claimed that DuPont was "ripe" with opportunity for the taking, so all interested should be at the *Employment Security Corporation (ESC)* come Monday morning at 0600 hours. I wish that I had saved copies of the advertisement to publish right here. The positions announced were highly sought after, since most would start at $50,000 a year. Once upon a time during the 1970s, DuPont hired routinely throughout the year, so it seemed, as those who stood in the line were keenly aware. The ad read nearly the same every time that it was published.

Keep in mind here that the ESC office was and still is a branch of the Federal Government that literally *rationed* out jobs based on their own political criteria and objectives, at least, from what I could tell; it still does ration out opportunity, but to a much lesser extent these days, maybe because a majority of the best paying jobs have been in-sourced and the production base at large has now already been out-sourced. That, at any rate, is what I observed that the organization actually did. I was so rudely told by employees on a number of occasions that their job was "to see that everybody who achieved opportunity stood inside the same line."

The very idea of an organization rationing out opportunity insults the Constitution and everything that our patriotic ancestors ever died for. The fact of people being denied opportunity by corporations, based on some sort of broad discriminatory agenda, was simply *assumed*, being used by the ESC to validate its status and position inside every community throughout America. (I say "*assumed*" since no company was ever taken to court and proven, beyond shadow of a doubt, to deny opportunity to anyone qualified to perform specific employment services during this time period, as far as I am aware.) If each individual company had been taken to court and found guilty of denying opportunity to qualified people based on personal or political assumptions, then existence of the ESC would have been rightfully justified, but such was *never* the case.

I deduce that the true purpose of the ESC, during the 1980s and 1990s especially, was to play one group of Americans off against another, creating a distraction in the form of a divisive appeal to emotion. The real (federally sanctioned) objective of corporations out-sourcing labor/in-sourcing highly skilled professionals and off-shoring the production base in general continued unabated. Most Americans failed to recognize what was happening and/or lacked the fortitude to denounce it en masse. Had the citizenry forcefully protested and opposed this massive fraud and sell-out, we might have been better off.

This tactic, using a distraction in the form of a divisive appeal to emotion, is one that has been used throughout the last 150 years at least, while government and big business literally stab the population in the back, one liberty after another and even infringing upon the Constitution itself— though no school history text dares speak of it.

Going back to DuPont deceiving job seekers and their own employees (with both federal and state government permission)... At 0600 Monday morning, the ESC office had a line winding all the way around it three and four times. According to their own telling, some 9,000 *people* a day put in for the supposed "opportunity." The ads ran for approximately three weeks, with people standing in this line six days a week, some even camping out overnight. That adds up to 162000 people!

I, too, stood in that long line. The DuPont public relations person right there at the ESC office claimed that this same scenario was played out in every community where DuPont had a plant. Many people from my local district actually traveled out into these areas. When the hiring period had ended at the first few events, only *twenty people* were actually hired; most in fact only to be laid off a year or so later, with one or two who were very well connected being allowed to remain for an extended time being.

Obviously here the claim of "real" opportunity was only a ruse to cause people to believe that opportunity existed, and to maintain the false suggestion that in spite of what people may hear, all was going to be well. By the time the mid-1990s rolled around, DuPont was only hiring "temps", according to all local reports. According to later reports from former members of management, the same held true everywhere that DuPont had a production facility. As time went on, even the management themselves were to a very narrow skeleton crew; with a near tripling of the work load, many complained.

"Temporary" employees work for much less in wages than regular employees, with few if any benefits and absolutely *no* job security [1] whatsoever. These abused individuals, right along with subcontractor employees in any of the highly regulated states[2], stand as the closest resemblance to outright slaves on American soil in our modern age (other than industrialized prison labor).

---

1 http://www.cnbc.com/2014/04/21/for-many-americans-temp-work-becomes-permanent-way-of-life.html
2 Working 12 hours a day for a straight wage, without the overtime bonus pay (paid at time plus one half).

Analysis of the Situation

The public needs to understand that the US production and manufacturing base was the backbone of the entire economy, the very fertilizer from which all other growth occurs[1]. As I understand it, the Swiss and the Germans still have laws on the books that prevent outsourcing of their production base. Back in the days when the EU was merging to form a currency and consequently, a government body, the idea of changing that law was investigated by heads of corporation and government. Both nations concluded that to change the law would dramatically hurt their economies.

On that basis, a very valid one, these nations refused to dismantle the law which preserved their positive national economic state. Both nations have more apprentice and trade opportunities per capita than any other industrialized nation on earth, as far as this author can tell. Their economies stand strong as the best in all of Europe at the present moment,[2] and now we Americans know why! Does the US leadership lack the common sense to arrive at the same conclusion, or are they working toward a different goal? Obviously they are pursuing some objective and have some motive, and that is what this work aims to show.

Now that the higher paying industrial jobs are continually being outsourced, the US has less income tax revenue. And then, US enterprises are granted exemptions from state and local taxes just to keep them from relocating, keeping at least some jobs in town. Otherwise, they cannot compete with those who have moved out. Having lost tax revenue, municipalities are downsizing,[3] and huge numbers of them are going broke[4]. Many states verge on complete bankruptcy; and we have more individual people drawing on the welfare system than ever before,[5] since little in the way of real employment opportunity still remains.

At the same time, the US government has sold Treasury Bonds—that is, has borrowed some $14 *trillion*[6] from the Chinese (and other nations that are not, otherwise, necessarily our closest allies) just to meet their national obligations; and all of this borrowing is done *without* permission of the American public, whom the leaders are forcing the indebtedness upon. The interest payments alone consume half of our gross national product!

---

1 http://cerasis.com/2014/02/28/manufacturing/

2 http://www.bbc.com/news/business-18868704

3 http://www.pewcenteronthestates.org/report_detail.aspx?id=56695

4 http://www.washingtonpost.com/news/wonkblog/wp/2013/07/18/detroit-isnt-alone-the-u-s-cities-that-have-gone-bankrupt-in-one-map/

5 http://www.thenewamerican.com/economy/economics/item/17367-welfare-hits-record-levels-after-50-years-of-war-on-poverty

6 http://www.forbes.com/sites/mikepatton/2015/04/24/national-debt-tops-18-trillion-guess-how-much-you-owe/

Just like any individual who goes too deeply into debt, or indulges in any type of excess, the US as a whole is on the road to ruin. Economic experts are already predicting a *default*, or "burp," as they say, on the national debt *this year or next*,[1] as a precursor to a much more massive *default*. This event can be likened to a quake that upsets a seaside city before the onset of a massive tsunami. And this tsunami may very well be intentional[2].

Response of the Citizens

Americans are catching on, and in large numbers, but not quite fast enough. A number of state governments are pointing the finger at the Fed to criticize this crass mismanagement. Some of these states, with the state of Texas leading the way, have even threatened outright *secession*,[3] as they would be justified to do.

If any state claims the right to self government, the legality of so doing will undoubtedly be challenged by federal authority, stating that such issues were put to rest well over a hundred years ago. The defense is that the original Tenth Amendment had a *clearly legible formula that allowed any state or states to vote itself out from under federal rule*, if that rule was ever imposed against the will of the people or against what was allowed in the Constitution. As commanded by the founding fathers, the people had an obligation to the Constitution, God and themselves to replace their [4]rulers if they began to impose laws without public support.

The problem with the Tenth Amendment, in its present form, is that it was illegally infringed upon and most Americans still don't recognize that, except those of the Southern states born of the generation who stood strong to contest it (unfortunately, they were smashed and could not stand long enough to see the job through).

I shall give proof beyond question of this claim as we go along in our reading. Of course, since the infringement was illegal, done as it was while the populace was distracted with the war and its aftermath, with fighting for survival, in complete absence of the people's broad consent, then any state's claim to self government remains solid and valid within Constitutional law, if we disregard the infringed Constitution euphemistically labeled as *The Amended Constitution To Preserve The Union.*

---

1 http://www.washingtonsblog.com/2015/07/governments-worldwide-will-crash-the-first-week-of-october-according-to-2-financial-forecasters.html

2 My personal bet is that the US government will stage an astonishing event as a distraction to the public from the fact of this coming default, and also incite divisions of the masses against themselves as further distraction designed to strike individuals much closer to home.

3 http://www.cbsnews.com/news/states-petition-to-secede-from-union/

4 See the fifth page, paragraph two

Proof that divorce from the union is justified also includes the federal government managing resources in such a negative manner that the health of individuals, states, and the population at large, are adversely affected. Our national debt margin alone is a terrible threat to our entire national body, currency values and the health of every American citizen. If the nation should go broke, by accident or design, where does that leave the citizenry and what does history tell us will be the relationship between the people and those in power?

For at least a generation now Texas state officials have complained to the Federal Government about the manner in which the illegal immigration issue has been managed.[1] There has yet to be an honest hard core attempt to stop unauthorized passage across the southern US border. Very finite state and national resources are forced to absorb an infinite number of consuming, demanding people.[2] This wave of illegal invaders began flooding the borders unchallenged in the early 1980s, and maybe to a lesser degree, involving specific states, much farther back[3].

Analysis of the Illegal Immigration Problem

Probably the greatest problem caused by excessive immigrant hordes, especially illegal immigrants, starts with US political leaders who allow these illegals to draw from the state system,[4] giving birth via the US welfare system and placing them in public schools, without having put any tax revenue into the system first.[5]

When these immigrants first arrive, they work for cheap wages[6] (*undermining the US wage base that protects American employees*) and for untraceable cash. Yes, some of this cash is spent on goods needed for daily life and some sales tax is paid, but these people tend to share living space in large numbers and to send the bulk of their earnings directly back across the borders to their own countries, without any benefit to the US. Some of these people purchase huge tracts of land with their cash, inside their own homelands, where they build large homes and start up businesses instead of

---

1 http://www.dailymail.co.uk/news/article-2965703/Texas-governor-claims-20-000-illegal-immigrants-crossed-border-Mexico-January-1.html

2 http://www.washingtontimes.com/news/2004/dec/6/20041206-102115-6766r/?page=all

3 http://www.endillegalimmigration.com/History_of_Illegal_Immigration_in_US/

4 Who instantly become US citizens

5 The mass numbers of them overwhelm the accommodating system, since it was never designed to process huge numbers

6 Of course, illegal immigrants have no choice but to work for anything they can get: less than the legal minimum wage and the union wage. Thus, they unfortunately undermine two of the few standards that help to limit the abusive power of corporations, who will pay the workforce just as little as they can.

in the US. They may retire after only ten years in the US system, having set themselves up for life in their home countries where costs are far lower. This is all done at the expense of the US public welfare system, through education, and drastically reduced medical care, while American citizens are forced to subsidize it.[1]

I honestly commend these industrious individuals for using the US system to their advantage, *since the US government allows and even encourages it.* They save their own money and possess the creativity to see the advantage in their own nations, then access resources for themselves that put them at a great advantage. But why does the US leadership allow them to exploit the system, that is, *to exploit us?* Why are US citizens required to pay up, to accommodate foreign invaders?[2] If we listen closely, we might hear the distant cat calls coming back across the border, laughing at US citizens who allow themselves to be exploited.

The answer can only be that the US government does not work for the average US citizen; it works for *itself and the prosperity of the large corporations at the expense of the average American.* The largest category of American people today exist as the *serf* category, in what amounts to a Fascist authoritarian rule of pro-corporation government; one that may be leaning more toward a corporatist tyranny. [3]

Maybe a One-World Government?

As some authors have alluded, there may also be a concerted attempt at forging the people of the world into a single unitary state, with the citizens of the West being the experimental subjects. There are facts that strongly suggest such a worldwide effort of government and corporation imposing itself on the whole planet, with the *behind closed doors* formation of a one-world government, religion, currency, etc.[4] that is beyond the scope of this work.

What I will venture to say is that the developments I will describe may well be part of such a concerted effort to reduce entire nations into subject states. Obviously liberty of the individual citizens will be sacrificed in favor of maintaining a one-world "utopian" society, where of course, the earth's corporations reduce humanity down to the level of an expendable resource. The "gifted" leadership will then own all of earth's resources, natural and

1 http://www.nilc.org/immigrantshcr.html
2 http://thelawdictionary.org/article/why-is-it-that-illegal-aliens-get-free-food-stamps-health-insurance-and-pay-no-taxes/; also see   http://cis.org/edwards/double-standard-obamacare-favors-illegals
3 https://en.wikipedia.org/wiki/Corporatocracy
4 http://www.thepropheticyears.com/reasons/The%20rise%20of%20the%20new%20roman%20empire.HTM

otherwise, and prosper to a level greater than any ever witnessed by mankind[1]. I use the term *"utopian"* sarcastically, since the only "utopian" experience will be for the greedy leadership and obviously not the rank and file citizens, who are most assuredly destined to exist only as the work horses.[2]

Many people who understand that the authorities are hell bent on imposing these restrictions and onerous conditions simply shrug their shoulders and, wishing to avoid negativism and show good character, say to themselves, "If I resist, I won't get anywhere, so it's better to get in line with the new reality, accept our fate with new resolve and fortitude, and get on with it. We have to do the best we can with what we've got."

My great fear is that the younger generations in particular, who never experienced what I consider "normal" life in America (and that includes immigrants, legal and otherwise, who may have grown up in countries were the individual never did have a strong position vis-à-vis the authorities), will easily give up on the notion of returning to those times of relative liberty, the liberties that America boasts about far and wide, the (now missing) liberties that are part of what draws people to this country in the first place. They seem ready to relinquish their rights, including property rights, at every turn. Go along to get along… allowing the huge rhinoceros in the room to stomp over them in the name of patriotism and harmony.

To be honest, I am not very much impressed with today's generation on the whole. I haven't seen that they possess the fortitude to stand up to their own government, whether federal, state or local, to protect their rights. In most eras it is the idealistic young people who are able and willing to brave a confrontation, to question authority, to challenge police excess, to push back against growing restrictions. Outside of the Occupy Movement, I haven't seen much evidence, yet, that this generation is willing to step outside its comfort zone and take a stand. What I have observed over the past 50 years is that an official appeal by the US leadership to the citizen's sense of duty and patriotism is enough to convince a short-sighted majority to sell out,[3] the Constitution. However, as the boot heel comes down, sorry to say, I think they may find enough motivation to get moving.

Trouble is, the boot heel is being placed *gradually*, so that the victim underneath doesn't spook. Lulled by stories about the need to help the disadvantaged minorities, the unfairly victimized, the poor migrants and other high-minded memes, and logical-sounding stories about technology changes, economic cycles that affect the job market, etc., which are all

1 http://www.prophecynewswatch.com/2015/November03/031.html
2 http://millercenter.org/president/bush/speeches/speech-3425
3 http://www.nytimes.com/2014/12/01/us/politics/clamor-rises-to-rewrite-the-us-constitution.html?_r=0

reasonable *up to a point*, the average citizen has remained seated long after he should have jumped up in outrage, in massive flaming nationwide protest.

Meanwhile, any organized response has been headed off long since as the leadership is well prepared and have been discretely positioning themselves and their minions to hold in check any such event in the future. The police, FBI, domestic "counter-terrorist" forces and others have more surveillance technology and military equipment that can be used against any potentially disgruntled citizen than ever before,[1] and they have been given Constitutional exemptions allowing them to use them against citizens here in their own country. Tell me again, what did we fight the Revolution for?

Just remember Jade Helm and other recent exercises. Clandestine military exercises in and around the state of Texas[2] and in the surrounding states, as well as the Northwest in general, are just the tip of the iceberg. Through the grapevine I have heard locals in uniform saying that people in the military high command are informing them of planned secret exercises in other states,[3] Virginia, Tennessee, and South Carolina as well. These true *heroes of the people* in uniform tell me that the economy is anticipated to collapse, and that a massive insurrection is anticipated. These units will work in concert with the local police to contain the expected rioting, looting, random shooting and killing that they believe will follow; but their masked men and SWAT teams have already killed many innocent people, barging into the wrong homes and shooting indiscriminately—when the supposed offence was only a minor drug infraction in the first place. What were they doing in New Orleans, driving around in military vehicles aiming guns at the Katrina victims who needed food, water, shelter, and transportation? What kind of "useful" and "proportionate" response will we see if the situation does erupt when the economy crashes? They may be training to respond with far more drastic measures to fulfill a clandestine intent dreamed up long ago.

Uniformed individuals whom I have personally spoken with say that they will refuse to fire upon their fellow Americans. That is what they say, now, in the calm of today, but how they will respond when things heat up is only a matter for conjecture. US troops and the National Guard have been known to fire on their fellow citizens, even college students,[4] during times of discontent, and they do so apparently with no sign of continence or compunction.[5]

---

1 http://www.counterpunch.org/2015/04/10/using-drones-against-protesters/. See also, http://www.defenseone.com/technology/2015/04/americas-police-will-fight-next-riot-these-stink-bombs/111430/

2 http://www.rt.com/usa/244969-texas-martial-law-army/

3 http://www.asheville/heritage/Un-CivilWar.html

4 https://en.wikipedia.org/wiki/Kent_State_shootings

5 https://en.wikipedia.org/wiki/Battle_of_Blair_Mountain

Make no mistake about it, the signs are all around. It's no fun to ponder such an eventuality, but shear survival as liberated individuals, free citizens and a sovereign nation depends on all of us doing thinking ahead and not being taken by surprise.

What are those signs? We have a failing government.[1] Maybe that is only an appearance of failure to mask a move to join the imperial consolidation of world government? If so, that is still a failure to serve the free-born US citizens.

Since it is natural for citizens to grab onto something that they feel will work, when a collapse is underway, they will begin looking toward an entity that fits with the US heritage plan. Doing so will feel perfectly acceptable. Right now, the only state that possess a skeleton of its own independent nation buried inside, presently being dug up and apparently being clothed in the flesh right before our very eyes, is the state of Texas—and the Fed knows this.

Where the Skeleton of a New Nation Lies

After Texas, the skeleton of a possible new nation based on a living tradition lies buried only in Southern soil, and maybe, the once-organized native nations. This author doesn't necessarily see the South being resurrected along the same lines as before (as some may imagine), but I do see fragments of it merging together, even with certain areas outside, to form a strong, economically and politically viable unit. There are demographic and political reasons why I do not see the South, as a whole, ever going back to its former glory, but the framework is still there to build on. Even to this day, its citizens have not forsaken their cherished heritage; changes would have to be made in the way in which rights were distributed, but the region was once wealthy and understood perfectly well the empowerment that true liberty can bestow, and deep down there still lies a strong subconscious desire to revive that divine endowment.[2] All that must be done is for the old framework to be renewed and the breath of life breathed back into it. And the US would see a new, effectively and efficiently managed, wealth producing, sovereign nation with appropriate checks and balances, one that prides itself on individual liberty and the right to excel in life.

The corrupt, collapsing US Federal Government knows this, as I can gather from recent actions taken and discussed, although only the most non-productive city and state governments (begging on bended knee for

1 http://moneymorning.com/jim-rickards-coming-great-depression/. See also, http://www.washingtonexaminer.com/gop-megadonor-us-economic-data-is-fake/article/2555693

2 http://www.cnn.com/2015/07/02/politics/confederate-flag-poll-racism-southern-pride/

federal handouts) are actually doing the dirty work of initiating a subverting attack against the independent heritage of the land.[1] What the federal and state governments have been attempting to do for over a century is to erase any memory of this old model, to call it a skeleton whose grave should be left undisturbed, should be eradicated from the citizens' consciousness, portrayed as entirely negative and now permanently and justifiably dead, to remain dead and eternally forgotten[2]. The good people of the South should take heart in this unjustified persecution of their precious heritage, since the persecution itself indicates a living fear on part of the US Federal Government and their own spiritually weak minions, a fear of a righteous determination that is most certain to prevail among those whom are determined to *live free or die, forever free!*

To be quite frank, when the Republic of Texas raises its banner of liberty, I highly anticipate a military move to its borders, by the federal government or some alien agent motivated by them, either internally or externally[3]. There will be a federal order and a command to disband all state or individual notions of separation and national recognition from any of the fifty states, I anticipate. The free individuals of Texas should prepare for this and develop an effective plan to counter such actions, including the coming semi-clandestine military exercises and the agents of destruction who have already been carefully inserted in its very midst.

I also anticipate that the Mexican drug cartel is being bribed with both money and weapons right now by the US government, as well as by a number of foreign entities, for the purpose of attacking Texas and/or surrounding states, should they ever make any serious effort at dividing the Union in the future. For all of the reasons mentioned and many more, the people should know the truth about what is really going on. One aim of this book is simply to open the eyes of those who will find themselves on a frontline of one kind or another, and the time may be not far off.

Another May Rise To the Call

Lastly, I see a possibility that the great state of Alaska could soon declare its own independence, more than likely following that of Texas. The land mass has the resources and the people possess a strong sense of the old call,

1 http://www.foxnews.com/politics/2015/07/09/south-carolina-house-approves-removal-confederate-flag/. See also, http://hotair.com/archives/2015/06/26/memphis-mayor-cmon-lets-dig-up-confederate-gen-nathan-bedford-forrests-remains/
2 http://www.huffingtonpost.com/2015/07/10/confederate-flag-removal_n_7769300.html
3 https://www.rt.com/usa/us-drug-cartels-mexican-489/.   See also, http://freedomoutpost.com/2013/04/mexican-drug-cartels-operating-inside-american-borders

live free or die, forever free! I have spoken with many Alaskans over the years who are *extremely* dissatisfied with the way the nation is being managed and the fact that they, as individual entrepreneurs, are forced to contribute into a failing, corrupt national system that works against their pursuit of a livelihood. Their complaints are very similar to those of Texas, with the exception of the immigration issue, and they hold a very valid position all on their own, when one closely examines all of the facts and details. Especially in the last five years, there have been whispers of a desire for separation, but not as overtly as the recent call in Texas has been.[1]

It takes courage now to stand up for maintaining what we had all these years: liberty, including the right to adhere to our religious convictions, to own guns, to proudly honor our heritage and uphold the Constitution. It may come at a cost, but that did not deter our honorable forefathers. Most surely the knowledge of being in the right gives strength and confidence to those who decide to take this stand.

The Final Warning

Finally, I wish to warn those who would actually consider *giving in* to the dawning, devastating new order to relinquish all personal liberty, heritage and Constitution. Few will recognize it now, but when it comes to the crunch a huge number will be turncoats, caving in when the struggle gets rough.

This could amount to a civil war, or a virtual civil war (one without clear front lines, without clearly designated parties, without battles that start and finish. It may even start out as complete chaos, seemingly all against all. But it will come down to two broad types. The *patriots* will be those who understand they need to keep their guns if they are to be able to defend any other rights, those who adamantly oppose legislation that sanctions conduct previously considered immoral, and who uphold the rights enshrined in the Constitution. They will be opposed by what I'll call the *pigeons*, those bleeding heart liberals who are willing to sacrifice their own well–being for the benefit of those who can't be bothered to provide for themselves— even if they could—those who think that food stamps, housing subsidies and Welfare payments are entitlements tied to no responsibility, for as long as life goes on, who like to think of themselves as world citizens first and foremost and who therefore would support any UN mandate over the US Constitution, and are open to all the new moral codes and lack thereof. Some of this cohort believe that the solution to racist discrimination is not to appreciate diversity and use education to find ways to work together, but rather to drop any distinctions, to erase borders and boundaries, to move

1 https://en.wikipedia.org/wiki/Alaskan_Independence_Party

people around so they no longer know which place was "home," to hold to no standards and to say "it's all good." Even cannibalism, I suppose.

THESE "NICE" NEW VIRTUES are, in fact, self-destructive. They serve the multi-national corporations by rendering the individual helpless and exposed. They weaken each nation's traditions and social cohesion, weaken religious centers any sense of community that could protect people's dignity, and sap the economies of nations where people still value doing a good job. If you have no roots, no group to identify with, no heritage to ground your morals in, and no one to turn to, then you are clay in the hands of the ones who sign the paychecks. You are totally helpless and on your way to becoming not only a slave but a robot.

The penalty of falling for this trend, as so many well-intended people are liable to do, will be most devastating, since the absolute authority will have no mercy. This is no joke.

Chapter 3. The Original Plan

The land of America was "discovered" long before Columbus, of course, by accident and probably also by plan. There have always been storms at sea, and ships were blown off course routinely. Through the ages, at least a few who crashed on what are now American shores[1] may have found a way to make it back home.[2] During Viking days there may have been attempted settlements, near the Great Lakes and also from the mouth of the Mississippi northward. Meanwhile, bold fishing expeditions scouted the East Coast.

Reports would have suggested that there was good agricultural land here, but the real problem was the impracticality of shipping products such a long distance. To take full advantage, one would have to develop a shore-based colonial effort with the task of producing and processing food and products for cash or trade. A fleet of ships would be needed to bring supplies and to ship the products back home from there.

The First Serious Efforts

It's not our purpose here to study in detail the early colonial efforts, but let us focus on the beginning of the English effort, at Roanoke, old Jamestown, and Plymouth. The more efficiently run the colony, the greater its chances of survival. This meant an effort based on trial and error, but one where the margin for mistakes was somewhat narrow at best. Another factor in success was to be able to accurately assess the opportunities and risks, including the weaknesses of

---

1 *Ancient Explorers Of America: From The Ice Age To Columbus*, by Aleck Loker
2 http://borderzine.com/2012/03/did-europeans-settle-in-the-arizona-desert-thousands-of-years-before-columbus-sailed-to-america/

the people who already occupied the area and then move to create strengths in the build from there. After a number of horrible setbacks, the English became quite good at this, obviously.

However, let's hold in mind exactly *what* the first successful English colony, Jamestown, really was. Founded in 1607 and reinforced with a new group of settlers in 1610, this colony was a *business venture* backed by investors brought together via influence from Queen Elizabeth, with supporting military at their leadership's disposal. It would have been foolish to imagine that such a colony could survive without military defense—from the natives as well as from a possible Spanish attack. England was at war with Spain and the Americas were still largely under Spanish rule.

Jamestown was intended to be an extension of the English Crown/ *government*, with the idea of processing raw materials into finished products and shipping them back into markets developed in Crown-held territories.[1] They came up with tobacco as the first profitable crop from America. The Crown was expected to handle administrative affairs and provide protection for the colony in general. As the shipping base was developed, the colony grew in population and organization.

The native people were attacked early by the alien diseases brought to their shores by these bizarre new people, and had already suffered such with the advent of the Spanish. Huge numbers died from simple diseases such as the common cold, for instance. Mumps killed hundreds more; but the greatest plague, that wiped out entire villages in some cases, was small pox, which slew tens of thousands.[2] These deaths meant all the more in a population that suffered a very low population growth rate due to high infant mortality.[3]

The English would have early on perceived and exploited these weaknesses in order to make their goal of expansion easier to achieve. They also attempted to enslave local people to make them work at extracting the valuable resources of the land, forcing them to labor in the absence of any incentive. They resorted to negative incentives: massacres that wiped out huge numbers of native fighting-age men, productive men and boys. At the same time the Native Americans also suffered losses due to their own inter-tribal wars, alcoholism, and loss of primary food sources; while English numbers grew and eventually exploded as they progressively adapted to their new environment, gradually filling the increasingly vacated land.[4]

---

1 https://en.wikipedia.org/wiki/London_Company
2 https://en.wikipedia.org/wiki/Patuxet_tribe
3 John Lawson's History of NC, The Indians
4 Except as a hunting ground with only seasonal hunting camps and an itinerant population

Here we can see that the amoral and impersonal corporate power would use anything and stop at nothing to achieve its goals: to obtain resources, no matter at whose expense, and to make money. The authoritarian order that ran Jamestown was well-organized and clear in its intentions.

That particular portion of land had not initially seemed especially necessary to the local natives, as it was wet and the ground water was not good to drink. They had maintained a low population within the colonial sphere of influence. But as the colony expanded, things changed. The newcomers were taking over better and better land, with no regard to the fact that the land was already, de facto, owned and used by other people. The corporate principle was that seemingly vacant land (hunting grounds, sources of important wild plants, mineral deposits) was to be occupied by foreign interests, regardless of how the local people cherished it.[1]

Remember, too, that the Jamestown colony existed under what amounts to a rule of a military colony, under martial law, with the sole primary purpose being to render profit for the Crown. This military authority served as the Court of Law with the mandate to administer arrests, trials and executions as deemed necessary. They collected taxes and enforced general codes deemed necessary for the well-being of the colony. Under military law, the general population had very few, if any, individual rights. The corporate owners back in London had all the rights.

It could be argued that the colony had to function as a unitary body[2], rather than as a bunch of individuals, as it was struggling for survival. It was a kind of war economy/war society, where individual rights of course had to be set aside for awhile or the corporate goal would fail and all the participants would have died. Like a military squad or platoon in action, to insist on one's individual liberties at the expense of the group would have been fatal.

Changing Personal Situations

After overcoming leadership failures and a variety of setbacks (gold and silver were hardly lying at the surface ready for the taking, and actual hard work was required to get any venture going), things began to look up. And in the new environment the people of the colony began to change their mental conception of themselves. They tended to be (1) transient unskilled laborers who moved from house to house and town to town, longing for the day when they could afford their own property; (2) property owners who

---

1 http://endoftheamericandream.com/archives/the-chinese-are-acquiring-large-chunks-of-land-in-communities-all-over-america
2 https://en.wikipedia.org/wiki/Jamestown,_Virginia ,Rising fortunes, Arrival And Beginning

eked out a living as small subsistence farmers on the edge of town, some of them owning and operating a general store or trading in various products; or (3) apprentice tradesmen who endeavored to master a skill or service highly needed by the surrounding society. Then of course, there were (4) the indentured servants and finally (5) the slaves, though they were few. There were also some (6) skilled tradesmen who worked in another person's shop or he might own and run his own individual production enterprise and mercantile shop.

The business *owner* most closely resembled today's dying middle class. Based on what I have observed in my visits to the colonial site and reading all I could about its history and archeology, according to eye witness reports of the day, the laboring transients basically lived hand-to-mouth while moving from place to place. The business owner lived very much like the renter, largely avoiding personal debts and producing most of what he consumed, except that he owned his home rather than rented, in a majority of cases. People had few personal articles, and whatever they had, they simply used until it completely wore out, then they reworked it or crafted it for another alternative use[1]—until it simply crumbled away into dust. When the business owners or tenants did need something, they tried to buy used, or they tried to find scrap and make the item themselves at no cost whatsoever.

Servants were not paid for their work; they were housed and fed. Slaves were a very expensive commodity: they had to be purchased, and this was essentially a non-cash system. Thus the slave owners at Jamestown and Williamsburg for the most part were top government, corporate and military officials. Also, the initial purchase expense gave the owner a reason to take care of the slave's well being, and the value of the slave's labor for his or her owner increased with the slave's skill level. All that the servants/slaves were required to do was simply work to earn their livelihood.

As time went on, the Jamestown colonists adapted; first by neutralizing the native threat[2] via rigid organization and calculating observation and foresight to avoid problems, then finally, by specializing in some needed skill or service that their developing society valued, such as carpenters, brick masons and silver smiths.

But after securing the survival of the colony, the town leaders had to look for products that could turn a profit for the corporate investors. Products such as wild rice, cotton and tobacco were developed for export and trade. A shipping base was constructed as the ship builders took advantage of

---

1 The author recalls playing in the ruins of a 30-year-old plantation, finding shoes patched up and resoled until they could no longer be worn, then used as wall filler in the basement, among many other worn out articles such as knife handles, broken glass articles, broken toys, shattered wine bottles, etc.
2 https://en.wikipedia.org/wiki/Indian_massacre_of_1622

the huge pine timber resources. Pitch pine tar, for example, was useful, and various types of rot-resistant timber were available. Trade goods were shipped from Jamestown all the way to Great Britain and back again. The US navy to this day still owns and manages huge tracts of timberland acquired in the colonial period.

Trade goods shipped locally and abroad included but were not limited to; tobacco, which without a doubt was one of the most valuable, yarn spun from cotton fiber, indigo and hemp, field peas and native butter beans of a wide variety in sorts, cassina or yuopon tea already processed by packaging the dried or baked leaves, locally made wine and spirits, sawn boards and wood, especially juniper, cypress and cedar, stone used for carving goods and building, even hickory-cured pork from pigs that had been fed on local acorns, and the list goes on and on.[1]

The point is that the profits from all this went to the corporate investors, not to the workers.

Growth of Fortune

It appears that working the land became so profitable that plantations arose outside of the city gates, and the native threat was gradually reduced due to the causes previously mentioned. Most of the servant class during this period were indentured laborers or those who had arrived on a land consignment contract agreement, and other similar but less well-known arrangements that let them unable to leave their employers. The indentured laborer was working to pay back the cost of his transportation to the new continent (prepaid by the employer), at hefty interest rates, and many never managed to do it. The terms of the land consignment contract agreement stated that if one agreed to labor on a farm, usually for seven years, then he would receive a good tract of land agreed upon ahead of time. The size was usually about 640 acres, according to all of my best information. The person in the land consignment agreement paid for his own transportation or was working for the merchant-marine and attracted favorable attention from the captain/ship owner. This was the case for one of my own direct ancestors.

According to my best information, most of the land acquired from the natives during this time was purchased outright or was simply land taken without discussion. The natives who agreed to the purchases did not always remain content with the deal, as they gradually understood better what was going on;[2] but at least at the outset there was a façade of fair dealing and the deals were consensual, legally binding, with surveys and documentation; at

---

1 John Lawson's *History of NC*, the people of NC , The Indians
2 http://www.coastalcarolinaindians.com/case-1-on-the-trail-of-tom-or-a-new-look-at-the-tuscarora-war/

least, that applies to purchases made by individual colonial settlers rather than the administration.

One way and another, the colonies were beginning to settle, grow and prosper as the individual settlers gained confidence and witnessed the general success of the colony. Raw, virgin territory came under cultivation, something that was long since impossible in England. Here, a man could view the manifestations of his own success right before his eyes. This not only increased his pride in his work but helped convince him more of his own potential to succeed.

But Jamestown and Williamsburg, right along with old Brunswick Town (now in North Carolina), for example, and a growing number of others, were not private estates. They were *imperial capital ventures*, or capital ventures indirectly related to the Crown. Their purpose was to produce finished products or raw materials cheaply for Crown-sponsored corporations, then resold abroad at a steep mark-up: a steal, as is the preferred business transaction.

Taxes on the colonists also brought in revenue. Since the revenue in product shipments was so vast, and the general tax on the average citizen so small in comparison, the rules for coercing payment were not as rigid later on as they had been in the very beginning days of the colonies. Most skilled tradesmen could either avoid payment altogether or simply recoup lost revenue through payment on the side in untaxed cash or *specie* payment; a technique would remain in place, off and on, until the 19986 tax reform bill mentioned earlier put an end to much of that. The governments across the big pond didn't like losing money, but when huge profits came in from other ventures, that was where they paid the most attention. It would have been non-productive to go after every two-bit player and so they allowed the system to go on as it was.

Many times, if lands acquired by the colonial governments were not immediately used, then the natives were allowed to occupy the lands again, but for a fee in hides and agricultural products (at standard price issued to the colonist in general). While there were no doubt incidents of fraud by corrupt collection officials, in a general sense, the rate of tax was about the same for the indigenous people as for the colonist in general, who also suffered from corrupt collection officials at various times.[1]

Life went on and the colonies continued to prosper and more were established. The people engaged in their industrious pursuits. There were problems, of course; this was no heaven on earth, and there were power struggles, bitter religious squabbles and other clashes. There were also

---

1 http://www.learnnc.org/lp/editions/nchist-colonial/1973

occasional witch trials[1]—but those often came down to abuses by corrupt leaders, officials and business associates who were persecuting individuals who were vulnerable and who inconveniently owned property that someone wanted. Sometimes personal feuds between families played out with one family seeking to confiscate the other's property for a rogue resale.[2] In the context of our theme, we can see that events like these were mini harbingers of a much greater negative future that is playing out in America now. The people who were persecuted in those days were individuals whom it would have been politically acceptable to persecute at the time—and they legally held title to something coveted, of hard value. The pattern bears watching.

Colonial Mentality Changes

Overall, the colonists grew, prospered and engaged in their own business enterprises, and for the most part, doing so was very positive. However, let's view the often-overlooked reality of another development in the mentality of the colonists. Back in the days of the English colonies in America, successful business people allowed what were known as shop stewards to apprentice in learning the trade or service. To get a good start in what we now call a career, one either went off to apprentice in the "trades" or to labor in the "services," which also provided on-the-job training. Most of these "educational" stints were five to seven years long. Apprentices to well-known business owners gained good reputations themselves. In the meantime, the business owner got increasingly skilled workers while paying the set rate for unskilled laborers for a number of years. Then the apprentice became certified and officially endorsed by the owner; so if all went well, everything balanced out justly in the end.

Sometimes laborers were allowed to learn the skills of the trade and how to run the business just by asking—and showing talent and hard work. Others were family members and friends of the family who were confident of the skill level that the apprentice potentially held. In other words, people could rise up if they applied themselves, since opportunity was abundant; or they could just choose to be idle or "lack-less," as they called it, although idleness was discouraged.[3] One only needed to *possess the desire to get ahead.*

With the passage of time, any man who appeared in the colony with nothing more than the clothes on his back, a clear sober mind and a good, practical idea, could find a position and work himself up into his own business, without being excluded from the opportunity or extorted of his

1 Wikipedia, Salem Witch Trials, Local Context
2 http://etext.virginia.edu/toc/modeng/public/SalVRec.html
3 "West Virginia Law Relative to Idleness and Vagrancy" https://archive.org/stream/jstor-1133743/1133743_djvu.txt

hard earned resources. Soon the colony was functioning more as a collection of industrious, independent individuals, rather than a collective and centrally controlled whole. The populace was made up of tradesmen who were employed by contractors who had once been tradesmen themselves, and who in most cases had risen up from simple laborers. They either got their starts as indentured servants or as adventurous colonist who assumed all of the personal risks of striking out into the unknown, often empty-handed when they started. In other words, these brave men and women became very confident of their independence and did not feel that they were in need of any handout from the authorities. The world surrounding them had been constructed by their own hands, the hands of their families or very close associates and friends!

With the passage of time, more and more of these hard working, brave individualists came to view Crown government as a road block to personal success. The governors and other officials, sitting way up there in their mansions on the hill, striving to serve a king far away and fill the coffers of corporate partnerships at home, at the expense of the population in the colony. They could see a need for a military, but one that was immediate and drawn from among people of their own peers when needed—not a standing military authority. These people came to see themselves as being perfectly capable of handling all of their own administrative affairs, legal affairs, and other public affairs. The Crown military and governor came to seem more and more irrelevant, and burdensome. They were seen agents representing a foreign corporate entity, serving some other interests, and parasites at that. People were tiring of an *absolute authority/martial government* who did not even represent their interests.

Colonial communities formed their own militia units and their own courts made up of people whom they knew would be fine stewards of their own concerns. With the passage of time, there were increasing conflicts, and rising emotions, as the corporate authority, looking out for the interests of the Crown via increasing repression and extortion,[1] were confronted by the authority formed of the people.

These people were growing their own food now, crafting their own products, gathering their own medicine from the land, making their own cloth from raw wild cotton all around as well as that which they grew on the plantations, and to a large extent, they were handling their own public affairs. Yes, the colonists had trade relations with Great Britain, but they had also developed others on their own.[2] These people also, by their own efforts,

---

1 https://en.wikipedia.org/wiki/Bacon%27s_Rebellion
2 http://www.encyclopedia.com/topic/Foreign_Trade.aspx. Also, since England drove out the French during the French and Indian War, France had to engage in trade to get any goods they wanted from the colonies.

had risen up from simple laborers to skilled craftsmen, tradesmen and professionals. They didn't see a real need for the Crown and its corporate enclaves.

When these questions were increasingly debated, the colonial authorities responded by sending in troops—which by now the colonists saw as foreign invaders. The colonists possessed weapons, could manufacturer their own[1], and they had learned how to fight guerrilla-style from the natives by retreating back into the "limitless" dense wilderness and making use of hit and run tactics.[2] They could also recruit from their own ranks to raise a military overnight to assemble forces of able, willing and vested fighting men.

These rugged individualists did not need any alien order lording over them, imposing some external authority while claiming that they were doing so in the colony's best interests—masking an attempt to repress people who were able to see and seize a business opportunity, in order to extort a tax on, or stamp out competition from, such honest hard work!

Why did any productive individual who had by now completed his apprenticeship, who now held the standing of quality in his own stenciled stamp and name, need the approval of any other authority—who did not even represent his own interests, be it born of the corporation and/or from a foreign authority?

Sometimes, somebody asks a good question and it's still valid a few hundred years later. Why did the colonists need approval to engage in honest business? All a thinking, investigative people has to do is to conduct the research to find the valid answers and that truth will be revealed.

The ability to analyze, observe, do a little deductive reasoning and anticipate what's coming, may well be what determines our survival in the near future, as both a free people and a sovereign nation.

Few average people of our day bother to practice this kind of thinking for themselves, using basic logic. This was apparent already when my children were attending school inside the US public education system: at the same time when education pundits were constantly stressing the need for students to be instructed in the art of critical thinking! Of course, the leaders failed miserably in giving even basic examples of effective, critical thinking and routinely reacted based on assumptions (invalid ones, at that),

---

1 https://en.wikipedia.org/wiki/Long_rifle
2 The Scottish clans would have a series of runners to carry a flaming cross through allied territory at mid night, during times of conflict. Where the cross came to stand on enemy territory, around it would rally all who had taken up arms and followed to form an army that would attack at the crack of dawn.

when dealing with students and their personal situations as well as staff. But our colonial forefathers *did* demonstrate this most valuable skill.

The Need for Divorce

As time continued to roll on, people increasingly began to suspect the need for divorce from Great Britain. Taxes tariffs on incoming goods, and revenues skimmed off exports were just siphoning off all the extra value produced by the people doing the work.

Now, England had fought a war with France over possession of new world real estate, and France lost the conflict[1]. France had been at war with England anyway for a quite a while over the years, nearly as much so as it had been with Spain, so fighting with France on American soil was no surprise. But then the payments for supplying the overseas troops came due. England felt that her American colonies should foot the bills for housing the soldiers, their food, and general accommodations, which more than likely had already come at colonial expense anyway with goods taken by foraging troops moving through the land.[2]

In addition, the English also were having problems in the diamond mines of India, since compelled labor tends to fight back from time to time. The diamond mines in India made that area a far more valuable possession than the American colonies, so more resources had to be sent in to quell the uprising there, in fact the best resources—including military leadership. That's a point not always mentioned in US history books.

As the desire of the British to extort the cost of billeting their troops from the Americans became apparent, a number of new laws were imposed.[3] My own research based on numbers available seems to indicate that this crass "extortion" amounted to only roughly 5% of colonial profit—which does not seem to be outrageous when we currently pay 10 to 12% nowadays, with 6% going to the Fed and 6% going to the state; but in the context then it struck many people as unbearable.

Additional factors worth mentioning that are directly in line with the material throughout this work include, but are not limited to; *The Currency Acts of 1751 and 1764*. As the colonies grew increasingly more independent in view of their own capabilities and world outlook, they soon determined that they could print their own currency based on the value of gold or silver, living underneath their own financial authority. In summary description, the

1 https://en.wikipedia.org/wiki/French_and_Indian_War
2 http://americanheritage.com/articles/magazine/ah/2005/6/2005_6_75.shtml
3 https://en.wikipedia.org/wiki/Quartering_Acts;   https://en.wikipedia.org/wiki/Stamp_Act_1765; https://en.wikipedia.org/wiki/Declaratory_Act;   https://en.wikipedia.org/wiki/Currency_Act; https://en.wikipedia.org/wiki/Indian_massacre_of_1622

decision of colonial leaders to allow this separated the financial rule of the colonies from the power of the English central bank. Since the colonies were limited in their possession of gold and silver because of limited access to it, through both of these acts the British banking authorities outlawed the making and use of colonial bank notes, with the exception being for personal debt, having little or no gold or silver to back it. In this manner the primary colonial finances were at the mercy of the British central bank, who could withdraw the backing in gold or silver, or simply insert more of it for the purpose of raising or lowering value to the benefit of the British Crown and it's well connected individual and corporate supporters.

The imposition of a fee or tax to cover expenses not geared to benefit the colonies, income generated by the colonists; own work, insulted the now fully developed colonial sense of independence more than it impoverished them. The colonists may have also felt insulted by having to pay for provisioning an army fighting for interests outside of their own, since they personally had no problems with the French. In the minds of colonists, they were already freeborn men and women!

The Unbearable Acts (not to be confused with the Intolerable Acts), the pressure to resist was mounting.

What About the Natives?

Although some Native Americans were still around, some even adapting completely and dwelling within the colony, intermarrying and interrelating within the social structure, the majority had simply retreated farther back into the countryside. While the British attempted to persuade the tribes to attack colonial outposts, and were successful to a large degree in some respects[1], many chose to cast their lot with the colonists since in a number of instances they were already married and aligned in among them.

The military order of the colony, working on behalf of corporate/government interests, had expanded the colony at the expense of a gradually retreating native population. The colonists simply just followed to fill the spaces allotted to them. While there is no doubt that many knew the land had been native tribal land, most felt that it was lying idle and was ignored by the natives, who had at their disposal vast amounts of terrain in relation to their low population; they seldom even drifted through. The natives, while they did not mind sharing the land to allow people the opportunity to gather food for sustenance, did imagine that a time would come when these visitors could be expected to simply move on. When these colonists refused to do so, then resentment built up. This resentment became the motivation that the British used to persuade the natives to attack.

1 The colony of Boonesboro, for example

Among the American natives, for example, it was not uncommon for a stronger, much more powerful tribe to take control of a certain region and allow the less powerful tribe to go on living there, in peace, as long as they paid tribute.[1] The military governments of the colonies could perhaps have tried offering the tribes some level of compensation as they expanded outward, for the privilege of using their land; the system was also not unknown in Europe. That might have reduced the number of conflicts.[2] Realistically speaking, however, sharing profits to any degree because it is the moral, even the most intelligent, thing to do, simply is not in the nature of the corporate beast. That is especially true when those behind the corporation can have a well armed, confident, highly trained military impose their decisions and protect their business interests.

Sadly, notions of morality, right and wrong, have seldom figured in the way any sort of *new world order* is imposed. What happened to the Native Americans can be seen to presage what citizens are observing happening in their hometowns now, and can offer realistic insight helping to make valid predictions of events hiding just ahead in the mist.

The Boston Tea Party

As we have intimated before, with the passage of time among the colonists found feelings of complete independence rising in themselves. Great Britain, due to a series of wars and economic setbacks, imposed a list of acts this author labels as *"Unbearable."* The result was a vocal protest at the capitol buildings of Jamestown, VA, Williamsburg, and other outposts throughout the now thirteen colonies. This resistance climaxed in an act of overt defiance called "The Boston Tea Party."

The Boston Tea Party was the first well orchestrated act of defiance against the British authoritarian rule. The protests defining their demands and allowed time for the authorities to respond in a positive way, but the lust for power and insatiable greed prevented such a response. What the colonists needed now was a more direct action. As a result the East India Company lost a complete shipment of tea into the Boston Harbor. This was a large economic loss to the East India Company, but also to the taxes received by the British Crown. Lacking this tea, the colonies simply switched to drinking yuopon tea or sassafras tea.

Cassina or yuopon leaf was a natural product related to the yerba maté used down in Argentina, even to this very day. The locals had made use thereof for hundreds, if not thousands of years prior. The caffeine content of

---

1 See note on *Lawson's History Of NC*, The Indians
2 See information on William Penn's Colony

this tea was actually much greater than that of even Spanish coffee, though the two were often mixed.

As more colonists used alternatives, corporate complaints and revenue shortfalls put pressure on the government, meaning the very offices of the Crown itself. It is a well-known fact that the ear of government listens when the hand that feeds it begins to lose revenue. How could the high government officials now restore the needed income? How were the authorities going to respond to the "threat" of the average person demanding the right of self determination? The authorities usually respond the same way to cries of injustice from an exploited people: with crass indifference; unless the move is calculated to fulfill a self serving purpose.

The British response was to marshal the colonies with more visible, inflexible authority. But the presence of this visible authority did not have the desired effect of intimidation. On the short term it may well have held the effect, but the increased visibly and imposing muster of arms present, served more to separate everybody into columns of "them" and "us." Such divisions served to build the feelings of camaraderie among those who were rallying to call themselves "patriots" and caused resentment against those who were labeled "loyalists."

The British forces were easy targets in their dazzling red coats and fine mass-produced weaponry, versus the rag tag look of the colonists in homespun battle dress and crude weapons, home-made "long rifles" eventually being among the most dominant.

As time passed and colonial resentment continued to build, eventually the swelling tension was destined to explode. In Boston, producers had been trading illegally, that is smuggling, for a while, in an effort to circumvent the British export tax. When the British began cracking down, they gave their regulators full authority to both prosecute and condemn, by court and law. Violence broke out between the colonists and the regulators, as well as the troops who were marshaled in at the time. The British responded by sending in 4,000 more troops, hoping to quell what seemed to be the beginning of a sweeping mutiny.

The entire colony of Massachusetts soon was threatened with trial for treason, but the colonists responded with more boycotts and refusals to purchase British goods. The huge London-based corporations, the East India Company (owned by aristocrats and merchants whose names are masked by corporate formalities) specifically, begin to lose revenue, the government they fed and their officials became enraged, and took senseless, violent action to intimidate the plebeians. What resulted was an event that in time came to be known as *The Boston Massacre*.[1]

---

1 https://en.wikipedia.org/wiki/Boston_Massacre

The Boston Massacre

As soon as the shock effect of the event ebbed, the air of intimidation subsided and the colonists began to crowd and group around; at least some, no doubt, plotting a response. In order to appear as though they had not condoned the action, the British indicted the troops who had fired on murder charges, but all were acquitted. Two were charged with manslaughter, only to be granted reduced sentences later on and released with just a quick branding of the hand.

Parliament, wishing to ease tensions, eased the tax on tea, while at the same time reducing the price of tea and appointing specific merchants to distribute it. Such action was anticipated to increase tea sales dramatically, but it also was anticipated to help restore the fortunes of the East India Company. Anger would be aroused again when the Governor of Massachusetts refused to allow the ships either to offload the tea on dock or to exit the harbor, and the same occurred in all of the other colonies. And in Boston, under a blanket of darkness, colonists in pseudo-Indian disguise swarmed on board the anchored ships to destroy all of the tea.

Tea was big money for the corporations of the day as well as for the British government. By directly attacking the source of that revenue, they were attacking the authority who lorded over them. Such action, of course, was one that would virtually guarantee an authoritarian response, since profit at expense of the people is what *always* matters to any corporate authority.

The forthcoming response was to expunge the colonial government in any form and to replace it with authoritarian emplaced royal officials. But rather than cower down before these officers and officials, the colonists were outraged, organizing to initiate their own action plans. The nascent First Continental Congress soon called for a repeal of all financial support for the Crown, including repeal of all taxes, but made allowances if the Crown would recognize certain concerns of the colonists. Recognition, of course, would mean loss of profit; so next time, there was certain to be a much more pointed response, to get the message across that any noncompliance would not be tolerated.

Naturally corporate and government interests want to neutralize all threats from the people and preserve their revenue income at the same time. The entire point of establishing and maintaining these colonies was to generate business for the Crown via their endorsed corporations who benefited from cheap labor in the colony (not to mention in India) and to reap the readily available raw products in great abundance. Then there was the farming tax revenue, although compared to later tax rates, in this author's humble opinion, those rates and policies seem very fair. But now, the British response was to abruptly impose a rigid, inflexible tax upon the people of Massachusetts.

The royal Governors of all the British-controlled colonies had removed any individuals known to be sympathetic to the Patriots and had replaced them with loyalists. In effect the Continental Congress had been outlawed, resulting in the average people having no representation and being forced to accept the order to pay up. This enforcement of the tax order infuriated the colonists and gave them that much more resolve to resist.

The problem with tax imposed in any form is that it demands rigid regulation and rigid, inflexible enforcement to be effective. If it goes beyond a token amount, such a tax siphons off and purloins any profit or benefit to the productive individuals who engage in honest enterprise. The all-inclusive word we use for this is *incentive*. And as soon as taxes, tariffs, permitting costs, obligatory insurance, etc., and other imposed fees remove the incentive, there is no motivation to do business in the first place. But the perception of unreasonableness, rigidity, and corruption can be even more discouraging than the fees themselves. It is quite possible that this rigid corrupt enforcement in the collecting of the tax may have infuriated the average colonist much more than the 5% tax itself.

Regulation generally means that individuals have to allow an outside agent to impose his own instructions for conducting the owner's business, from afar, many times at the jeopardy of the enterprise itself[1]. The inflexible, inconsiderate nature of tax collection agencies down through time has an overwhelming tendency to disregard local realities, as they all apply to the business, the owner's family or the business owner himself; never mind the fact that the individual owner who possesses the property in full understandably feels he possesses a basic right to profit from that property, no matter what mortal authority attempts to tell him otherwise.

Likely, the Patriot colonists figured that if they allowed the tax and its inflexible, corrupt enforcement to go forward, the appetite for revenue would have no end, increasingly turning to outright extortion, backed by a flagrant abuse of authority[2]. Official high school or even college level textbooks may not mention it, but regulatory abuse of royal authority in its collection techniques and otherwise[3] was a primary reason why the colonial Patriots stood their ground. Another possibility one can deduce is that the corruption was actually a Crown-endorsed part of the British tax collection plan for the American colonies, so that government officials could publish the measly 5% tax rate while collecting much more revenue via unethical

1 http://politicaloutcast.com/2015/05/another-irs-robbery-of-a-small-business-owner/
2 http://lfb.org/the-sordid-history-of-irs-political-abuse/
3 http://www.breedshill.org/there_will_be_blood.htm

means,[1] even to the extent of extracting the collection agent's salary from the individual colonist to save the Crown itself from having to pay him!

History is written by those in power, and it would be no surprise if US history as taught is even now skewed to suit corporate interests, twisted to paint the authority as the liberator and depicting those who might oppose it as villains. Those with power have always been aware that the same collection techniques may have to be applied again. Evidence of this great cover up is readily available to the diligent researcher.

Why the Facts Were Twisted

Most official accounts simply declare that the colonists resisted paying the tax, at best only alluding to the heavy-handed way it was collected. The question is, "Why would the official record omit this part of the story?" or only allude to it vaguely, then move on?

Let's look at the facts. According to all of my research, the percentage amounts demanded were only 5% at best. [2] Evidently some very offensive enforcement techniques must have been used just to collect this meager 5%. Did the authorities who later recorded the history feel that taxes and enforcement would never again be a problem? Obviously not, and when much higher percentages were demanded, even more ruthless, inflexible enforcement techniques would be needed. In other words: let's not make heroes out of those who resisted the enforcement, when one day in the future much higher taxes[4] and more insolent measures may be needed, with a far more abusive authority enforcing it.

The colonists by now had a near 200-year history of industrious, self-serving independent living. They had demonstrated the ability over the course of time to govern themselves, defend themselves and take care of all their own needs. Even though the British did provide well-organized administrative services and protection from foreign threats, the colonists felt themselves now well adapted to providing these services inside the boundaries of their own communities and states. All that they needed were their own resources to do so. To these rugged individualists, submitting to an authority that for a few generations had already felt alien was uncomfortable, undignified, and unjustified. The benefits of this overlord were not worth the constant and often dishonest tax collections and the presence of troops.

1 https://en.wikipedia.org/wiki/IRS_targeting_controversy
2 Thomas, *British Politics* 47- 49
3 https://en.wikipedia.org/wiki/Townshend_Acts, section on American board of customs commissioners
4 State and Federal taxes take in 43% of a person's pay check

Life was tough enough without submitting to a host of measures reminding the colonists they were there to be exploited.

The Battle of Lexington

The great defining moment came on the night of April 18, 1775, when the British general Gage sent 700 men to Lexington to seize the munitions of the Patriots. Just as this author hopes to awake and arouse those who need warning, Paul Revere rode out, as legend has it, to warn the colonists of the threat and raise the call to arms.

And these grand Patriots rallied to meet the well-armed British soldiers in Concord, to engage in battle at first light in the morning. British troops entered the city early on August 18, to find 77 armed and ready minutemen regulars eager for battle—or for the complete surrender of the enemy.

Shots were exchanged and several Patriots lost their lives. The British then rode on into town, where a detachment of three companies was engaged and routed at the old North Bridge by a force of some 500 minutemen.[1] As the British turned tail and ran toward Boston, small, well-concealed detachments of minutemen and Patriotic colonists attacked them guerrilla-style, generating numerous casualties. The panicked retreat continued until fresh British reinforcements arrived on scene to save the day.

Thus with these two engagements, the great war against corporate government and its efforts to reduce men to the level of an expendable resource had been initiated. This battle was never expected to be the end of the story. It was a response only to the immediate demand of accommodation to a 5% tax. The original contention of Thomas Jefferson and his allies has unfortunately been proven right, that unchecked greed bears no limitations.

While this study is not intended to be a retelling of the Revolutionary War, there are telling moments what show it was in part a war for the individual versus the corporation and its government backing. Bear in mind that the historical record was made and later rewritten to conceal the intentions of government and corporations to impose their will on the working people. History even today is written to save face for various parties. What power wants to give fodder for another resistance movement from the rank and file?

Authority always seeks to reinforce its importance, so as to cause the average people to feel that rather than purloining what is rightfully their own, the authority holds the people's best interests at the fore and deserves to be paid and supported for its benevolent work. By convincing the people to feel that government serves them, then when extortion is imposed and liberty eliminated, the people are willing to go along.

---

1 The large number suggests there was some sort of night-time rallying technique, other than Revere's ride alone.

People generally enjoy stability and security, and will avoid conflict even to the very last, in silent hopes that the situation will abate all on its own. The sad truth is that when the first negative signs appear, that is the time to act. Once the conclusion materializes, there is little room for maneuver.

Not only does this work point out specifics that the official version of history attempts to cover up, it also points out historical details of an effective measure to take in response to the imposition of unwarranted demands, limitations of liberties, and other unreasonable infringements of rights.

Why Did the Colonists Win?

The colonists won because they never did face the full strength of the British power. As mentioned, the main British concern at the time was the diamond mines in India and the insurrection there. The loss of those mines would have been much greater than anything they stood to lose in raw materials and the relatively few finished products from the American colonies. In other words, the *potential loss of revenue was the primary concern*. The best generals and equipment went to protect the mines in India, only third rate generals and equipment were used to defend British interests in the American colonies.[1] Business is business. From what history tells us, British generals were actually sent to the colonies in America as a punishment for incompetence.[2] But even then, the American colonies were forced to work with foreign allies,[3] despite the folklore/official historical record and any tall tales told by veterans-turned-frontiersmen, drinking in the local taverns or boasting around their camp fires near some remote trading post.

With French assistance,[4] colonial forces met the British at Yorktown, Virginia, and a great battle for liberty from the imperial corporation took place. The French, who had lost a huge portion of their land holdings to Great Britain earlier, were eager to reestablish a trading base with the colonies to the anticipated ire of the British. The hope was to gain the ability to negotiate, rather than to fight, for establishment of that base. There was also the obvious motive of revenge.

When the British General Clinton retreated back into New York for reinforcements there in anticipation of an attack by sea, he unwisely left General Cornwallis and his army shadowed by Patriot forces, and pinned with his back to the sea. Cornwallis, being only third rate himself and less

---

1 John E Ferling; *Almost A Miracle, The American Victory In The War Of Independence*, 2009 pp. 562- 80
2 Wickwire, pp.134-137
3 The French as well as other, often mercenary, allies.
4 Already well established trading partners who purchased raw colonial product

than competent as a commanding general, abandoned his fortified position at Yorktown prematurely under the patriot bombardment, soon surrendering his force of seven thousand on the same day that reinforcements were arriving at sea to relieve the embattled British position there resulting from the Battle of Chesapeake. This single move, no doubt motivated by intimidation from the artillery assault and the heavy 16-day bombardment, effectively placed Cornwallis and his forces in check. He then had no other realistic option but to surrender.[1] To demonstrate his own opinion of his performance as general, Cornwallis apparently feigned illness, using it to avoid appearing at his own surrender ceremony and facing his comrades in defeat.

With the surrender now being formal and documented, so that it had to be recognized by the British authorities, the struggle for true independence had in reality just begun. The common people were free, but what were they going to do with this freedom? How were they going to reestablish validity among their trading partners, convincing them that trading with them would still be a profitable venture? How were they going to organize their own government? Would it be one of their own design and model, or would it be one very similar to the model that they had already known for so long? Either way, how were the going to prevent a corruption of the new authority and the repression of the average people via extortion and intimidation?

Individual Responsibility for Liberty

These questions were very valid and demanded to be answered by the dawning government. The answers to these questions would affect the society yet to come and all of their descendants. As we shall see, the effort was bold and many wise decisions made that helped to prevent abuse, but unfortunately, the predictions of Jefferson were to haunt future history like a terrifying banshee, as they gradually materialized into an astonishingly degree.

The iron fist was closed *slowly*, like a leaf of the Venus fly trap (the "fly," in our case, being the epitome of freedom in its greatest glory, and the leaf representing forces of collusion designing to ensnare and enslave him. Note carefully how the leaves seldom miss without direct intervention of one type or another.

What the founding fathers asked us to do was to provide that intervention, in the form of the new Constitutional laws, through a system of checks and balances. The method we use to determine the degree of transgression would be via violation of those checks and balances. Even a small slide away

---

1 Wilcox, p. 493

from individual liberty would serve to justify protest from the people, since in Jefferson's own words, [1]

> The natural progress of things is for liberty to yield and government to gain ground.

This is so because those who gain positions of power tend always to extend the bounds of it. Power must always be constrained or limited else it will increase to the level that it will be despotic.[2]

Thus corporate and government intent toward citizenry would *always* be to dominate and extort, and the duty of a free people would be to step up in protest. They must defend themselves by demanding that this natural imposing move of government to subordinate liberated people be halted and those forces step back behind the lines of legality, the lines outlined so vividly in the original document of our sacred Constitution, live and active until the year 1860.

In other words, the responsibility of maintaining individual liberty *lay with the people themselves* in the end, no matter what preserving actions were decided upon by the founding fathers at the time of the Constitutional debates. The future would be directed by the people's own course of successful action, or inaction through *complacency* and outright ignorance of their own history, and a prevailing lack of fortitude born out of a weakening corrupting submissiveness, to speak the truth even when it is so obtrusively self evident.

The analytical prophesies of the great visionary, Jefferson, began to emerge all too soon. The urge to impose upon individual liberties began as small, seemingly insignificant infractions, only to emerge some 90 years later full blown, as a bloodthirsty, blatantly illegal infraction of the Constitution, a move to allow an outright corporate takeover of all privately held resources and to establish the future corporate bondage of the entire US population, in one form or another. Note that this would be relatively easy to accomplish at any time, so long as the people remain in a state of seductive contentment and mind-numbing ignorance of the events emerging all around them, as well as to the truth of events locked away deep inside their own national history.

Maybe this work will serve to chop a wide hole in that thick wall of pompous presumption and allow the bright light of a new dawning day to shine through, waking up the public to the danger all around us now.[3]

---

1 Thomas Jefferson to Edward Carington 1788
2 http://fee.org/freeman/thomas-jefferson-liberty-and-power/
3 For another look at the sinister collusion of banking (*the Federal Reserve*), huge corporations and their inside government backers, see: http://www.eagleforum.org/publications/column/no-wonder-obama-wont-let-us-read-tpp.html/

Chapter 4. The First Ninety Years in a Nutshell

The most important part of the nation's beginning, in fact, was not the Revolution (although of course without the physical break from Britain, our sovereign nation would have never been born[1]). The debates that then issued, the thought and imagination that went into the building of a new nation, would bear fruit in a system that was uniquely wonderful and at the same time held the seeds of a very detrimental development.

Most Americans simply do not realize that the design of the Constitution, with its checks and balances, did not come into form instantly, but every clause was hotly debated, even to the point that some delegates suggested that it might take another war to settle the dispute as to how the new nation would be governed! One camp actually wanted to reimpose a monarchist/highly centralized Federalist government, while the others wanted what we would label today as laissez-faire government, or as little government as it is possible to have, with solid checks on the value of currency and the mechanics of government, to prevent any collusion that might endeavor to purloin the earnings of the hard-working plebeians.

Most of those who favored the centralized, absolutist federal government, which would resemble the old monarchy, were either in the employ of corporate interests or were among the extremely privileged, corporate industrialist aristocratic class themselves.[2] Those who were most in favor of a liberated, individual-enterprise society favored greatly a system governed by the people at large, with solid checks and balances to hold back the tendency for power

---

1 http://www.bbc.co.uk/history/british/modern/endofempire_overview_07.shtml
2 See: https://en.wikipedia.org/wiki/John_Jay; and: https://en.wikipedia.org/wiki/Alexander_Hamilton

and wealth to corrupt.[1] This led to often heated intellectual debates, but finally a compromise was developed.[2]

A Travel Assignment

The old Independence Hall in Philadelphia, and the Liberty Bell, are well worth visiting. I learn something new, especially concerning the occurrences at Independence Hall. Upon walking inside, I behold what amounts to a courtroom, if one might conceive the picture. Since accurate minutes were recorded with clear notations, we not only know the exact chairs in which the delegates sat, we even know what the weather was like and the very expressions and demeanor of each person present! We know where the chairs were positioned at the time in relation to the room, the clothes that the delegates wore, as well as the specific details of the presentation made by each person.

In honor of the moment when the Constitution was formally adopted, most of the original chairs have been placed in the exact position they were in during the time of the delegation. One may view reenactments of the delegation made in strict accordance with the minutes. These people tell all as it was described and do not attend to any notions of "political correctness" or later government intent to keep the public from knowing the truth by twisting the facts (unless the original record was distorted even during its initial transcription, which seems unlikely).

The Concerns and Corruption

In the end, even those who were rigid in their belief that centralized rule of government, with the states and the people subordinate, were convinced that moderating that stance would be best for the nation at large; but even so, with the checks and balances developed and written into law, there was a catch. Most of the delegates who favored rule by the people also favored true *democratic* rule by the people. The catch was that the nation would be divided up into voting districts, and that specific districts were to be represented by a single publicly-elected official, versus a direct plebiscite of any sort.

This was part of the compromise required to gain acceptance for the checks and balances in the first place, since half of the delegates did not want

---

1 https://en.wikipedia.org/wiki/Thomas_Jefferson
2 Known as the Great Compromise, or the Constitution itself born from a series of compromises. https://en.wikipedia.org/wiki/Connecticut_Compromise

any form of hard, impartial check to be placed on the arm of government authority.[1]

However, from the very beginning it was well understood that this "representative" could be bribed, since high level government officials and representatives of the corporations, who also were aligned with the wealthy business gentry, could easily afford to pay off the officially-endorsed "people's representative" to pass laws that would favor corporate endeavor at the expense of the same people who voted them into office!

These bribes, of course, were never publicly known as such, but were known by a number of political euphemisms such as campaign loans, campaign contributions, miscellaneous appropriation funds, rainy day funds, even public education funds at the state level, public works funds, and the list could go on and on. In our own modern day and age, we could also throw in the social security fund, the Medicare and Medicaid funds into which money is appropriated from anonymous sources, and so on, since so much has been extracted from these funds to support high end corporate and government self serving intentions that the people on the ground will never know about.

As a contemporary example, out of the blue, the IRS hit my wife with an automatic extortion of $400 a month, directly from her pay check, for over two years, with no precedent. We traced it back after missing work, going to their office and waiting hours just to speak with an inflexible official who treated us both like we were criminals; and finally, after weeks of trying, we discovered the truth. The IRS had made a mistake!

They said we did not owe the money and were kind enough to even give us a statement on official letterhead stating so. That meant that they, or her state government agency of employment, owed us $10,000! Needless to say, we are still waiting, years later, for the refund.

In short, the US *does not* have a democratic government, to everyone's shock and surprise. Every school history text has told us that we have a deity-ordained democratic government from the very beginning, but the shocking truth is that we don't! We actually have a representative republican government, but few anywhere dare to mention the fact of it.

Furthermore, if it has been deemed by the legislative branch of government[2] that certain states or communities do not have enough delegates to give thorough representation in any presidential election, then the vote goes to the *Electoral College*, specially selected (not *elected*) delegates who hold the final say in any bid for presidential election. Keep in mind that when

---

1 https://en.wikipedia.org/wiki/The_Federalist_Papers, the Federalists did not believe in a bill of rights

2 We have no way to determine if the need really existed or was manufactured simply to hand the vote over to the Electoral College.

enough money is passed, *anything* is possible, and the rest is a masquerade. It is very possible that presidential candidates may be literally *"purchased"* by corporate interests via the Electoral College, and other avenues.[1]

There have been cases where the nationwide vote gave one candidate a winning margin of 100,000 votes, only to be over-ruled by the Electoral College. While it might require a high-security clearance and exclusive personal government contacts to track down the details, common sense logic betrays the obvious: someone with enormous influence, or some corporation(s), must have played a huge part in that. The person who actually took the seat of president was *most definitely* the champion of certain families[2] the ultimate owners of the huge corporate conglomerates.[3]

Money gets what money wants, and we live in a system designed from the very beginning to allow such to be so. It was part of the original Constitutional delegates' compromise. I offer these modern day examples just to demonstrate how the public and historical direction is still affected by the decisions made over 200 years ago.

Because of the power found in collective funding, the public should always raise questions when the people *demand* one move, and the government literally *forces* another.[4]

Don't the Tenth Amendment and the Preamble in the Declaration of Independence state that the federal government is delegated its authority **by the states** and the **consent of the governed**, not the other way around? Who does the authority in question represent? Who is it that stands to benefit from luring the majority of the public into believing the false message? Whose payroll are their spokes-people on, who are entrusted with the task of justifying the promulgated conclusion?

The motivations behind this, like anything else, are self serving for someone on one level or another. When we set out to analyze the situation, just follow the money trail (like the Yellow Brick Road) to see where that great Wizard sits to manipulate, and the question of *how* it's done is soon revealed.

Life on the Home Front

After the Revolution, things went along more or less as usual, except that Great Britain had ceased to ship goods into the colonies, obviously

1 https://en.wikipedia.org/wiki/Al_Gore

2 http://www.tetrahedron.org/articles/new_world_order/bush_nazis.html

3 http://www.rense.com/general14/bushsformer.htm

4 Two examples readily come to mind: "Wisconsin to join U.S. healthcare lawsuit, says Walker". Westlawnews.thomson.com. Retrieved2012-03-29; and http://www.cnn.com/2015/06/26/politics/supreme-court-same-sex-marriage-ruling.

hoping to punish the colonists. However, this just made the colonists find or create alternatives, or simply make do without. Outside of the established port towns and cities, most people had been doing without much in the way of imported or fine manufactured goods anyway. This experience is where the term "Yankee" was born, or "Yankee Doodle" as he was known in many jurisdictions. Both terms were originally British epithets, referring to a country bumpkin, but the colonists re-purposed them to mean a self-sufficient and resourceful person who doesn't need to be coddled.

Basically life assumed the picture of late eighteenth and early nineteenth century farm life over the wide panorama of the nation, but in other areas, some different developments were occurring. In the Southeastern states, specifically, families had been acquiring huge landed estates and many were building themselves a lifestyle of solid, elegant wealth. Slave labor, unfortunately, was universal throughout the United States, but in the Southeast primarily, where it was particularly profitable. In the Northeast, the growing season was limited and most farms very not so large; families and a few hired hands might be able to manage them. However, slave labor was used to a greater degree than Americans realize, in timbering, ship building, iron yards, brick making and so forth, as well as on some farms; but nowhere near to the degree that they were used on sunny Southern plantations. That being said, in the year 1800 slaves made up less than 20% of the US population (just over 5 million total) and it went down from there. The situation in the Caribbean was another story.

In the Southeast, a person with nothing but the clothes on his back could simply live in a camp situation, and save any money earned by selling the surplus of what he grew, caught or produced. Taxes were minimal and food could be found all around him in many instances. He might invest in land, then begin working his way up by farming a few acres himself. He would then invest in more farm land and then, finally, in slaves once his estate became too much for him to handle alone. By this means, and not only by inherited wealth, huge estates were constructed from "out of nothing," or "thin air" as the saying goes.

Children were raised with the virtue of improving upon what the generation before them left. Most married and moved back onto the estate, if they were male. The females married and moved off with their new husbands, which was why it was so important not to marry beneath one's own economic status. Usually the man added a room to the house to accommodate his new family, especially the children, as they grew older. Such was the way that huge country mansions were developed, beginning with nothing but a great idea, a willingness to work, and raw determination to succeed.

In those days there was no income tax at all and the real estate tax was minimal. In short, there were very few officially imposed limits on the natural desire to excel financially. One's only limitations were those of nature, as the original Constitution had intended. That being said, however, the pervasive corrupting hunger for power and a regular eternal source of revenue could not be kept at bay for long.

The First Transgression—The Whiskey Rebellion

The "Whiskey Rebellion" is the colorful name given to the first noteworthy case of heavy-handed control in the interest of big business. The federal government needed to raise money to pay off debts incurred during the Revolution. Alexander Hamilton, the original corporate hack, was head of the treasury. And when it comes to corrupting power, the devil is in how the tax was structured. A tax was instituted, to be paid out either in coin or by the gallon, but the rate favored paying in cash. Large corporate distilleries in the East sought to dominate the whiskey market at the expense of smaller distillers, when in fact whiskey was the only cash product some areas could produce. The trend began in the east and moved westward. The large distilleries could hand over cash, but the small backwoods distillery[1] could only pay in kind. Many farmers in the back country had very little coin to begin with, so whiskey effectively was their medium of exchange. In their eyes, this tax appeared to be intended to pay off other people's debts anyway, and it amounted to an income tax.

At least part of the resistance to this tax, as others before it, was stirred up by the way that that tax collection was enforced. One tax collection official was George Clymer. Clymer basically played the locals for fools, haphazardly disguising himself and threatening the locals in an effort to intimidate them into compliance,[2] some of the same fallacies attributable to the British in their tax collection methodology. Of course, his ruse didn't fool many, nearly landing him head first in some really deep kimchi at the conclusion of events.

Another individual named General John Neville had vowed to enforce the tax at all costs, no matter what the plebeian response. He was owner of a substantial distillery and more than likely had political connections as well. In the beginning, he had opposed the tax, but when he saw the advantage to be gained by eliminating the competition, he quickly changed his mind. In August 1792 he rented a room in Pittsburgh for his tax office, but the landlord turned him out after being threatened with violence by the Mingo Creek Association.[3] It seems that the tactics for resistance changed from

---

1 Slaughter, 148; Hogeland, 69
2 Slaughter, 125–27
3 Hogeland, 97, 102

only targeting the tax collectors to targeting anyone associated with them; all observances being splendid analogies to make note of here, as far as this author is concerned.

John Neville became the main target. He was a prominent politician, a large scale distiller, and was in charge of collecting revenue for the newly formed American government. This individual was about as close to being a member of the local aristocracy as any person could get[1]. He arrived in the area of Pittsburgh with a US marshal, bearing the intent of forcing the locals to comply with the order to pay and intending to round up those who refused to do so, forcibly taking them to the nearest courthouse. His association with the large distilleries is what led Neville to become such a hated a target. Not only was he shot at, but some five hundred protesters assailed upon his estate, *Bower Hill*, burning it to the ground; and there were other nearly identical incidents, such as the experiences of a collector named Wells.[2]

The end result was that 13,000 militiamen were sent out by Washington to quell the rebellion. All of the insurgents prudently went back home, giving up the fight—with the exception of minor pockets of resistance. After all, avoiding the tax outright was much easier and made much more sense than fighting about it on a field of battle against well organized federal troops. In course of the next six years, 175 small distillery owners in Kentucky were indicted for not paying the tax, according to the court records,[3] and there were numerous court records of resistance in other places.

No one really knows how many small distillers refused to pay the tax and got away with it, but in this author's opinion official numbers probably only represent about 5% of those who refused to pay up. In this case, going home and simply ignoring the tax altogether was the wisest move.

This rebellion against taxation was a pivotal event in US history. The young republic had barely begun its existence when the forces of wealth and corporate power commenced to impose their demands upon the public, targeting specific isolated, relatively politically powerless people. Many whiskey-makers managed to slide out from under this one, but already the message was being broadcast: *You little people labor to pay OUR bills, contenting yourselves with working in OUR enterprises, and let us sit back to reap the golden rewards from your efforts. The playing field is ours alone, and you live only to serve us...* This is *our* land, and you plebeians had better be satisfied just to exist in it!

---

1 https://en.wikipedia.org/wiki/John_Neville_(general)
2 http://www.saylor.org/site/wp-content/uploads/2011/03/Whiskey-Rebellion.
pdf, page 3
3 Rorabaugh, W.J. *The Alcoholic Republic: An American Tradition*, 1979. Oxford University Press, 53.

The Transgression Continues—Northwest Indian War

At nearly the same time, the US government had begun to impose its authority on certain other independent groups inside its own territory. That is how the US corporate-backed government has worked, all the way through its history, even to this very day. The confrontation with the Branch Davidians in Waco, TX, illustrates one aspect of this inclination.[1] The nationwide campaign to prevent people from opting out of public utilities and avoiding inspections and permits and other intrusions is another.[2]

The next incident in our history was called the "Northwest Indian War." According to the official history, the French, and certain Indian tribes together with the British, had already fought over this territory for over a hundred years. In the end, the British held claim along with the tribes, who were virtually granted autonomy under British rule. A notation made by this author is that by the time of this conflict, the area was not yet officially under American rule. A series of conflicts came out of this incident in which the Americans did not fare well at all. The indigenous tribes won huge victories in the beginning. In the conclusion, however, they were forced to sign a treaty that ceded to the US government [3]an area that now contains several entire states. Why was this war fought? Why the use of force, when negotiation could possibly have secured a much better deal?[4] The real answers to these questions we shall learn by reviewing future events of a strikingly similar nature.

These indigenous people were free and independent, living according to their own traditions and laws. Many of these tribesmen had personal trade relations with both the British and other native tribes, on US soil and Canadian soil as well, outside of government control. Not only did the US government wish to own the land these native people were using, they wanted to have a hand in any transactions (at that time, primarily trading furs). By isolating the tribes on specific, finite parcels of land, controlling their food sources, giving them cloth and trading coveted goods to them on highly favorable (for the traders) terms, US government traders—working for large corporations—were able to establish a new market that benefited both the government and the corporations by eliminating competition from outside agents, such as the British, for example.

---

1 https://en.wikipedia.org/wiki/Waco_siege - Controversies section. At the trial, Government officials claimed that the metal door that proved the ATF had initiated the assault *"mysteriously"* had been lost.
2 http://www.al.com/entertainment/index.ssf/2013/08/history_channel_mountain_man_s.html
3 https://en.wikipedia.org/wiki/Treaty_of_Greenville
4 https://en.wikipedia.org/wiki/William_Penn

Not only that, but the land of these tribes had not been *officially* surveyed, making acquisition perfectly "legal," or rather, legal enough, for whoever were the first people to conduct the survey. Understandably, once the "first Americans" got used to these trade goods (especially iron pots, ax blades, cloth, knives and guns), they quickly considered them indispensable, eventually even forgetting the skills of producing goods outside of the trading system. Thus the intrusion of federal traders virtually made the Native Americans *enslaved consumers* living at the complete mercy of the corporation and government, a great lesson for modern-day Americans. And keep in mind as we view our lesson in history, *what is pushed as "progress" may actually be designed to enslave.*[1]

This identical intent to control the people at their own expense soon became self-evident in the economic policies of the federal government. Alexander Hamilton, who steadfastly backed the interests of big business, designed a central bank that foresaw the use of a centralized currency with no other entity having the authority to control how much currency was being issued.—Each state was producing its own currency up to this point.

This was to be a bank owned by the federal government which would issue loans, manage currency and do the general things that banks do. In honor of the Federalist agenda, this bank would operate without outside checks and balances, allowing the government to rule financially and without any concern for the interests of the plebeians. And government would be free to raise taxes through tariffs on imported goods and liquor.

The First True Citizen Hero

Thomas Jefferson (second Vice President 1797–1801; third President 1801–1809) had no desire to see a national or central bank/centralized currency, fearing that it would lead to corruption. Jefferson believed that any central bank should be kept on a leash by having checks and balances to prevent corruption; otherwise, the natural tendency would be to evolve toward outright usury. Remember, *the US Constitution does not mention the idea of a central bank in any way.*

He also feared that large well-organized foreign entities would eventually dominate the bank to control all business enterprise on American soil. He idealized independent free-thinkers supported by their own economy and compared the alternative to servants, or contract workers who were bound lifelong in debt to the company store.

---

1 http://www.nationofchange.org/make-no-mistake-you-are-american-debt-slave-1389886420; also, http://www.raptitude.com/2010/07/your-lifestyle-has-already-been-designed/; and http://kfor.com/2015/04/22/automakers-fighting-to-prevent-car-owners-from-working-on-their-own-vehicles/

George Washington had intended to remain neutral on this issue, so the official account goes, but he wound up giving most of his support to Federalist policy in the end. George Washington worked in the name of big money and the corporation's desires to dominate. Washington's actions during the Whiskey Rebellion more than revealed where his heart lay.[1] This author contends that Washington's family had access to a level of wealth on par with many in the British aristocracy, and as a lad growing up in Virginia he had access to many aristocratic accommodations

Federalist aims continued to reign supreme until the election of Thomas Jefferson in 1800, but those who endorsed Federalist policies had been in the driver's seat for three presidential terms already, backed and supported by the corporations. When Jefferson took office, the opposing forces were already aimed against him, although we must admire Jefferson's genius in navigating to push the virtues of individualism in spite of Federalist/ corporate domination of the governing house. Much as it pains me to say it, however, I cannot deny that there were corporatist undertones even in the actions of Jefferson. Even the most determined intellectuals are forced to concede in the face of rising power, no matter what its intent. The only exception would be one of a perfect altruistic self-sacrifice on the altar of Liberty, a splendid exemplification of the patriotic call to live free or die, forever free!

Examine Jefferson's policy of exploring the territory of what amounted to the Louisiana Purchase, in search of a Northwest Passage to the Pacific Ocean, as a first example. If such had been discovered, trade and commerce would have been greatly improved. Quite likely, Jefferson intended to place some sort of checks and balances on how corporations would have conducted affairs in use of such a passage; yet over time, that system of checks would have deteriorated with the election of other presidents with other loyalties, and their personal cabinets with their alliances. And this was seen years later from the Lewis and Clark expedition and the presidency of Jefferson.

One of Jefferson's most admirable positions was that he felt a strong need to eliminate national debt. He insisted that it only facilitated corruption, deterioration of all other areas in general, eventually climaxing in revolt of the masses. He felt that a nation could exist perfectly well without running up a national debt, a belief that ran completely contrary to that of the Federalists (who, after all, were servants of corporate interests, including centralization of a currency with a value dictated by government elites). Jefferson believed that government could function in absence of taxation, obtaining revenue solely through customs duties and other fees.

---

1 He was primarily of British gentry descent and he inherited most of his wealth, Alden (1993, pp. 3–4).

Jefferson also decreased the size of the military, correctly asserting that maintaining a huge standing military would unnecessarily drain the resources of the nation.[1] *He felt that an armed citizenry could more than adequately repel any foreign forces.* There is also a risk of corruption from within, among those in high government, backed by corporate interests, who might endeavor to use a large standing national army against the very people who had voted them into power. Wasn't that what the British had done?

Jefferson was attuned to the dangers of corruption. He was highly suspicious of judges who were appointed by those who preceded them. Such a practice could only promote a system of patronage and cronyism, eventually leading to corruption that would spread until virtual serfdom was forced upon the population. As an antidote to some of these risks, he advocated the Bill of Rights which, he argued, would give power to the judiciary for them to analyze one another, taking specific action when the facts suggested and supported doing so.

Jefferson also argued to strike down the Judiciary Act[2] that had founded a strong federal court system. He objected to the tendency of the courts to fill the bench with life-time appointed Federalist judges. Such appointments, with their salaries included, were very expensive to maintain, so abolishing them would save the nation much needed revenue. Abolishing the permanent appointment of Federalist judges also led Jefferson in his fight against development of Hamilton's First Bank of the United States.

Let's hold in mind that Jefferson was very obviously concerned, consciously and subconsciously, to ward off the development of tyranny in the future. One of the ways that a tyranny comes to power is by controlling a nation's money, giving it the power to dictate prices and forcing the population into debt via centralized banks owned either directly by government officials or indirectly via people allied with government officials.[3,4]

On this note, let's examine the specifics of Jefferson's battle with the First Bank of the United States. Jefferson led the argument that the bank was unconstitutional, in that it would serve the interests of merchants and investors at the expense of the majority of the population. In other words, it would serve the interests of large business enterprises and wealthy people at the expense of the average people. Keep in mind that those who made up the Federalist Party were primarily the sons and daughters of large corporate owners and government elites, so it would only be natural for them to seek

---

1 A primary maxim in Sun Tzu's "The Thirteen Chapters" or "The Art of War."
2 https://en.wikipedia.org/wiki/Judiciary_Act_of_1789
3 http://www.forbes.com/sites/jimpowell/2013/02/05/how-dictators-come-to-power-in-a-democracy/
4 http://beforeitsnews.com/economics-and-politics/2013/06/how-money-drives-the-cycle-of-tyranny-2454186.html

to allow themselves absolute control of the nation's currency and the liberty to dictate its value.

Jefferson also objected to the development of a national mint. He and his Cabinet believed that local banks local banks could serve as a counterweight to centralization, putting the brakes on possible corruption from a single faction having absolute control. They felt that having a national mint solely responsible for generating money was dangerous to a sound monetary system and was most beneficial to business interests in those areas of the nation [1]that were already well developed commercially—specifically in the Northeast, by the way. It would certainly not be in the interests of the nation's productive landed estates, in the South or even what was then considered the West. They argued that the very right to own property would be infringed by catering to these corporate interests, an idea that time has more than validated. The development of a national bank was also unconstitutional, since the Constitution stated specifically that Congress was to regulate weights and measure to issue coin money, rather than mint notes and bills of credit [2]that could be inflated and deflated to the benefit of the elitist few running the centralized bank and their corporate-backed government-insider connections.

To understand how this centralization of currency in the form of a national bank would threaten basic property ownership, read a statement from Wesley's PDF, notated in the footnotes at the bottom of this page:

The context in which these debates were going on was quite specific. The government had borrowed from, or run up debts to, the citizens to fund the War for Independence. Now, in an age when most people had little cash at all, many average people, former soldiers for instance, could not afford to wait; they had to collect what was owed sooner, rather than later, even if it meant accepting a steep discount. Enter the group of financiers led by Robert Morris. They created the Bank of North America, which agitated successfully for debt-holders to be repaid at par. But many of these debt-holders had only recently purchased the debt from the original, smaller debt-holders, at a significant discount from par—precisely in anticipation of such an outcome. The politically-connected insiders made fortunes as their distressed assets were suddenly revalued by political fiat.

In other words, land speculators could purchase land at discount, sell it at that presumed rate, and then revalue the mortgage on a different scale of repayment. This inevitably led to eventual foreclosure, with the land being

---

1 http://www.mmisi.org/ir/45_1-2/westley.pdf
2 Westley, Christopher (Fall 2010). ""The Debate Over Money Manipulations: A Short History"(PDF). *Intercollegiate Review* 45 (1-2): 3-11. Retrieved February 28, 2011.

reclaimed by the same banking interests who had sold it to begin with. Then they could repeat the process and make a fortune in doing so.

This was one of the principles at work even in the earliest days of our nation! If we read a bit farther down in Wesley's PDF, we can see where the same policy was prevalent during the 2008 economic downturn:

> Such policies did not simply begin during the financial crisis of 2008, which was characterized by holders of various forms of mortgage debt being similarly paid off at par due to political interventions in defiance of market forces. In both instances, we witness an example of a class of people who benefit from money creation and who will therefore agitate for the establishment of institutions that maintain such practices, together with a counter-class that does not benefit from the inflation and, in fact, is compelled to pay for it in the form of higher prices.

History affects the present generation in more ways than the average American can even imagine. Before we continue with the story of Jefferson's presidency, let's read on in Wesley PDF to learn of the bill's most immediate outcome when the First Bank of the United States was formed:

> The bank immediately began inflating, to the extent that producer prices rose at an annual rate of 7 to 12 percent a year for its first six years of existence. This inflation, which financed spending on military programs and interest on existing debt, had the effect of enlarging the number of classes that came to depend on government inflation and benefit from it. The bond between monetary and foreign policies has roots running to the founding of the nation.

The bill to establish the bank passed in the first house, but floundered in the second house. One of the more interesting challenges made was by James Madison, declaring "that all powers not endowed to the Congress are retained by the people or state authorities." Madison also ventured to say that if Congress had been intended to have such power, then the original authors of the Constitution would have clearly stated it. But Hamilton argued that the idea of a centralized bank was *not ruled out* by the Constitution, and he asserted that the Constitution applied to non-person entities in the same manner that it did to individual persons! (This presaged the highly contentious Supreme Court ruling in 2010 that extended the concept of "corporate personhood" to allow corporations to make political campaign contributions, that is, to buy elections.) In the end, the person with the final word was George Washington[1,2], an ardent Federalist, and the bill was ultimately signed into law.

Even at this early point in US history we can see that corporate interests were given priority at the expense of the individual. George Washington, the high commander of the Patriot army during the American Revolution, fought in the name of individual liberty against what was essentially a corporate tyranny working its ways via government-imposed laws. But once the British Crown was out, he now favored corporate interests, even while acting as the superior authority within the new system.

While Jefferson understood the importance of corporate development to the development of the national economy, he also strongly believed that a system of checks and balances would be necessary to safeguard against excesses. Corporate power inevitably rubs up against the rights of individuals, up to and including the basic Constitutional right to *own property*—that includes land and other resources. Even in the early days of government, wealthy individuals and big business enterprises were clearly stated in their intentions to *dominate* the progress of government, without a doubt aiming to eventually dictate many aspects of the daily lives of the citizens, to their own extortionist advantage, at some point in the future.

To further give explanation with far closer relevance here, as well as to explain Jefferson's concerns in regard to defending the common man from possible future tyranny, let's look at Wesley, page 7:

> The appeal of monetary inflation is obvious to political classes that must be able to redistribute wealth in order to remain in power. Modern governments have only three methods of finance: taxation, debt, and inflation. All three encompass the problems associated with wealth redistribution, in that resources are expropriated from private hands for the use of public bureaus that carry with them significantly different incentive effects, as well as the problems associated with the introduction of extra-market force to ensure that redistribution occurs.

As we can clearly see here, the policy of corporate initiative endeavoring to establish control, for their own profit, still holds its head high after more than 200 years, right in the face of a new nation heralded as the home of individual liberty.

Reclaiming the boundaries of America for corporate exploitation by newly formed American corporations and their old European corporate

---

1 Alden (1993, pp. 3–4)
2 Washington was of primarily English gentry descent, https://en.wikipedia. org/wiki/George_Washington, early years.

allies appears to have been an unspoken objective of those actors behind the scenes who used Patriots to wangle this land out of Crown control. The problem for the corporate interests and their allies was that the new group of land-owners already felt that they had a rightful heritage to unfettered freedom secured by a timeless, inviolable Constitution. (Obviously, I refer here to the citizens of the new nation, made up of immigrants and the children of immigrants, not the original Native Americans who were, in fact, increasingly insignificant from a political standpoint.)

Now we can begin to observe the manner in which corporate interest has prevailed all throughout the history of America, from the earliest beginning right on up through the reign of the third president, who in fact was the first real hero of the American people at large, no matter what his critics might say.[1]

Jefferson had strong influence in Congress and strong backing, but still he did not have the power to overcome the interests of banking and its big business cooperatives. The bill for establishment of the First Bank of the United States was signed into law by none other than the ambitious George Washington, who worked to establish himself as a member of the wealthy landed gentry. Acting in defense of multinational aristocratic interests would have been natural for Washington. Remember that establishment of the First Bank of the United States really was designed to centralize all US currency so it could be controlled by one power group.

Centralization of currency thus bore the heavy possibility of future corruption. The only method of eliminating this obtrusive possibility of future abuse would be to set some limits on the decision-making of that group. The primary means for limiting the possibilities for such abuse would be the requirement that the values stated on banknotes be supported by an equal value in gold, held in reserve.

The problem with checks and balances, however, is that the elite who stood to accrue all the benefits from the system understood they would be hampered by such a system. The only valid check would be a system of alternative currencies for states and individuals to fall back upon, when the

---

1 The wide publicity given to the fact of his having a Creole concubine can be considered in view of the common use of a negative appeal to emotion to tarnish a person's reputation. This should bear no relevance to the esteem he earned by his concerns regarding liberty of the plebeian masses, his contributions to the Constitution or the sacrifices that he made for them. While the facts do bear the conclusion that Hemings was indeed Jefferson's concubine, the DNA evidence was only present in a single line of Hemings' direct descendants, the cross with the Jefferson line traced to occur some forty years after Thomas Jefferson's death. The suggested conclusion in this author's observation is that no children between Sally Hemings and Thomas Jefferson ever existed; the fact of such a possibility remains inconsequential in his celebration, and overblowing this circumstance is a crude tactic used to diminish his anticipated reverence..

value of a primary currency abruptly dropped or when the people lost faith in it, whether by design or simply as a result of movements of economics in general.

Present-Day Examples in Reflection

A fine present day example of establishing a check on national banking can be seen with the State of Texas, which moved to demand its gold back from the Federal Reserve in 2013 and initiated the production of its own currency in silver[1],[2], as we shall discuss later on. Many other states are contemplating the same sort of move, but the forces aligned to prevent that are overwhelmingly strong.

It is the contention of this author that such moves as those initiated in Texas are valid and perfectly legal but will be seen as the seeds of a future political conflict, one that may turn into a serious physical confrontation between the people and huge corporate-backed banking interests (CBBI), since the CBBI are the ones who stand to lose the most if this goes through.

One solution would be for corporate and government interests to simply admit that the off-shoring of the US production base was an experiment that damaged the US economy to an unsustainable extent, even while it did create a new (very small) class of super-wealthy families. Reversing this policy would be tantamount to an indictment of the US corporate banking-backed approach in its entirety. [3]

Why doesn't the Fed promote the individual's right to engage in free business enterprise by supporting a looser regime of regulation combined with a real *tax reduction* incentive (or do away with the income tax altogether) in lieu of allowing large corporations to relocate offshore? There must be a self serving reason for this.

One of the main points in this text is to explain why such a conflict may be in the offing. When mild-mannered street protests fail to make an impression, desperate citizens may find a way to finally get their voices heard; but when the power actually feels threatened, that is when history has seen thousands of citizens lined up in front of the "big guns." In that kind of conflict, the entire society is in jeopardy, not just a single group or specific minority groups. In such times, anyone who can be accused of having dared to resist in any manner, intellectually or physically, becomes a target.

This was the kind of danger that inspired our ancestors to declare their commitment to *live free or die, forever free!*

---

1 http://www.cbsnews.com/news/texas-law-first-state-gold-bullion-depository-federal-reserve/

2 http://money.cnn.com/2012/02/03/pf/states_currencies/

3 https://www.thetrumpet.com/article/6456.24.118.0/europe/germany/resurrecting-the-holy-roman-empire-of-the-german-nation

The ability to adhere to this guidance is limited since Americans have already long been victims of self serving, callous deception designed to manipulate. Let's examine just *how* the wicked wave continued to swell, as it prepared to move against the people and their Constitution.

Madison, A Turncoat Follower

With the election of James Madison (President 1809–1817), originally a Federalist, he seemingly changed his stance, aligning with the great intellectual Jefferson and his view that checks and balances were needed in all authoritative affairs of government. While Madison opposed the reinstatement of the First Bank of the United States for the purpose of financing the War of 1812, he reinstated the charter in 1816 upon its demise following twenty years of existence. Conventional history tells us that the presidency of Madison was hallmarked by Jeffersonian concerns and policies, while few dare point out the relevance of Madison's last act while in office, which was to veto the *Bonus Bill of 1817*.[1]

Provisions in this bill would have allowed for development in the Western states of roads and general infrastructure financed by tolls and individually collected fees. States dominated by banking and corporate interests feared that creating a system of accommodation to travelers would drain both manpower and economic resources away from states already under corporate control and the lording arm of what amounted to the first national bank. Some may still attempt to argue that the veto truly was an act in the best interests of the entire nation, but questions arise when we look at Madison's publication that soon followed.

Madison published a report entitled "Views of the President of the United States On Internal Improvements[2]." In this report he declared that Congress had the power to appropriate public funds at its own discretion. In his own contention, the president had no power to question any Congressional appropriation of funds. Simply speaking, if corporate and banking interests held sway over the Congress, then Congress was in its rights to tax citizens and appropriate funds however it chose to do so.

So in the end, Madison returned to his original loyalties, that is, to the banks backed by the corporations and their elites. Take notice as well that Henry Clay's *American System*[3] (which reflected renewed nationalism after the War of 1812) was flagrantly endorsed by Madison, and it played a prominent role in US internal policy during the early years of the nineteenth century. This benefitted primarily the corporate and banking headquarters

1 https://en.wikipedia.org/wiki/Bonus_Bill_of_1817
2 http://www.presidency.ucsb.edu/ws/?pid=66323
3 https://en.wikipedia.org/wiki/American_System_(economic_plan)

in the industrialized sections of the nation, by promoting the Federalist policy of centralized currency and development via the issuance of currency to contractors from the industrialized areas of the nation.

Both the West and the South objected to its provisions, obviously seeing no financial benefit to themselves. This regional conflict of interests did not go away.

Monroe, No Friend of Natives

James Monroe (President 1817–1825) continued the same anti-Federalist, pro-Jeffersonian plan of moderating the rule of government via checks and balances. However, some of Monroe's policies in regard to Native American land rights most definitely raise eyebrows today. Upon acquisition of Florida from Spain, rather than seeking to accommodate the Native Americans there as new fellow citizens, he labeled them as being in the way of progress (as he saw it). He had other designs for the land that these people possessed, and those plans had to do with accommodating the interests of banking and the corporations. Madison faced little opposition since the Native Americans had no political influence anyway, of course.

The Panic of 1819

A "highlight" of the Monroe Presidency is an event known as the panic of 1819. The issue of centralized currency via the establishment of the First Bank of the United States, and the fears of Jefferson concerning the manipulation of such currency when in the hands of an elite few, came to the fore. This panic was an economic crash that came about due to excessive speculation in public lands, fueled by the unrestrained issue of paper money.[1] In other words, the bank intentionally flooded the market with "easy money," inducing people to invest in real estate on mortgage; then when interest rates went up the banks foreclosed on the loans, and the land prices collapsed. Then "big money" scooped it up, and when prices started to recover, they sold it again.

A few direct quotes give a better grasp of what was going on:

> The Second Bank of the United States (BUS), itself deeply enmeshed in these inflationary practices[2], sought to compensate for its laxness in regulating the state bank credit market by initiating a sharp curtailment in loans by its western branches, beginning in 1818.[3] Failing to provide Metallic currency when presented with

---

1 Malone, 1960, p. 416-417, Wilentz, 2008, p. 206, Dangerfield, 1965, p. 87
2 Malone, 1960, p. 416, Dangerfield, 1965, p. 12-13, p. 86, Wilentz, 2008, p. 206-207
3 Ammon, 1971, p. 465, p. 466, Dangerfield, 1965, p. 82-83

their own banknotes by the BUS, the state-chartered banks began foreclosing on the heavily mortgaged farms and business properties they had financed.[1] The ensuing financial panic, in conjunction with a sudden recovery in European agricultural production in 1817[2] led to widespread bankruptcies and mass unemployment.[3]

Was this panic by accident or was it by design? A quick examination of the events leading up to this moment suggests the strong possibility that this event *may well have been very intentional.*

This author's personal bet is that the elites in control used the "crash" to pick up some sweet deals in real estate for themselves or their business cronies, or campaign contributors.

I would also contend that corporate interests were not satisfied with Monroe's simply giving them unchecked access to certain lands formerly held by the Native Americans. Their ramped up greed knew no end; they wanted that and much more, in the form of prime real estate. Not only did the centralized bank move to intentionally crash the economy so their corporate partners could lay their hands on prime real estate at rock bottom price, this move was also done in an effort to intimidate the President himself into simply allowing these interests to take whatever it was that they desired, any Constitutional rights of plebeians be damned!

John Quincy Adams: A Hero of the Infected Collusion

The administration of John Quincy Adams (1825–29) is certainly worthy of close examination, for here we find very strong evidence to support the contention of corruption at a high level, at the expense of the ordinary citizens. Here, when citizens had lost property such as farms, small land plots and small business property, we have what appears to be large scale property investment going on. Apparently once the currency had been inflated by over-producing bills, there arose a sudden desire to purchase property and develop roads.

The claim of systematic purchase due to currency manipulation is proven by the fact that Adams had endorsed a wide range of internal improvements and embraced the "American System"[4] that we described earlier on. As readers may recall, the American System was embraced by the Federalists who desired that Government act largely in absence of any checks and balances. This system, so appealing to corporate interests, was only applauded in those areas where corporations were headquartered. For the most part,

1 Malone, 1960, p. 416-417, Hofstadter, 1948, p. 50
2 Parsons, 2009, p. 59, Ammon, 1991, online source
3 Wilentz, 2008, p. 208, p. 216, Dangerfield, 1965, p. 82, p. 84, p. 85
4 https://en.wikipedia.org/wiki/American_System_(economic_plan)

in the other areas of the nation, individual interests took precedence, and rather than manufacturing and trade corporations there were enterprises that controlled vast tracts of vacant land, or mineral resources and other natural resources.

This dichotomy was already separating America into two factions. *The First Party System* descended directly out of the Federalist Party and labored on behalf of corporate interests. *The Second Party System* descending from the efforts of Jefferson, who believed in advancement of business and government but not without checks and balances to secure the Constitutional rights of the citizens. The second group was the one embraced by artisans of individual enterprise, particularly in the sections of the nation not dominated by the banks and large corporations.

Some of the areas accessed and controlled by government office[1], the First Party System and its policies; were the Ohio and Cumberland Road area, The Chesapeake and Ohio Canal.[2] the Chesapeake and Delaware Canal, Louisville and Portland Canal, Falls of the Ohio and the connection of the Great Lakes to the Ohio River System. Massive construction projects were organized in these areas and obviously to the profit of a specific few.

As mentioned earlier, this author finds it just too striking to be mere coincidence: the huge construction projects initiated in previously undeveloped areas, coming on the heels of a massive *inflation/deflation* that followed the development of a central bank. The facts supported Jefferson's view, and the scenario all played out promptly. The very fact that such a sequence of events could take place in direct succession, even inside of the official mainstream historical account, points to the cause and effect. The only difference in this account and the official one, right along with most mainstream records, is that here we extend just the barest intuitive insight in order to read the writing.

There is another major sign that corporate interests were being served in the election of John Quincy Adams. He did not receive a majority of the people's votes. The House of Representatives voted Adams into office, since, according to observation, there were not enough representatives in proportion to population in some areas to constitute a fair vote. At least, that's what was said by those who supported the vote between Adams and Jackson in the first place.[3] Although official proof is hard to come by, common logic strongly suggests that certain interests essentially paid the house delegates for a final decision, should a vote between Jackson and Adams be seen as needing recall. The situation was this. The First and Second Bank of the

1 https://en.wikipedia.org/wiki/General_Survey_Act
2 https://en.wikipedia.org/wiki/Chesapeake_and_Ohio_Canal,   note   the president attending the ground breaking ceremony of C&O canal company
3 https://en.wikipedia.org/wiki/Corrupt_Bargain#Election_of_1824

United States had been established; Jefferson had warned that consolidating control of the currency would invite corruption in a way that favored big money and government collusion; the currency had indeed collapsed and then the country saw the acquisition of huge tracts of land and development projects started that obviously amounted to corporate collaboration. Look at who won in the end, and you might get an idea who set the rules of the game.

Andrew Jackson, who was now in the same position as Jefferson earlier, also stood strong in support of his main constituency, the individual enterprising citizen, and he was all in favor of the individual's freedom of choice. Jackson stood in strong opposition to Adams, who favored big money and open-ended corporate extension via government manipulation at the expense of the civilian population; this fact can be read even in the official history, although such wording has been tactfully cast to the side in favor of more euphemistic language.

The Tariff Act of 1812

For what strongly appears to be the purpose of weakening the economy of individuals who thrived by the virtues of entrepreneurialism and property ownership, John Quincy Adams passed the *Tariff Act of 1812*.[1] This tariff was designed to prevent individual enterprise interests from affecting those of corporation and government, at the expense of individual economic progress in those areas where large corporations had not yet dominated. Other corporate and banking protections were being imposed here as well.

The primary effect of this tariff was that it weakened the economy of the areas controlled by large land holders/individual enterprise practitioners, while it built up the economies of the areas controlled by the large, hungry corporations and consolidated banks. This was done by a tax[2] on products coming in and going out to primarily European nations. This tariff also forced the large land holders to purchase needed goods produced in areas controlled by corporate interests and banks at inflated prices, weakening them economically even more as well as rendering the leadership vulnerable to future exploitation.

This author also senses, as alluded to earlier, that there was a growing government-sponsored corporate reach to take over lands and resources controlled by small yeomen farmers aligned with the large land holders in general. The vast land tracts under individual control in the parts of the nation where the land owners dominated were resource rich and ripe for the taking, especially since those who controlled the corporations also controlled

1 https://en.wikipedia.org/wiki/Tariff_of_Abominations
2 Some elders have claimed as high as fifty percent, according to word passed down to the author

the government and the corrupt financial system. Keep in mind that this negative development *could not occur* with a hard system of valid checks and balances in place, as the great intellectual Jefferson so vehemently advocated.

In response to popular insistence in the areas of large land ownership as well as a blatant refusal to endorse the law imposed in certain states, this tariff was finally reduced in an act entitled *The Compromise Tariff of 1833*,[1] but not without much bitter debate and more sporadic contest, some continuing on for the next twenty years.

Andrew Jackson

The next president of real consequence who came onto the scene was none other than Andrew Jackson (1829–37), whose style was to dominate via raw determination. Andrew Jackson stood on the same ground as Jefferson in the face of a huge and growing banking/corporate conglomerate, what is now known as a *cartel*. Like most cartels, they observed no standard of ethics when it came to imposing its own rules. Any basic rights of the plebeians, Constitutionally given, moral or otherwise, were only to be viewed as impediments. It would be interesting to know how Russians, British or other historians label these financial manipulations in the US currency system.

Even though Jackson was in favor of a system of checks and balances, his actions in regard to Native Americans suggest that *even he* fell under the powerful sway of banking and corporate influence. While Jackson truly did champion the average citizen at large, he allowed government-backed, wealthy, influential individuals and corporations[2] to make gains at the expense of certain American citizens. It was universally accepted as politically correct, at the time, to do so; speaking primarily of the Native American population, who existed on the societal fringes anyway, just like the persecuted did who were labeled as witches in earlier times.

In other words, by his actions Jackson spoke to corporate interests, instructing them to forbear touching the majority of Americans, but when it came to *these* specific categories of Americans, the moneyed interests could simply do as they pleased with them. He well knew that he could get away with doing so and perhaps he had no choice but to give the collusive partners something in return for laying off on the mainstream US population for the time being.

1 https://en.wikipedia.org/wiki/Tariff_of_1833
2 Note as well that Jackson was backed by the Federal government in passage of the law that infringed on native land rights

Adams and Jackson

In sum, Adams had championed Native Americans in the lands of the West, as we know from the official history. His actions angered settlers in the West, no doubt. But these actions also paved the way for future Native American removal in the East, especially the Southeast, territories that were relatively easy to access and that were *part* of the total lands coveted by big money and corporate interests. In other words, Adams *indirectly* supported Native American removal in the Southeast by appearing to give them special recognition and rights in the lands of the West (in a disguised effort to make those lands appealing to the Natives' best interests). The lands in the East broadly speaking, and extremely resource rich South-lands specifically, were highly coveted for development. Official history refuses to recognize that obvious connection. Instead the blame for future removal/repressive actions is placed solely on those who demanded that all banking and corporate endeavors should be subject to some reasonable oversight, some limits set, to protect the citizenry at large.

With the presidency of Jackson, the issue of central banks manipulating the currency reached a much higher plateau. At the beginning of Jackson's presidency, all of the states were still issuing their own currencies, although banking conglomerates were seeking to centralize those currencies into a single national currency. One hallmark of the Jackson administration was his "war on the national banking system," a predecessor of the future Federal Reserve System. Other hallmarks include his highly controversial "Indian policy" and a number of decisions that defined the society of the time and set the course for the future, eventually leading to all-out political and physical war between the two opposing factions.

History as conventionally presented conveniently twists facts, swaying public attention away from the actions of big money, corporations and their government collusion. Then we get the divisive appeal to emotion[1], demonizing slave-holding and placing a negative label on any system supporting of slavery as being obviously and abhorrently immoral (applying social standards retroactively to condemn a practice that was at the time widespread). It so happens that a majority of the individuals who called for checks and balances on corporate and banking endeavors (endeavors which were most developed in the Northeast) also embraced what was then

---

[1] See the above reference to John Quincy Adams

a Constitutionally endorsed right for individuals from any demographic to own slaves, as has been documented many times.[1,2,3]

As revealed within the footnotes immediately above, the reality of the times certainly raises serious questions that demand answering in their proper capacity.

Casual Review of Jackson

Jackson's personality, domestically and abroad, was that of a conquering warrior. He had triumphed personally, rising to above the life of a subsistence farmer, hunter and gather, to that of lawyer, then finally President of the United States. On the battlefield he had won battle after battle, first against the British (as a young lad and as an adult), then the Native Americans, even to the point of crushing the entire Creek confederation.[4]

Presumably Jackson held a conviction that he was always "*right.*" His outstanding self confidence and his anti-Federalist stance alone earned him many enemies who were more than motivated to prove him wrong. More than likely, they went to greater lengths than usual to do so. His hard anti-Federalist, pro-check stance on the banking system (and government in general, by this time), simply aggravated this determination among his opponents. His stance against the banking system, however, was something that even in hindsight stands out as a high-water mark, a view that has been shown valid ever since. The events that followed, during his presidency, more than validate the fear that the currency of the US banking system was being manipulated for the purpose of achieving political and business objectives for an elitist few at the top end of the system, to the detriment of all others.

Even Jackson was influenced by banking and corporate conglomerates. While his presidency was hallmarked by a concern for the welfare of the common man, still he favored nationalism and protested loudly when states questioned corporate-backed banking influence via tariffs and threatened outright secession in response to such usury. We can also detect the interests of corporation and big money in his Indian policies.

As we discussed earlier, James Adams Quincy had already worked to make the lands west of the Mississippi seem appealing to Native interests, to encourage voluntary relocation for as many as possible. His primary intentions were to acquire the vast non-surveyed Southeastern tribal lands

---

1 http://americancivilwar.com/authors/black_slaveowners.htm note that this truth of history is conveniently omitted from the official public record
2 http://www.theroot.com/articles/history/2013/03/black_slave_owners_did_they_exist.3.html
3 http://uncpress.unc.edu/books/T-8697.html
4 See: http://www.ncas.rutgers.edu/center-study-genocide-conflict-resolution-and-human-rights/creek-war

and some in the Northern Midwest, for banking and corporate interests, giving construction contracts to specific government-endorsed contractors and land companies. These construction/contracting companies were owned by congressmen or their very close associates.

Once the government surveyed the lands, the speculators and land companies could purchase these tracts from the government 'in bulk, at excellent discounts. These lands could then be cut up into smaller, but still significant, tracts to be purchased by the developer. This provided a substantial profit for the speculator or land company and even so represented an excellent deal for the developer. The speculators and land companies could also cut these parcels up into tracts for sale to prospective settlers via easy-to-access bank loans (at deceptively high interest rates). Those settlers expected to engage in subsistence farming for the most part, while others had in mind building and maintaining plantations. All of this money came back into the hands of government via campaign appropriations and miscellaneous contributions, which brings us back to the point of Jackson's interest in accommodating these interests without endangering his political constituency among the plebeians at large.

The Natives themselves constituted the only wall that stood in the way of this (and a few caring settlers in the surrounding settlements). All concerned stood to make a substantial profit, except the people/true owners of the land. It is not unreasonable to conclude that state and federal representatives were paid off just to send in the military to forcibly remove the Natives from their own land. Just consider *the Indian Removal* act passed by Congress on May 6, 1830.[2] This bill had many supporters in both the house and the senate.[3]

The Indian Removal Act

To view the influence of banks and corporation on Jackson's decisions regarding Indian Removal, here is a direct quote given by Jackson in Congress:

> Humanity has often wept over the fate of the aborigines of this country and philanthropy has long been busily employed in devising means to avert it, but its progress has never for a moment been arrested,

---

1 Wilson, Woodrow (1905). *Division and Reunion*. Longmans, Green. p. 91.
2 https://en.wikipedia.org/wiki/Indian_Removal_Act
3 Notice how the official history misplaces the primary blame on those who supported checks and balances on banking, corporate and government authority, coming primarily from areas of the nation dominated by individual enterprise and large land holders. Notice the divisive appeal to emotion by tactfully labeling those who hailed from these areas *"slave owners,"* even though owning slaves was a Constitutional right open to all demographic groups, and less than 10% actually did so.

and one by one have many powerful tribes disappeared from the earth. ... But true philanthropy reconciles the mind to these vicissitudes as it does to the extinction of one generation to make room for another.... Philanthropy could not wish to see this continent restored to the condition in which it was found by our forefathers. What good man would prefer a country covered with forests and ranged by a few thousand savages to our extensive Republic, studded with cities, towns, and prosperous farms, embellished with all the improvements which art can devise or industry execute,[1] occupied by more than 12,000,000 happy people, and filled with all the blessings of liberty, civilization, and religion.[2]

For proof that the average subsistence farming settler was against the bill, just take a look at how the bill was audaciously opposed and by whom. Probably David Crockett[3] was the most famous participant here. He was the Representative for the average settler inside his home state of Tennessee during the period under discussion. The state legislators were staunch supporters of checks and balances on government, banking and corporate interests; yet by Crockett's representation and challenge to the Removal Act, he was saying that the overwhelming majority of his fellow citizens were vehemently *against* abuse of the Native people and outright government theft of their tribal land.

I would venture to say that *most* of the Cherokee[4] and even the Five Civilized Tribes were more "family"[5] than opposition to the average subsistence Anglo settler. Their interests largely coincided. The interests served by the Act were not theirs. But as often happens, the official record seeks to displace responsibility for abusive crimes from the guilty onto the innocent.[6]

Another interesting opponent of the bill was Theodore Frelinghuysen, US Senator from New Jersey. He gave a six-hour speech to Congress in opposition of removal. What astounds me is not his opposition to the bill, but what is almost a prophetic message for all "lower class citizens" today:

> Let us beware how, by oppressive encroachments upon the sacred privileges of our Indian neighbors, we minister to the agonies of future remorse.

1 The sentences following the notation betrays the self serving interest in Jackson for development of these lands
2 Columbia University. Retrieved March 21, 2014 "Statements from the Debate on Indian Removal"
3 https://en.wikipedia.org/wiki/Davy_Crockett
4 http://nativeamericannetroots.net/diary/249
5 https://en.wikipedia.org/wiki/John_Ross_(Cherokee_chief)
6 http://www.breitbart.com/big-government/2015/07/11/memphis-city-council-votes-to-dig-up-grave-of-confederate-general-sell-his-statue/

In other words, the laws that endorsed to purloin our Indian neighbors' resources may well be applied to us at a future date. How right he was and how right he will be proven yet again, as we continue to move down the stairway to tyranny in the United States.

It seems to me that by the time of Indian Removal, the forces of banking/corporate/government collusion were so great that Jackson had *no choice* but to appease them in one way or another. While he refused to bend by infringing upon citizen rights to own property when it came to mainstream America, he did so when it was politically acceptable to do so, against those who lived on the fringes of society. Jackson simply removed the check that prevented their abuse and then looked the other way; a hard, bitter lesson that modern day mainstream Americans should consider.[1]

Another of Jackson's most important policies was his veto of the re-charter in the Second Bank of the United States. This incident became known as Jackson's war on the banks. Jackson's justification for refusing the veto was that he believed the bank to be a fundamentally corrupt monopoly [2]whose stock was owned by foreigners, and that favored the wealthy. He also stated forthrightly that he believed the bank to be an organization for the wealthy.[3]

The National Republican Party[4] launched an attack, claiming that Jackson was attempting to use class warfare to gain support from the common man. The NRP were mostly ex-Federalists who opposed checks and balances on the affairs of government, banking and corporation. The Democratic Party was the party that descended from Jackson's efforts and views. The NRP primary goal was to further the interests of banking/corporate/government collusion for the purpose of acquiring resources by manipulating the currency (or any other means at their disposal), acquiring land and reselling it back to their contractor supporters, who would then funnel money back in the form of contributions in various forms and under a variety of pork barrel labels and via other nefarious means.

Jackson sought to eradicate corruption from the bank by removing federal deposits, whose money lending capacity was taken over by large numbers of state and local banks, thus vastly increasing speculation. Three years later Jackson introduced the *Specie Circular*, an executive order that required buyers of government lands to pay in solid gold and silver coins. The result was a huge increase in demand for the specie, which the banks

---

1 http://www.thecommonsenseshow.com/2016/05/16/fema-slave-labor-camps-are-becoming-operational-the-first-prisoners-have-arrived/
2 MacDonald, William (1916). *Documentary Source Book of American History, 1606-1913*. The Macmillan Company. p. 359. , land purchasers used notes not even back by any form of real currency.
3 Latner 2002, p. 112
4 https://en.wikipedia.org/wiki/National_Republican_Party

---

did not have enough of due to an obvious intentional retraction, leading to the Panic of 1837.

It has been said that between the years 1834 and 1836, the sales of public lands increased over five times! Many times these purchases were made with notes that were not backed by legitimate coin; so Jackson was right, the banking system was a corrupt monopoly that favored the rich.

The families and friends of government officials could simply walk inside the bank, ask for a loan and get it, even receiving a note to make the purchase that was not backed by any sort collateral; an IOU/promise to pay later, apparently.

Here is another "Panic" that shows signs of having been manufactured, this time in an attempt to destroy Jackson's presidency, while, at the same time, some people got fabulously rich. Once the order was made for payment in gold, all that the monopolized banking system had to do was remove the gold and silver coins from circulation, knowing full well what the outcome would be. The economy would crash and Jackson's presidency would suffer; and then the forces of corporation and banking could allow their own candidate to rise to the fore, promising to reverse the collapse. And then the minions of corrupt power would lord over the system once more, being repaid for their deeds in reduced prices and development contractor deals on foreclosed real estate when the loans were not repaid.

One may also suspect that Jackson's call for the specie may have been a calculated strike at the NRP on his part, anticipating a withholding of the gold and silver backed coins. His call for it was one of the last domestic moves during his administration; so the blame for the Panic fell mostly on Martin Van Buren.

The true blame lies with corruption at the Second Bank of the United States, not Jackson's attempts at neutralizing their manipulation and corruption. There again, let's keep in mind who Jackson was and who he represented, as well as reminding ourselves who his opponents were.

The Great Propaganda and Jackson

There were other considerations during the Jacksonian presidency that would have far ranging implications. First, we have the Missouri Compromise debates. The Missouri Compromise was about whether Missouri would be allowed to join the nation as a slave or free state, as there was a concern over upsetting the balance in Congress. A compromise was reached: Missouri would allow slave ownership, but Kansas would enter at the same time as a free state.

As these debates were ongoing, propagandists from the Northeast, where the seats of large corporations and banking interests were, began sending out literature designed to enflame opposition to slavery by appealing to emotion. The truth is that if corporations, big money and government could keep the citizens side-tracked, at each other's throats, with a heated, emotionally-charged argument, then no one would see the knife being stabbed in the back of entire nation by what they were doing on side. Jackson was forced to play both sides in order to prevent the dissolution of national unity, and to prevent outright turning the banks against himself, probably forcing him to exit his position of office. In time a bill was drafted that would have stopped the "incendiary literature" from being delivered, but it did not receive enough votes to pass. Postmasters in the areas where the literature was being sent simply refused to delivery it, as a result.

Thus, those who had an interest in opposing the effort to set some rules and limits for banking and corporations set out to demonize those from the large landed estates by changing the subject of discussion. They sent their propagandized appeals to end the practice of slavery to representatives in Washington DC, obviously in an effort to distract a majority while, down some other corridor, they could move ahead with legislation favoring them. Jackson, who was wise to their devious intentions, eventually issued an order to table all of their propagandist notes in a law called *The Gag Rule*, and as a direct consequence, such actions to deceive were repressed.

Such notations here are very important since they will be a hard deciding factor in the outcome of the future, just as soon as all checks are removed to allow imposing action from the banks and the corporations via government backed by raw unchecked force.

In brief, the wealthy gentry and their business associates worked without end to consolidate US currency, without rules and limits on how the bank would manage it. That was supposed to be the mission of the First Bank of the United States. This bill was signed into law by George Washington himself. The bill was opposed by Thomas Jefferson, who hailed from outside the area dominated by corporate and government interests (being ruled instead by the right of individual enterprise—with checks and balances on government, banking and corporations, to protect the rights of the individual and his ability to move from one economic stratum to another). Jefferson's personal prediction was that consolidated currency, without checks and balances, would have its value simply manipulated to the advantage of an elite few, at the expense of the majority. His predictions held true, leading to a series of economic depressions—but I'm not saying they were the result of errors or of "business cycles." Two of them were followed by large scale corporate property investments, and one was intentionally designed to crash Jackson's presidency.

Jackson's presidential decision-making served to appease corporate and banking interests by removing the legal barrier which prevented them from purloining the land of native people, leaving them at the mercy of those forces holding the "monopoly on power," i.e., the government and those with insider contacts. In Jackson's mind, we are told, he was doing them a favor and acting to save them; but such a statement is simply a justification to his personal supporters, many of whom were intermarried with the Five Civilized Tribes by this time.

Another reason we may deduce is that he may have removed that barrier because he foresaw that if he demanded government land purchases be backed in gold and silver coin, the Second Bank of the United States would remove the currency from circulation to crash the economy and his presidency. He made sure to issue the order that loans be backed in gold and silver *at the last stage* of his presidency, so that when the economy did crash, responsibility would fall on the NRP member whom he was sure would be elected next—thereby crashing *his* presidency. If that was the calculation, it was pretty astute, but how sad it was that the innocent citizenry had to suffer and even die for reasons of politics, general corruption and greed.

Martin Van Buren

If we are to know the truth, we need to study the powers who forced the nation to make the moves it did; and those are the powers of banking via government collusion. With the crash that followed Jackson's presidency, the figure of Martin Van Buren enters into the office (1837–41).

Van Buren began as a candidate with strong Federalist beliefs, but to his good judgment, changed those beliefs upon observing the corruption of the national banking system, which was infecting the system at large. Van Buren was well aware of the corporatist effort to fan the flames of division with the emotional approach to the issue of slavery, judging by his clear effort to suppress inflammatory literature in a ruling that subjected mail to state laws. This effectively locked the literature out of states who favored checks and balances on banking and government that would favor the individual's choice. He also refused to recharter the national bank, another sign that he was well aware of the corruption previously mentioned.

Van Buren basically continued the policies of Jackson, executing the order to carry through on the effort to forcibly remove the Native Americans from their lands, in accordance with the Congressional order that denied them the right to own the non-surveyed land issued under the presidency of Jackson. He was against slavery in personal conviction, but viewed the individual's choice to own slaves as being a Constitutional right. His belief was that government should stay out of the affairs of the people at large.

However, his beliefs were blamed for the continuation of the depression resulting from the Panic of 1837, according to the official historical record. But it should be clear to the reader by now that the official account of the Panic is merely a propagandist twist, intended to conceal the truth.

Having studied these events and the related decisions in order to deduce the true intent behind them, one can see that in the backrooms those favoring unchecked banking and government, and who opposed Jackson, also secretly desired that Van Buren would be a turncoat and change his new stance, seeing what had been done to Jackson by the collapse in the economy. They hoped he would be intimidated into embracing a more liberal attitude toward the banking/corporate/government partnership that would thrive all the more, in the absence of any oversight or moderating influences.

They also hoped that Van Buren would further develop the divisive appeal to emotion, splitting North and South over the slavery issue, taking attention away from the real issue—which was whether to take care of the average citizen or to allow the banking/corporate/government collusion to proceed unhampered. If the economic system of the Southern representatives who favored checks and balances could be completely destroyed, they would be economically helpless and vulnerable to federal seizure of their land and even more privately-held resources which could be developed by the banking/corporate conglomerates. This pattern had existed all along that was destined to hold for some time being.

Another interesting point from the presidency of Van Buren is that he refused to incorporate the land of Texas into the United States. Even this refusal was a way to pacify the interests of big money in collusion with government, while coloring it as a protection for those who felt that the individual's freedom to choose should remain open. The individualist referred to Van Buren's refusal to accept national endorsement of Texas as a cop out. By not endorsing the new state of Texas, he also hoped to create a positive future relationship with the nation of Mexico.

Tippecanoe and John Tyler Too

With the election of William Henry Harrison (1841), enthusiasm was running high among the forces of unfettered banking and corporate activity. No doubt, Harrison intended to meet their demands, since he planned to approve the application for renewal of the Second Bank of the United States, and also to allow them to issue loans in the form of non-backed paper notes. What Harrison had in mind as far as huge property developments designed to benefit Congressional corporate contributors, this author cannot detect a clear reference. Harrison died of fever[1] (probably typhoid) after just a month in office.[2] Perhaps Harrison's unspoken intentions may be revealed in the outcome of the next appointment and the actions taken by this appointee.

Next in line was none other than John Tyler, who was then Vice President and who became president via constitutional amendment. John Tyler was one of those who supported an effective program of checks and balances, but with his refusal to endorse the charter in the SBOUS, he was destined suffer serious avenging repercussions. To add to his woes, the economic depression was simply allowed to continue and was even exacerbated, the forces of big money hoping to force his hand into signing the SBOUS charter. A majority of Tyler's cabinet resigned following the collapse of a speculative bubble from 1836 to 1839.

Tariff Bill of 1842

When the 1842 deadline neared, his situation deteriorated even more. Tyler soon capitulated and signed the Tariff Bill of 1842, which taxed goods coming into the country and going out at a whopping 40% rate! The bill was applauded loudly by the corporate industrialists but obviously scorned by those who produced and traded abroad in durable goods. The economy in those areas of small production suffered, as suggested by the scornful title of *black tariff.* Some say the true purpose of the tariff was to protect the corporate industrialists at the expense of individual producers, in hopes that with a dive in profit margin, the system would starve to death. The banking/ corporate/government forces sought to weaken the individual producers, create a diversion so that their political influence could be eliminated, then move in to seize control of their resources, thereby destroying the economic system in the areas that supported checks and balances in the financial system and the government at large.

---

1 This author questions these examples of sudden death, which are especially common among the political class and political commentators to this day. Poisoning by Democratic Party interests is conceivable, or even by his own party for not acting enough in their favor, or suspicions of hypocrisy, as the following notation suggests. Suggestions of public support for the NRP, but honestly supporting the DP in the dim light of the back room are apparent as well.

2 It has been noted that Harrison had supported an extension of slavery in the Northwest Territory and the establishment of large landed estates. Such areas would no doubt support a continuing representative base in congress. The cartel held high hopes in his presidency, but may not have trusted him enough to make any solid bets.

James K. Polk

The election of James K. Polk (1845–49) ended the tariff of 1842 by enacting the Walker Tariff of 1846. This tariff dramatically reduced the tax percentages set in place in 1842. This elimination of the protectionist security base angered the corporate industrialists, banking and other big money interests, as well as their government sponsors. Polk also reestablished the Independent Treasury System that eliminated the policy of federal funds being connected to state and private banks.

Was the *ITS* created specifically for the purpose of appeasing large banking's corrupt interests? Keep in mind who fueled the self-serving programs of corporation and government, after repealing the tariff of 1842 which was set in place to protect those same interests. The treasury funds [1]also allowed for indirect contributions via anonymous deposits when and if they were necessary, from any supporters inclined to do so. Depository and content information concerning the treasury fund could be accessed only by a select few sources.

Zachary Taylor

The next administration was Zachary Taylor's. (March 1848–July 1849) Taylor was a staunch supporter of unchecked government and banking interests. This individual had made his career inside the military fighting for the national interest, while being employed by the US Federal Government. While he did not publicly endorse the divisive appeal to emotion in the condemnation of slavery, his actions advanced the interests of the banking/corporate elite by placing limitations upon the interests of slave owners, with the State of Texas being admitted into the union. All other states brought in from territory claimed after the war with Mexico (a much larger potential population base), of course, were to ban slavery, and were subjected to rulings that disadvantaged the small farmers and small enterprises. In other words, these territories were handed over to the rule of the big corporations and their collusion inside government and national banking. Taylor's actions showed him to be a hypocrite, possibly provoking the Jacksonians into a clandestine action for the purpose of neutralizing his sleight-of-hand policies[2].

The presidency of Zachary Taylor was novel in that he hailed from an area of the nation that supported checks and balances. Further, Taylor was

---

1 https://en.wikipedia.org/wiki/Treasury_Note_(19th_century) the motivation behind their issuance was always funding federal expenditures rather than the provision of a circulating medium.

2 There again, this author suspects poisoning by the Jacksonians, maybe in revenge for the poisoning of Tyler who in secret may have supported them.

a loyal government employee who had made his career in the military, as well as holding a number of important offices. He was used to accepting absolute authority and submitting to directive rule, even when that rule was counter to his own benefit as an individual, in favor of any entire group at large. Maybe a few of Taylor's policies would have made a positive difference in the course of the nation's history; but alas, we shall never know, since he died [1]after approximately a year of being in office, his death coming after drinking iced milk and eating fresh cherries on a hot, muggy day—cholera may have been involved.

To review the issue of slavery and place it in perspective as it relates to the issue of big money and corporate interests aiming for complete domination of the national system, let's carefully observe how the process of limiting slavery evolved in certain states. While the official historical record notes this issue from a moralistic perspective but not that of economics, the educated, unbiased observer cannot help but note both the political and the economic intent in limiting slave-holding to the territories where it was already practiced at the time.

Bear in mind as this issue is discussed that large property owners who held steadfast to the ideals of individual enterprise were slave owners in a number of cases, but some of these individuals acquired vast wealth and held influence in government as a result of that wealth. The basis of that wealth was the liberty to generate produce on an unlimited scale, and that liberty in many cases stood on the Constitutional premise that allowed the individual to make use of slave labor. Private lending also facilitated a huge increase in wealth for property owners and producers.

To attack that Constitutional premise allowing slave ownership and to attack the liberty to own vast tracts of property and use it for large scale agricultural production was to attack those who sought limitations on the rights of corporations and banking interests. Thus, this author deduces, the intent of the banking/corporate/government mob was to destroy these opponents and dominate the system in totality.

Again, let me say that the divisive intent behind the appeal to emotion in condemning slavery also provided a distraction to the citizenry of the nation, with one sector viewing the issue with moralistic condemnation and the other sector viewing it primarily in terms of a Constitutionally endorsed right.[2] And such it was, unfortunately. It comes as no real surprise that eventually the two opposing sides might be pushed to take up arms,

1 Some of these events almost suggest what amounts to a civil war inside the halls of congress and the White House
2 http://teachingamericanhistory.org/library/document/the-constitution-and-slavery/, pay attention to the articles

and while these two groups were grappling, the banking and corporate interests could simply move straight ahead and infringe the Constitution for the purpose of serving their own interests, as their competitors were being destroyed.

Upon reviewing the speech of Frederick Douglass, we can see that the institution existed and was supported even in the areas later totally dominated by corporate and banking interests. It was only in the course of time, when the corporate industrialists coveted more raw land for development, that slavery suddenly became an issue for concern. While it is true that slavery in these territories had already waned or completely died out by the time that slavery as an institution had became a heated political issue, still the hypocrisy of treating the subject solely as a moralistic bone of contention becomes self evident. Much more was at work here than today's students of history are told. Basic foundations of US history are suppressed history.

To know the truth, we must follow the trail of money. The forces that were about to collide were *not* two deep-seated differences between sections of the general population, expressed on the floors of Congress, but the forces of banking/corporate/government, big money, seeking ever more privilege at the expense of individual liberty and the individual's personal freedom of choice. The interests of corporation and big money were set against those of every individual in the entire nation. The political support for those seeking to limit the banking/corporate/government collusion happens to have come primarily from one section of the nation, the section whose political position and economic base gave them the insight to see through the haze and recognize an attack on property rights and economic rights that had been uncontroversial just decades before.

Thus the attack on the financial system that supported that contest was directed only toward one section of the population, specifically those individuals who owned large landed, productive estates and exercised their Constitutionally-endorsed right to run their productive estates via slave labor.[1] The issue was twisted from a legal/economic/political question into a purely moral question for one simple reason. Emotions are inflamed by moral questions, whereas politics and economics may leave the public yawning. In every modern political campaign, we see that emotional issues run the contest, far more than any substantive issues do.

Millard Fillmore

The thirteenth president of the United States (1850-1853) was Millard Fillmore. He ran on what we, today, might label the "independent" ticket.

1 https://en.wikipedia.org/wiki/Uncle_Tom%27s_Cabin

Whose interests he truly represented were revealed in the actions that he took.

Unofficially Fillmore was a member of the Whig Party, which was a descendant of the old Federalist Party. Thus he supported the same old policies of favoritism toward corporations searching for cheap land and new big-money building contracts, and colluding with them to access low prices and easy money via the corrupt banking monopoly.

Fillmore also supported high tariffs, the black tariff specifically, which if you'll recall favored the large industrialists at the expense of landed estates controlled by individual producers, who were primarily the ones forced to pay the tax on produce exported and needed goods imported. There again, we may detect an active continuing economic attack on these enterprising property owners. It may be safe to conclude here that the backroom intent was to weaken their economic base, so that small-scale entrepreneurs by and large could be taken down, and prepared for the next phase of an insidious hidden agenda.

Fillmore designed to cut off the financial support of the opposing Jacksonian party, the party of those who owned productive, landed estates, by opposing the admission of Texas as a slave state. That would have allowed more representatives into the halls of Congress who would have demanded checks and balances on currency values, and in the governmental system at large, to protect plebeian interests. He also advocated outlawing trafficking in slaves between states,[1] in an obvious effort to further reduce the ability to make the land productive, thus reducing the wealth behind those who were unyielding advocates of checks and balances against banking and corporate interests in the name of Thomas Jefferson.

At this point in time a number of compromises were proposed, such as the Compromise of 1850[2], and a few other concerns of a similar nature[3]. But all of them sought to repress the choice to engage in business in a way that had been accepted as endorsed by the Constitution. If this was a moral issue, it hadn't been one before: it was manufactured as such. And these gradually encroaching acts of repressing freedom of choice resulted in an ongoing reduction in the numbers of Congressional representatives[4] who supported checks on the banking, corporate and government conspiracy. Meanwhile, those who flagrantly opposed the idea of checks and balances gained representation in Washington.

1 Secretly designing to quash slavery on a state by state basis in this author's humble opinion
2 https://en.wikipedia.org/wiki/Compromise_of_1850
3 https://en.wikipedia.org/wiki/New_Mexico_Territory
4 https://en.wikipedia.org/wiki/United_States_Senate_elections,_1850,   note that the rising *"free soiler"* party aligned with the dying Whig party had three representatives.

Fillmore appointed his men as governor and supreme court judges, men who supported the same old Federalist/Whig agenda of serving the banking/corporate/government collusion. We see this readily in his appointment of Brigham Young as Governor of Utah, who developed the state under the same corporate pretext of unrestricted access to money and land for profit and pleasure. We see this again in the appointment of Benjamin Robert Curtis into seat two of the United States Supreme Court Justice. If any new laws needed negotiation, then they would be designed to serve Whig interests above all others. (It is interesting that one of Robert Curtis's decisions allowed the federal government to dictate interstate commerce when this was a national issue on a par with the issue of slavery, like other issues related to protecting the corporate profit base and eliminating government responsibility at the expense of individual freedom many years later.)

Robert Curtis *walked out* on the decision of the Dred Scott case, in favor of slavery (securing an economic base for the landed producers, who also favored checks and balances on corporate and banking interests), because he could make more revenue in private practice,[1] no doubt in personal collusion with the corporate interests[2] he had served. Even his walking out heightened the emotion now surrounding the issue.

Millard Fillmore appointed four federal judges, one of whom was John Glen, an ardent supporter of the Whig agenda. Another appointee was Nathan K Hall, who had worked under Fillmore and was a staunch supporter of Fillmore's corporatist political agenda. He was also appointed as Post Master General, a position he held until the time of his death. That was an enviable appointment, heading up what was essentially a huge corporate venture married to government management (as, arguably, it still is at the time of this writing).

Ogdon Hoffman Jr. was also appointed as federal judge by Fillmore. His father had worked for the firm of Hugh Maxwell, who was district attorney in New York (the center of banking at the time). Maxwell was appointed by Zachary Taylor as Customs Collector of the Port of New York, a plum job for sure. Henry Ecford, a famous shipbuilder and entrepreneur of the time, was tried by Maxwell for multimillion dollar fraud against insurance companies, private citizens and even banks, only to get off on a hung jury. Could this light rap on the wrist reflect a bit of collusion with the powerful ship-building industrial interests at the time?

The next individual of interest appointed by Fillmore was a Southerner from the state of Kentucky named James McHall Jones. He was appointed to the United States District Court for the southern district of California.

---

1 Dickerman, Albert. "The Business of the Federal Courts and the Salaries of the Judges", 24 *American Law Review* 1 (Jan.–Feb. 1890). p. 86.
2 Great American Lawyers, an encyclopedia, volume one, 3rd paragraph, pg. 161

He made a fortune in property speculation, to which he gained title for as attorney for Hispanic land grant holders.[1] This man held strong Whig loyalties and, just judging from the method that he utilized to make his fortune, we may presume that he coveted the expanses of undeveloped land farther south. Unfortunately for him, the scourge of tuberculosis took him out of the conspiracy at the young age of twenty-seven.

Millard Fillmore backed the corporations, industrialists and banks in pursuing their agenda of land acquisition by any means and bestowed development contracts on his political supporters, benefiting only an elitist, chosen few. Fillmore appointed governors and federal judges who colluded with corporate industrialists and were certain to interpret upcoming debates regarding laws/Constitutional law along lines that made sure no checks and balances could be instituted. Big business was beginning to hold all the cards.

Franklin Pierce

Next up was Franklin Pierce. (1853–57) He came from that part of the nation ruled by corporate, industrial and banking interests but had the wisdom to recognize the increasing threat to the system at large, as well as the fortitude to act to curtail the growing threat to rights (Constitutional and otherwise) concerning the individual American citizen on the ground.

Judging even from the official history, this president was aware of the fact that the practice of allowing the federal government to manage state infrastructure improvements (which meant giving construction contracts to their supporters) was setting the stage for the same corruption nationwide. He also felt that not having a system of measures in place to forestall such corruption was inherently unconstitutional, a conviction that this author shares.

To repulse the attacks on those who advocated checks on the banks, government and their corporate collusion, he understood that the heavy appeal to emotion[2] used by the propaganda attacks via inflammatory literature, now with more of a religious[3] bent, had to be effectively quashed—and soon.[4] Pierce also acknowledged that the states held a Constitutional right to vote for secession and foresaw that secession would be the standard for the future if action to cease the attacks (their policies, language and *tariffs/acts* of extortion) from big money and their friends in government were not promptly initiated.[5] It was on these grounds that he supported

---

1 *Founding The Far West; California, Oregon and Nevada*, by David Allen Johnson, pg. 259.
2 Wallner (2004), p. 92
3 https://en.wikipedia.org/wiki/Calvin_Ellis_Stowe
4 Wallner (2004), pp. 57–59
5 Wallner (2004), p. 67

the gag rule. He nominated a candidate to the Supreme Court, Archibald Campbell,[1] who was a staunch advocate for checks on big money and their government collusion, seeking to preserve the rights of individuals and their Constitutional liberty to choose their own direction in life.

Pierce also opposed the use of federal government to support private industry, obviously sensing the opportunity for corruption, so he did not ratify the Gladstone Purchase[2]—which was ratified anyway; a testament to the power of banking interests already in place.

Pierce sought to eliminate corruption in the national treasury, which advocated a single depository for funds relating to government over privately held banks. With a solid system of oversight, this system of management would have been very effective and efficient. The Whigs, those who still desired to function only in accordance with their own uninhibited desires, still held those government funds inside of private banks that they knew would conceal deposits and withdrawals. James Guthrie was appointed to reform the Treasury, being assigned with the task of rooting out various forms of corruption, such as treasury employees and tariff collectors who withheld or failed to collect funds that were due the government (suggesting the possibility that they were colluding with the corporations). Guthrie also sought to prosecute these criminals, but he had at best only mixed success[3]. This suggests again that the connections of these criminals ran very deep and very high, high enough to penetrate to the very heart of The Hill.

In the name of Jefferson and the supporters of his checks-and-balance style of government, Pierce believed in structural progress but not without a system of supervision to eliminate the natural turn toward supporting one's personal constituency where there was a financial gain to be had.

Pierce appointed Jefferson Davis[4] over the Corps of Topographical Engineers.[5] In later years, Davis would have a very pivotal part to play in the looming conflict between those who stood for the individual's freedom to choose and those who sought to push the self serving interests of banks, corporate, and industry via government collusion.

The most trying event in the presidency of Pierce was the *Kansas Nebraska Act*. The purpose of this act was to allow development into the territories, with part of the territory being pro-checks and balances and the other part in favor of the forces of banking/corporate/government collusion.

The parts that would have checks favoring the individual and those that would be without checks, to favor the industrialists, would be decided by

---

1 https://en.wikipedia.org/wiki/John_Archibald_Campbell
2 "Article 3 – No Title" . *The New York Times*. April 25, 1854.
3 Wallner (2007), pp. 32–36
4 https://en.wikipedia.org/wiki/Jefferson_Davis
5 https://en.wikipedia.org/wiki/Corps_of_Topographical_Engineers

the settlers of the state territories themselves. But such a decision would violate the Missouri Compromise of 1820, since most of the territory was north of latitude 36°30'—the line that the Missouri Compromise had set to demarcate the area that would be free from checks, in favor of the industrialists.

The people in favor of individual rights had argued that the Compromise of 1850 already annulled the Missouri Compromise by admitting California as a free state. In other words, the economic base in the state of California could never be organized to support small producers in a campaign for representation. The candidate would not be supported by the corporations directly or indirectly. And small businesses could never achieve the financial clout to support any individual's campaign without unpaid labor; so therefore, not making the Kansas-Nebraska territory open to slavery would limit and reduce representation from the landed estates dominated by [1]agriculture-based enterprising individuals.

Opponents to the bill soon arose,[2] igniting a distraction in the form of the divisive appeal to emotion as settlers from both factions began pouring into the open territory. Harriet Beecher Stowe (author of *Uncle Tom's Cabin*) was a vocal member of a salon comprising leading citizens of Cincinnati in this period. Incidents intending to halt the infecting spread of propaganda also occurred[3],[4]. Once emotions had been fanned to the point of combustion and the propaganda was spread, perhaps overtaking the majority, this infection spread into the halls of government[5],[6], seeking to outnumber those representatives who favored checks on the banking monopoly and government collusion with the corporate leaders.

In the areas of the nation where the main headquarter offices of the large corporation and government sat, those that supported checks on the system to safeguard the interests of individual concerns had lost nearly every seat; thus the only states where those interests still held the seats of government were those where the economic system was based on individual enterprise and property ownership.

The propaganda intended to destroy the economic base that supported checks on big money was also moving to impose itself upon the "free choice"

---

1 https://en.wikipedia.org/wiki/Pacific_Railroad_Acts, land grants now given directly to private corporations, rather than to states, facilitating the corruption and potential for it, since checks and balances to neutralize the corruption had now been expunged.
2 https://en.wikipedia.org/wiki/Salmon_P._Chase
3 https://en.wikipedia.org/wiki/The_Philanthropist_(Cincinnati,_Ohio)
4 https://en.wikipedia.org/wiki/Bleeding_Kansas
5 https://en.wikipedia.org/wiki/Know_Nothing
6 https://en.wikipedia.org/wiki/Free_Soil_Party

citizens of the new Kansas territory.[1] This move was certain to create the greatly desired *distraction* in the form of conflict between those citizens who cherished individual rights and those who were led by their emotions. As a direct result of the inflammatory literature and the dysphemism designed to cast a negative light on the entire economic base of those who supported individual rights, the situation soon deteriorated into violence.

By this time, the emotional argument had even reached the halls of the Senate,[2] with a speech that fomented dissension in ways that had previously only been heard in the street. According to Hoffer (2010),

> It is also important to note the sexual imagery that recurred throughout the oration, which was neither accidental nor without precedent. Abolitionists routinely accused slaveholders of maintaining slavery so that they could engage in forcible sexual relations with their slaves.[3]

I believe that the sensation caused by speeches like this has filtered down to our own generation and it still influences the picture that we have of plantation life in those days. It is also used to smear the entire social order of those who eventually stood up to face the forces of the opposing cartel on the field of battle. The power of emotional appeal, and the distraction provided by the ensuing conflict, must never be under estimated. Such images still serve the same ruling cartel very well, when individuals stand to speak of the Constitution and our birthright to move from one economic stratum into the next, without authoritarian repression, via accumulation of our own private resource base.

Thus the forces of big money (a sort of banking "aristocracy" in collusion with the new "corporate aristocracy"), and those factions in government that they support, now gained a secure hold on an increasing proportion of public opinion. By attacking the economic foundation of the small producers, who happened to be the people who favored implementing checks on the self serving interests of the corporate and banking aristocracy, they could cut off the source of campaign contributions to any candidate that would work to implement such a system.

In the run-up to Kansas applying for statehood, *Free Staters*[4] moved into Kansas and set up a shadow government,[5] which in and of itself constitutes an illegal government. They also imposed the illegal *Topeka Constitution* on the

---

1 https://en.wikipedia.org/wiki/Topeka_Constitution
2 https://en.wikipedia.org/wiki/Caning_of_Charles_Sumner
3 William James Hoffer, *The Caning of Charles Sumner: Honor, Idealism, and the Origins of the Civil War* (2010) p. 62
4 http://en.academic.ru/dic.nsf/enwiki/2506617
5 As defined by wiki encyclopedia: A government run by an unelected bureaucracy, also known as a deep state or state within a state.

citizens of the territory, labeled by Pierce himself as an act of rebellion. Pierce continued to recognize the individual's Constitutionally-endorsed right to own slaves because he was well aware that those who called for checks and balances against the banking/corporate powers needed representatives in the Senate and Congress. Having these checks and balances in their proper place was all that would guarantee Constitutional liberty of the individual American citizen in the face of a growing, hungry self serving corporate and banking tyranny. Pierce felt so strongly about the need for checks and balances to preserve freedom of the people that he sent in federal troops to break up any backroom meeting of the *Topeka Government*[1].

By the time just prior to Pierce leaving office, this kind of provocative propaganda demonizing the economic base of those who supported checks and balances on banking, corporate elite and their government insider friends had not only infected the population but had also gained ground in the Senate and Congress.

The result was outright bloody violence, pitting two factions at each other's throats right there inside the halls of government.

James Buchanan

James Buchanan followed Pierce into office. While Buchanan was aligned with the Federalists indirectly via the parties that had evolved out of the old Federalist Party, he acknowledged the Constitutional endorsement of individuals' right to own slaves and to own and operate the large estate-based business entities, and was committed to resolving divisive issues stemming from the Kansas–Nebraska Act (that called for the decision for or against slavery should be made by local settlers, not outsiders). So again, while he personally opposed slavery on moralistic grounds, he acknowledged the *Constitutional rights* of individuals residing in states still allowing slavery to practice it freely. Slaves in one form or another were absolutely necessary to efficiently manage huge estates before the advent of mechanization. Keep in mind as well that this Constitutional right was available for all demographic groups, and they exercised the right—and that includes free Blacks. How often does the official history show us such an acknowledgement to be made by presidents?

In other words, in this author's humble opinion, President Buchanan clearly saw the economic link, that owning slaves (that supported labor on the landed estates) inherently supported those voters who favored candidates who represented the side supporting checks and balances on the banking/corporate cabal, whose inside government collusion constituted just over half of all those in government at this point! He knew that to infringe

---

1 Wallner (2007), pp. 195–209; Gara (1991), pp. 1, 11–20.

upon the Constitutionally-endorsed right to own slaves would destroy the economic system of regions not yet totally under the thumb of that cabal, the economic system that enabled those sectors to finance representative candidates of their choice. To destroy this economic system would render the citizens living outside of that control as having *no escape* from corporate influence or manipulation, and no protection against potential flagrant abuse of the individual citizen.

Take note of Buchanan's own words:

> This question of domestic slavery is the weak point in our institutions, touch this question seriously... and the Union is from that moment dissolved. Although in Pennsylvania we are all opposed to slavery in the abstract, we can never violate the constitutional compact we have with our sister states. Their rights will be held sacred by us. Under the constitution it is their own question; and there let it remain[1].

Buchanan also was also well aware of the incendiary propaganda issued by the supporters of the industrialist and banking elite and the damage that it was doing. As technology and the world economy were changing, conditions were already shaping up to favor a peaceful progressive end to the use of slavery anyway.

Problem was, peace was never the intention of this corporate collusion with government. With evidence reaching back to the early 1800s, they already had in mind destroying those independent producers who sought protection from [2]the largest pools of concentrated wealth and influence.

The corporations sought absolute control over the banking system from the very beginning, seeking to create a system where the value of a centralized currency could be *manipulated* to favor themselves and their government collusion without even a *hint of opposing position,* at the very expense of the citizenry.

And bear in mind exactly *who* Buchanan was: He represented the half of the Democratic Party under absolute rule of the corporations and the banks! His political stance gives *more* verification of the Constitutionality of the individual's right to ascend into wealth via real estate ownership and choose his own course of direction in general, which conflicted with the desires of the industrialists and their government constituency (just as the individual's freedom of choice does in our present day[3]). Bear in mind the true purpose of the tariffs that we discussed earlier:

---

1 Klein 1962, p. 150
2 https://en.wikipedia.org/wiki/Mexican_Drug_War#Casualties
3 http://www.offthegridnews.com/current-events/court-rules-off-the-grid-
   living-is-illegal/

Buchanan condemned both free trade and prohibitive tariffs, since either would benefit one section of the country to the detriment of the other. As the senator from Pennsylvania, he thought: "I am viewed as the strongest advocate of protection in other states, whilst I am denounced as its enemy in Pennsylvania."[1]

Buchanan did support the United States enlarging its territory, but he felt that the issue of slavery was best left to the people for their own resolution, aligning with Constitutional ideology.

The federal government had left this issue alone, and by 1885 it truly would have resolved itself, since nearly everywhere inside the Western world had abolished slavery anyway by that time. [2]The economic incentive behind it was evaporating fast, and if that had been a significant driver behind the Civil War, the war would have been avoided.

But this was not allowed to happen—which should prompt the obvious question, *Why not?*

Let's hear again from Buchanan, who actually recognized the abolitionist literature as inflammatory and having a negative effect, as it was clearly being used to bully people into giving up their rights;

> Although in Pennsylvania we are all opposed to slavery in the abstract, we can never violate the constitutional compact we have with our sister states. Their rights will be held sacred by us. Under the constitution it is their own question; and there let it remain[3]...

> Before [the abolitionists] commenced this agitation, a very large and growing party existed in several of the slave states in favor of the gradual abolition of slavery; and now not a voice is heard there in support of such a measure. The abolitionists have postponed the emancipation of the slaves in three or four states for at least half a century[4].

We can clearly see an allegiance here to the value observed in checks and balances, expressed by a man who hailed from those states that were already under the absolute control of the banks and corporations.

In such a period of heated conflict, how was the US national bank to respond, if it was going to respond at all? How had it responded in the past? The answer to that question should prompt the conclusion regarding to what occurred in the historical record.

---

1 Klein 1962, p. 144
2 https://en.wikipedia.org/wiki/Abolition_of_slavery_timeline
3 Klein 1962, p. 150.
4 Klein 1962, p. 150

The Panic of 1897

We call this period of time in the western financial record the Panic of 1897. True to their own history and the prophesy of the master intellectual himself, Thomas Jefferson, the consolidated bank manipulated the currency again, attempting to invalidate Buchanan's indirect call for checks to remain on the system. This caused him to appear incompetent and destroyed his presidency, by making it appear that allowing the banking/corporate cartel to operate with a free hand would be better for the economy. This was the impression left on the rank and file plebeian, and it was also a hard shot at the economic base of those representatives calling for checks on the interests of the corporate and banking aristocracy.

It seems that the Panic of 1897 resulted from a worldwide conspiracy of banking, the very first of its kind, to manipulate currency values and create a system of banknotes that were not backed by gold and silver. It had happened in Great Britain with Parliament circumventing the requirements of The Peel Banking Act of 1844[1], which was developed to demand that all notes be supported with gold or silver. Internationally, the situation did not last all that long, but in the United States the situation was extended due to other events.

Great Britain stood as a primary trading partner of those states favoring checks and balances on the corrupt forces of corporations and centralized banking in the US; but obviously the corporate and banking powers in Great Britain anticipated that they just might be able to reap a larger harvest by offering assistance to the corporate industrialists on the American side by facilitating a crash of the economy of the Southern States.

When the British banking collusion failed to see a real benefit to itself from the deal, or the American side failed to come through on its agreed specifics, the British side simply deposited more gold to back its banknotes. The values were manipulated to stabilize the economy in Great Britain; and the Southern states went full steam ahead to regain their profit margin and flourish through trade with the British —to the continued exasperation of those designing to destroy them.

SS Central America

Now the interests of the corporate elites, those of the centralized banking institution working through their government collusion, were forced to take hard action to facilitate a more destructive panic; at least on the US side of the water, since the British had obviously backed down on their offer to help destroy the Southern US economy, especially when they could readily view where doing so would not serve their better interests. How were they

---

1 https://en.wikipedia.org/wiki/Bank_Charter_Act_1844

going to initiate this act of economic warfare? Examine the sinking of the ship *SS Central America* in September 1857, which contributed greatly to the economic panic on the US side, according to the official historical record.

This ship has been called the "ship of gold" and for good reason. The ship was carrying 10 tons of gold from California and 477 male passengers. The banks of New York were waiting for this gold to back their banknotes. The ship left the port of Havana after a brief pause, heading toward New York City. On September 9th the ship was caught up in a category 2 hurricane. By September 11th the 105-mile an hour winds and heavy seas had shredded her sails and she was taking on water. About the same time, her boiler was threatening to go out. The next morning, the 12th, a uniquely positioned seal leaked and caused the boiler to shut down. The hold filled with water after the hurricane eye had passed and the second half of the storm struck. At 2000 hrs, the ship went to the bottom. In the end, 425 of the 477 male passengers died. This figure calculated to only 52 adult male survivors, just in case anyone missed it.

In this author's view, this sinking may very well have been due to sabotage by someone who worked on behalf of the centralized bank, government and the corporate elites, in order to intentionally cause the currency in the US to crash. While I have not yet found any hard conclusive evidence, the patterns in the circumstantial evidence are too suggestive to ignore.

Eastern US banks had refused to make loans to the Western states due to the issue of banknotes not backed by gold or silver. The railroad industry had boomed due to the Westward migration of Easterners, especially in Kansas, and the corporations gained huge tracts of government land due to inside currency manipulation.

Soon the railroads became an extremely profitable industry. The banks consequently seized the opportunity to make huge loans in near worthless notes to the railroad companies, who no doubt were part of the political constituency—colluding via campaign contributions[1], if not by making government officials actual share owners in the railroads. As noted before, during the Presidency of Jackson, the specie (gold or silver coin) was withdrawn; according to the official historical record, this was because of over speculation in the railroads and purchase of products to sell offshore due to reductions in the tariff tax. All of this suggests there had been an intentional withholding of gold and silver, especially in light of future Constitutional developments, as will be later noted.

Gold and silver were being withheld from the banks, although official history claims that this contraction was due to over speculation and a vastly increased demand. At the same time, the *SS Central America* went under

---

1 Klein 1962, p. 338

with 10 tons of gold ($50,621,429 in present day currency) destined for the banks of New York, which would have allowed the US currency to rally. A category 2 hurricane is not such a strong storm, in fact: I personally rode out such a storm in a small, antiquated wood-framed home once upon a time, and without a single scratch to the home nor myself). Captain Herndon was extremely competent and had just come off duty on a steamer patrolling the Caribbean, following what was apparently a furlough. He must have navigated through numerous hurricanes in the past. The idea that he could have lost the ship without some other interference strains credulity.

There is some evidence [1] as to what may have caused the ship to go down. An inconspicuous leak in one of the seals between the paddle wheel shafts and the ship sides (an easy hole to punch out while in port) seems to be one of the primary culprits, since her boiler could no longer hold fire. For a person who knew anything about steam mechanics, such a hole would have been very simple to make with a good long-bladed sailor's clasp knife or marlin spike. Steam pressure then dropped, shutting down both pumps that had been keeping the water at bay and keeping the paddle wheels moving so that her bow could be kept into the wind. No other ship was near enough to come to her rescue promptly, and she was now aimlessly adrift in the howling wind and torrential rain.

A bucket brigade was formed that labored all through the night, but their battle against the rising water was to no avail. The storm died down briefly, with the passing of the eye, but then picked back up. The ship still had no power and could not keep its bow to the wind. The next morning two ships were spotted, and they paused to save some passengers, primarily women and children. The intense storm prevented a majority of the company from being rescued, and the ship went down at 2000 hours. We'll never be sure of the details.

The Most Likely Suspect

Then there is the captain himself, William Lewis Herndon[2]. Herndon was born in Fredericksburg, Virginia, a great choice for a target from those ambitious to impose their ideas on American society. He was assigned in October 1855 as commander of the SS *Central America*, which was owned by the Atlantic Mail Steamship Company. The ship was on the New York to Aspinwal–Colon, Panama run. Such mail steamers were operated by companies under contract to the federal government. In the past, mail

---

1 The steamer Georgia law/SS Central America, was only two years old in 1855, when Herndon took command.
2 https://en.wikipedia.org/wiki/William_Lewis_Herndon

steamers had been assigned to transport huge quantities of gold from the California gold fields to cities on the East Coast and the mint in Philadelphia.

In total there seem to have been 575 people on board and 152 were saved out of the captain's "unusual concern" for his passengers and crew. The last reports had Captain Herndon in full dress uniform, standing by the wheelhouse with his hand on the rail, hat in his hand, his head bowed in prayer as the ship lurched and headed downward; obviously terrified of the disaster that he confronted, knowing that the ship's sinking would cause economic chaos, on top of the terrible deaths that he was witnessing.

In this author's humble opinion, the Captain's overly attentive behavior[1] appears highly suspicious. Herndon would have definitely been in a position to know about the mechanics of the steam engine, the boiler, the paddle wheel and the seals. He would have been able to calculate the deadly effect of such a leak. Since he had a strong connection with the federal government and the banks, he might have been instructed to engineer such a disaster. In addition, if the Captain was not the one compelled to do the deed himself, then he was coerced into allowing someone else to do it, and to prevent corrective action in time. It could have been done at the port of Havana on that cloudy day in order to sink the ship between Havana and New York Harbor. Possibly those behind the event insured that the dear Captain would follow through, perhaps by a death threat to his entire family should he fail.[2]

Either way he was doomed: should he survive, he could not have lived with himself knowing that so many innocents perished because of his action (or inaction), and he would have probably been murdered for his knowledge of the event anyway, right along with his entire family. The only logical way out would have been for him to show this extraordinary concern for his passengers as his own way of apologizing, then simply commit suicide by going down with the ship; also serving very well to eternally silence him in the matter, which must have pleased his paymasters very much.

An Evil Design Continues

When the panic ended, those states that favored the individual's freedom of choice fared *better* than those that did not (following a rather brief spell of suffering), to everyone's shock and surprise! No doubt Buchanan helped in this deal by lowering the tariff taxes, thereby opening up foreign markets, especially those of the French and the British, to trade. This was a boost for states engaged in growing produce and in shipping, states dominated by

---

1 Reeves, Thomas C. (1975). *Gentleman Boss*. NY, NY: Alfred A. Knopf. p. 20.
2 One account states that Herndon had relocated with his family to New York State in 1856, which would give even more credibility to the suspicion of a subtle threat from the interests of centralized currency and banking.

the landed estates [1] rather than industry and corporate production. Thus it appears that the only way large scale manufacturing and huge corporations could prosper to the degree desired by company and corporate owners was at the expense of all possible competitors of any sort, and on any level.

According to the official historic record, Buchanan left office with a federal deficit of $17 million (that would be about $340 *million in today's currency, by this author's estimation*). The total national debt for the time was $80 million in 1861. Now consider that the *SS Central America* went down with $2 million worth of gold [2](rounded out in 1857 value). This amounts to 2.5% of the total national debt in 1860 and 12% of the final $17 million incurred by the close of the Buchanan administration. We can see the large scale implications of the ship sinking.

Although the record is scanty, more than likely most of the $17 million debt was incurred by Buchanan attempting to appease the large corporations [3]and banks who had apparently suffered most during the Panic. For the time being, he had also achieved the ultimate objective, which was to forestall the break-up of the nation.

Buchanan's presidency ended with one more divisive appeal to emotion made for the purpose of gaining support for the position of the corporations and banks above those of individual rights, to condemn any remaining persons pushing for checks and balances on corrupt corporations and centralized banking, operating through their government collusion. This appeal to emotion was the final report of an organization called the Cavode Committee. [4]

The Cavode Committee

The Cavode Committee was designed to investigate Buchanan's administration for corruption and then to push for impeachment. Though some corruption was discovered, the Buchanan administration managed to pull through. Unfortunately, emotions were running higher than ever.

Placing the Details in Perspective

So here we are at the year 1860. The influence of the corporate aristocracy was in place from the very beginning. Christopher Columbus and his

1 Baker 2004, p. 90
2 Some accounts state that the amount of gold being transported was eight million dollars worth in 1857 currency value.
3 Grossman, Mark (2003). *Political Corruption in America: An Encyclopedia of Scandals, Power, and Greed*. Santa Barbara, CA: ABC-CLIO. p. 78.
4 https://en.wikipedia.org/wiki/United_States_House_Select_Committee_to_Investigate_Alleged_Corruptions_in_Government

whole enterprise were an extension of the Spanish Crown, financed by the big trading concerns and the nobility, being the forerunners of the large corporations arising later in time. We saw how when big money is put on the table, governments make promises in order to get the big reward; and when their promises cannot be met, they—with the backing of a state-sponsored military, *always* turn on the people to extort privately held resources in order to fill the gaps—up to and including torture and mass murder of the civilian population.

This trend has never wavered. The corporate powers organized in the United States and called for consolidation of the currency in disregard for any checks on how the value of the currency might be set, how it would be used, and to the benefit of whom. We saw vividly that when the opposition demanded some checks on corporate/banking power, along with the very valid justification for such, they were ignored and the abuse of authority in making use of these funds could be traced right through the past ninety years, up to the year 1860.

We have discussed the malfeasance and abuse of power that followed in the wake of this corruption, and the horrifying lengths that the corporate industrialist power goes to impose its will. It appears that nothing is too extreme for them; and the will of the large corporation *shall always* be served first, everybody else be damned.

We have discussed the manner in which currency has been manipulated to crash the economy, with the intention of destroying the presidencies of men who refused to bow down before the corporate and banking interests in order to steadfastly protect the principle of an individual's freedom of choice. We have seen how even entire shipments of gold totaling a value of more than three percent of the national debt, right along with over four hundred innocent passengers, were sent to the bottom of the sea in order to crash the currency and the economy—just to destroy those who refused to submit to the will of big capital, including the people of those states who supported government representatives who called for reining in this corrupt collusion.

All of these events are still relevant today. The self serving intention of big money has never faltered, that being to rule the United States and maybe even the earth itself[1], enslaving every nation[2]. Even men of fortitude and determined tenacity, such as Andrew Jackson, have been forced to appease it. This was the real reason why the tribal lands of the East were sold out from underneath the people of the land—because it was politically acceptable to do so and because the banking/corporate elite and their friends inside the government demanded it. Jackson was well aware of the destructive force

1 http://www.prophecynewswatch.com/2015/November10/101.html
2 http://therothshow.com/2012/02/new-coming-holocaust-christians-and-conservatives/

of the mighty wave that threatened to come down on him, should he refuse. And when the specie was pulled from the second national bank, the resulting crash nearly washed him away. The big money elites were sending a loud message: Give us something out of your presidency, or else we will destroy you and your legacy.

Buchanan was in the same boat as Jackson. The wave was far too great, the power in it by now much too entrenched to fight. Eventually he was forced to submit, even though doing so went directly against his personal principles and convictions. He was compelled to side with the power of money, banks, corporations and the industrialists against the individual American civilian.

In the end, the individual citizens themselves had to take sides in the matter, both sides choosing either to accept the position of the other, or choosing to allow the blood crucible of conflict to decide the matter.

By making this into a highly enflamed emotional issue rather than a rational difference of opinion, based on different but legitimate interests, they forced the issue. All of the people, both high and low, had given in, promising to sacrifice their flesh and blood before the ancient god of war: dead set on preserving the individual's freedom of choice above the will of gold, corporation and government, or dead set on imposing an extortionist system over all the nation.

While the people were at each other's throats, dealing with the horrors of war and its wake of destruction—the elites would commit the supreme blasphemy against every free-born citizen in America and all that the Constitution stood for.

The citizen civilians and soldiers on both sides were only pawns in a cruel game of chess; and on top of that, their very history was twisted so that the villains who infringed upon the goddess Liberty and the sacred Constitution became the great "liberators" for those who were labeled (by corporate-sponsored propaganda) as oppressed[1] and those of outstanding fortitude and superlative visionary wisdom, insight, creative intellectuality and solid steadfast conviction, those who stood strong in the face of the tyranny imposed by banking/corporate/government. And even as the years passed, many among their own seed eventually submitted to the power of a perverted, twisted propaganda masquerading as valid historical record, hanging their heads in shame at their own history,[2] something that had been an accepted and conventional economic model up until that moment, whatever we might think of it today.

---

1 http://www.southernheritage411.com/truehistory.php?th=094
2 http://bittersoutherner.com/from-a-distance-you-cant-leave-the-south/#. Vmb-Pv76X_U

A Sudden Recollection

As a young child this author vividly recalls a certain honored preacher proudly standing before his congregation on Sunday mornings. His name was Meachum—Preacher Meachum. Preacher Meachum had been a career army chaplain, a multitask missionary and world traveler in general. He had called many nations home, back in his day. He had helped turn head-hunting natives on the island of Formosa into peaceful Christian citizens and had many an interesting story to tell as a result of the experience. He had also lived in Germany during the rise of Adolf Hitler. He would tell of the changes going on in Germany during the days of Hitler's rise[1], how the government of Germany forbade people to gather to protest the authoritarian rule (one might see some parallels to the way the peaceful Occupy Movement was handled here at home...)[2]. Meachum spoke about the persecution of intellectuality and an authority that imposed itself everywhere,[3] even inside the Church!

Most moving of all, one could see the heads of the congregation shake *"no"* as the preacher spoke of this intrusion on personal liberty and hear the applause accompanied by a rousing cheer when Preacher Meachum shouted out that such a thing would *never* happen in this great country, just as long as our nation never forgot who its heavenly creator was! And all in that congregation of housewives, school teachers and young children, hardworking farmers, tradesmen, individual enterprise people and ex-soldiers called out in a chorus, "Amen! Give all glory to God in the house! ... America will surely remain free forever and ever!"

---

1 https://www.aclu.org/top-ten-abuses-power-911

2 http://www.huffingtonpost.com/2013/01/05/fbi-occupy-wall-street_n_2410783.html; see also   http://www.prwatch.org/files/Dissent%20 or %20 Terror%20FINAL_0.pdf

3 For some contemporary insights into the situation, try this: http://www. allgov.com/news/top-stories/senate-bill-allows-indefinite-imprison-ment-of-americans-without-trial?news=843654; See also   http://cryptome.org/ 2015/03/NSA_surveillance_program.pdf;   http://www.wnd.com/ 2012/09/persecution-of-christians-on-rise-in-u-s/;   http://www.the burningplatform.com/2015/10/09/when-the-bride-of-christ-becomes-a-whore-for-the-state/; and   http://www.prophecynewswatch.com/2015/ September30/304.html

Chapter 5. A Contest of Wills

The Push for Centralized Currency Started with Hamilton

We have discussed the administrations of the presidents from the founding of the nation to the year 1860. With that discussion comes the topic of banking and the influence of big money on the national system, as the presidency and the influence of big money are unfortunately inseparable. Now we will discuss the money trail itself, to clarify how big money has influenced US policy and thus how it has influenced the events and outcome of US history itself. While it is not the intent of this work to discuss how big money has worked through corporate industrialization to dominate the world for the purpose of extortion and indenture, it is very relevant to this work to make at least a casual reference to that possibility. World banking and its collusive practices are definitely in the process of gaining an ever tightening grip on the individual inhabitants of earth[1]. I would also contend that one day American national, economic and even religious policy shall be directly influenced [2]by some sort of united world financial and political policy[3], if not absorbed outright by it.

When it comes to history, it's hard enough to establish exactly what really happened, much less why; but when a consistent pattern shows that one group of interests always wins, it makes sense to add up the facts and make the best deduction we can. How else can we interpret the past in order to understand

---

1 http://humansarefree.com/2012/03/christian-church-is-biggest-financial.html
2 If not completely consumed by
3 https://www.thetrumpet.com/article/6456.20.0.0/resurrecting-the-holy-roman-
empire-of-the-german-nation

the present and assess what may await us in the future? After all, words spoken by individual men alone can be very misleading, but when they accumulate we can begin to see what they truly stand for. And this work is fully committed to closely examining the specific words and actions of specific 'men, and matching them up with outcomes that appear to serve as signposts toward our future.

To effectively reach this end, we must recapitulate what we've covered so far, the involvement of big money and its influence over government was seen in America from the days of the very first explorations and settlements, and that influence never waned. Whether under the Crowns of European powers or the banner of free-born patriots chanting "liberty" and "freedom," this influence simply continued to grow. The result has been a continuous trend toward rigid conformity...and toward corporate/banking control of more and more aspects of American life.

The families of most of our Founding Fathers were well off. Washington himself inherited a sufficiently privileged and connected background to establish a career as a trained land surveyor, and he invested in land, endeavoring to make that land productive in order to sell the output on the open market so that he could become even wealthier. He established a flour mill, a distillery and other cash-producing businesses. Owning a plantation was absolutely the best way for an individual to increase wealth and make a place for himself among the gentry. The Constitution would later on be written to ensure the individual's right to thrive and not be crushed by government policies that served only corporations and centralized banks that serve their interests..

It has been said that the poorest Charleston rice plantation generated *eight times* more wealth than the wealthiest Boston mercantile operator in those years. Technological changes altered the economic benefits of trade and shipping compared to agriculture in the next several decades, but at the time of the American Revolution other places, too, such as the island of Hispaniola (known as the Gem of the Caribbean, once the wealthiest colony in North America), were flourishing on the basis of agricultural exports. In the Caribbean, settlers grew sugar cane to convert the juice into sugar and molasses, ferment the molasses, and distill it into rum. The rum was sold practically worldwide, even being transported to West Africa in exchange for people who were enslaved and transported back to Hispaniola and eventually sold to the plantations (as well as to plantations, farms, factories and iron yards of North America).

The British, on the other hand, were developing productive micro-engines and hoped to use them on the American mainland for the purpose of crafting

---

1 Luke 6: 42-43, every good tree is known by its fruit

products desired by the British people and those throughout Europe, hoping to eventually reach those markets of Asia. They also modeled practices that clearly were destructive rather than a service to the population.[1], [2]

The main point, however, is that much as we admire Washington for his role in establishing the "free" United States," his business was big enough to be helped by the banking elites; his interests were the same as corporate interests; and like them, he benefited from government practices that supported the bigger operators more than the individual. Washington himself showed his true allegiances by making a *single tainted signature*, when the final say was his[3]. Now the forces of big money and their collusion with corporate-backed government could rule with a new, legitimized impunity and a hard fist to impose its way in what amounted to an outright *rape* of the US economic system and its plebeian citizenry.

Let's observe a direct quote from the source at footnote 222, as to *specifically what* the opposition had to say concerning the push by government to centralize the nation's banking. This part of the lesson is very critical, if we are to see through the twisted propaganda of the official history:

> Jefferson and Madison also opposed a second of the three proposals of Hamilton: establishing an official government Mint. They believed this centralization of power away from local banks was dangerous to a sound monetary system and was mostly to the benefit of business interests in the commercial areas of the nation, not landed individual interests, arguing that the right to own property would be infringed by these proposals. Furthermore, they contended that the creation of such a bank violated the Constitution, which specifically stated that Congress was to regulate weights and measures and issue coined money (rather than mint and bills of credit).

Note that the words "North" and "Southern" have been effectively removed from this record in most instances, since those terms are a part of the divisive appeal to emotion made by the author of that particular work, effectively demonstrating to readers here where his alliances went; and they were most definitely not with the rank and file citizenry. The use of emotionally-charged words is only one of the devices used to deceive by distracting the reader, to blind him. As time transpired, these divisive appeals made to raw plebeian emotion would also serve as negative labels

---

1 Westley, Christopher (Fall 2010). "The Debate Over Money Manipulations: A Short History" (PDF). *Intercollegiate Review* 45 (1–2): 3–11. Retrieved February 28, 2011.

2 For a view on how banks and government *create* poverty, see: http://www.georgewashington2.blogspot.com/2009/06/other-reason-for-american-revolution.html

3 John Marshall, *The Life of George Washington*, (1838)CHAPTER 28: Defense, Finance, Foreign Affairs— and the First "Systematic Opposition" (1790 to 1791)

into which to assign critics of the message who dared to make a stand for the truth.

Understanding the pitfalls of allowing a centralized bank to be established in the absence of checks and balances is of utmost importance when taking note of future events. Has it not been said long before that the debtor is *slave* to his lender[1]?

If the value of money can be manipulated, then the wages of workers and the profit of producers can be dramatically reduced. That means mortgage payments cannot be made, except by those with the deepest pockets—and that leads to foreclosures. Then the banks or other lenders receive the property; and again, all but those with the deepest pockets need to sell it as quickly as possible, which even further reduces the value of the property, while the sheer number of properties available saturates the system at large. The largest, most well-connected corporations know the real score and they have access to unlimited amounts of cash or credit—especially once the government has learned to call them "too big to [be allowed] to fail" and is willing to prop them up until the crisis is under control. Now those "giants" can step in to buy up properties that once were privately owned. Later, the value of the currency can be raised again, as the demand increases, allowing those who benefit from government collusion to sell these thousands of properties back into the market at prices far higher than the bargain-basement prices at which they had snapped them up.

If the system possessed any kind of controls, limits or alternatives to that currency—for instance, if individual states possessed their own currency, based for example on whatever their most valuable product was, then any rise or fall would be confined to those single specific areas. Of course, collusion within or among individual states can occur just as well, but everyone would have the option of "shopping around." An equal amount of corruption and an identical set of harmful practices is unlikely to be endemic to the entire nation at large. Such is what was meant by having checks and balances on any system of currency and economy.[2] The system would not have been perfect, but with such checks in place, at least individuals could have demanded better from those who ran the system. [3]

Follow the Money Trail

Once we fully understand the concerns of the opposition, we may use them as an analytical basis as we seek to extract the truth from the perverted

---

1 Proverbs 22:7
2 http://www.foxbusiness.com/personal-finance/2012/11/15/half-your-pay-check-to-government-in-2013/
3 http://www.idahopress.com/opinion/bestread/property-taxes-are-uncon-stitutional/article_15aa942c-9f1b-11e1-a6dd-0019bb2963f4.html

historical record. Just as we follow the "yellow brick road" in the story, *The Wizard of Oz*, we can follow the gold bricks, that is, follow the money—to find out who is behind the curtain arranging the strange mysterious occurrences we see in our world.

While some of our forefathers sought to create a paradise for the liberated individual to pursue his heart's desires, constrained only by the inherent limits of nature, others, with other views, were already at work, having assumed the power behind the throne inside the king's own castle and only masquerading as supporters of liberty for the people. In reality, this group stood only for their own enrichment, where they still stand to this very day—but now they hold much more power, backed by a brute force greater than any rule before.

The marriage between government, corporation and currency began in the United States with the establishment of The First Bank of the United States[1], which morphed from the Bank of North America established barely ten years earlier. This bank was championed by the "great" Alexander Hamilton[2]. To understand the bank, one must first know and understand who Hamilton was.[3]

Alexander Hamilton, the illegitimate son of a Scotsman and a married British woman living in the Caribbean, was acutely intelligent and extremely ambitious. He became the first US Secretary of the Treasury and an avid believer in Federalist policy (in which the government and capital, that is, big money, work hand in hand with no other office having the power to set any limits or rules for their conduct). As readers may recall, the Treasury was the fund or account into which flowed all deposits made to the government and out of which all government money flowed. This account could be accessed by only a chosen few. Other officials and the citizens at large have no idea how much is in the account, how much flows in and out, and most important—from and to *whom*.

In short, Hamilton insisted that a national bank (*centralized currency*) was necessary to stabilize and improve the nation's credit and improve the handling of financial business by the United States government. There is no doubt that the bank *was* beneficial for the health of the nation—*but not without checks and balances* to prevent corruption.

Hamilton proposed and supported four major financial innovations, namely:

Have the federal government take over the debts each state had incurred during the Revolutionary War.

Pay off those war debts.

1 https://en.wikipedia.org/wiki/First_Bank_of_the_United_States
2 https://en.wikipedia.org/wiki/Alexander_Hamilton
3 https://en.wikipedia.org/wiki/Secretary_of_the_Treasury

Raise money for the new government.

Establish a national bank and create a common currency.

This may look good at one level, but these "noble" aspirations primarily meant that the states would automatically become indebted to the federal government, subject to tax in amounts dictated by the federal government. and locked in to a currency that only the feds could manipulate—and that they would manipulate, for the benefit of an elitist few at the expense of the citizenry.

The primary function of the bank would be to manage credit issued to government and private interests for internal improvements and *"other"* economic development, per Hamilton's system of public credit. The system was rife with the potential for abuse. The phrase "other economic development" is a bit too broad a term to be left open to interpretation, but it was precisely the same government officials who would have the right to interpret it, if no other authority had the right to regulate banking activity.

Let's look at what was meant by the term "public funds."[1] The United States government had amassed huge war debts while financing the Revolutionary War against Great Britain. This money was borrowed from France[2] to establish the Bank of North America,[3] and was sold to US citizens in the form of stock / IOU notes that passed for currency. This idea was accepted for the sake of financing the war effort.

The US government at that time lacked the means to finance this debt as it had not yet been granted the right to impose income tax or any sort of duty tax on imports. As a temporary measure the Continental Congress resorted to printing money and bills of credit, causing rampant depreciation. In other words, the currency collapsed. To technically avoid bankruptcy, the Continental Congress eliminated $195 million of its $200 million debt, by fiat.[4] Thus the currency, called a *Continental*, was rendered nearly worthless.

During the years prior to the war, the national legislature cast its debts off onto the individual states. When most states failed to meet their required quota amounts for war materiel, the patriot army began confiscating supplies from farmers and traders, essentially giving them IOUs whose value was impossible to ascertain—and whose value dropped mighty quickly. By the end of the war, the states owed over $90 million.

The solution to the problem, as determined by Congress, was to service the debt and cover government operating expenses via tonnage duties and

---

1 https://en.wikipedia.org/wiki/First_Report_on_the_Public_Credit

2 Paris and Amsterdam bankers loaned the Continental congress huge sums of money to finance their war effort

3 https://en.wikipedia.org/wiki/Bank_of_North_America

4 Currency with value dictated by government regulation rather than gold or silver.

tariff taxes. On July 4th 1789, a tariff act was passed.[1] An interesting note is that $40 million of the domestic debts were owed to the soldiers of the patriot army and to citizens who had made loans to cover war expenses; they had been given IOUs (of undetermined value, that is, of practically no value at all).

Many of these people had been unable to wait to be repaid, and in order to support their families and cover urgent expenses they had to relinquish their notes of IOUs to speculators at sharply reduced rates. It was proposed that the government would eventually pay back the original holder at full value, and pay the current holder (speculator) of the IOU whatever price he had paid for it, as well. But that would mean that the federal government would be on the hook for combined pay-outs that would exceed the original value of the note.

James Madison proposed that the current holders (speculators) be reimbursed whatever they had paid for the IOUs, while the original holders would receive the balance. That way, the federal government would pay just the amount at which the note had been set.

Hamilton rejected both plans and insisted that the original creditors be left penniless while the current holders (speculators, which he considered "investors") should receive the full value of the note – *with interest!* The justification for this was that, in his own words, it would *"create a favorable climate for investment in government securities*, transforming public debt into a source of capital" (what a euphemistic obfuscation! What is really meant was that the government ripped off the veterans in a shameful fashion).

Rather than seek to eliminate the national debt, Hamilton sought to trade government securities on par with currency notes as legal tender, assuming the same value as currency. Of course, that meant that the public debt would continue to rise, eventually demanding to be repaid in full. Who was going to pay it? First, let's see *who* the speculators were and specifically *who* Hamilton was looking out for. It was most definitely *not* the rank and file family, neither the soldier nor the citizen who had sincerely contributed to the war effort; those would lose wages and their lifetime's investment revenue.

Those who could afford to buy up the notes were the well-to-do (many of whom possessed inside connections and were alerted to the fact that these would be redeemed at face value) rushed to "help" their poorer brethren by buying them out. More than three quarters of these notes had been purchased at ten cents on the dollar, but were selling at 20 to 30 cents before Hamilton's advertisement effort announcing them[2]. Here lies the strong suggestion of

---

1 https://en.wikipedia.org/wiki/Tariff_of_1789
2 Without a doubt these delays were well planned in advance, and intentional.

corporate connections benefiting from secret government relationships, but there are more suggestions of sleight of hand here.

When Hamilton's report finally came out, speculators from Philadelphia and New York (centers of national banking) came into Southern ports by the shipload to buy up these securities/ IOU notes before that section of the country became aware of the plan. The value of the notes continued to fall for months following Hamilton's report, leading to the conviction that Congress would halt Hamilton's proposal of redemption.

James Madison was convinced that Hamilton's program of redemption was a cruel scheme to defraud the Revolutionary War veterans of wages owed to them and represented a handout to those who did not need it, some of whom were members of Congress themselves! Madison's proposal of "discrimination" was a sort of "check" designed to correct these Congressional-sanctioned abuses, but it was frowned upon by Congress (which supports the theory that they themselves were seeking to benefit).

Hamilton argued that concentrating the wealth into fewer hands would *strengthen commercial investment* and encourage constructive economic growth, enlarging government credit available to business enterprises[1]. Allowing access to government funds in the absence of provisions to ensure fairness would also open the door for more corruption at the expense of former soldiers and individual citizens who lost property to finance their states' tax burdens to the federal government, being repaid in worthless IOU banknotes.

Interesting to note is that Congress rejected Madison's proposal by a vote of 36 to 13. Already the influences of big money and their collusion with government were stomping on the sweat and blood sacrifices of the average American citizen.

The First Sin Against Our Vets

Back before the Revolutionary War even began, the Continental Congress had gone into debt to the French government to finance the war effort. To pay that debt, they flooded the market with notes that were not backed in gold or silver, just hoping to pay it off when the situation improved after the war. During the war, as well, the soldiers who fought, risking limb and life, were paid via the same notes of highly questionable value yet carrying the implied worth of the face value printed on the notes.

When the war ended, the debt was shifted back onto the states. But the states could not pay. Now the same soldiers who had fought went out to the farms and the tradesmen's shops to take what they needed—confiscating products, if you will—work tools and raw materials, in the same value

1 Another euphemism to justify the great fraud.

as the notes. Efforts were made to pay the right amount in notes or IOUs promising repayment in equal value golden coin/specie. So in the end, all of the individual citizen soldiers and ex-soldiers, farmers and tradesmen, shop keepers and the like, were left with box loads of essentially worthless government IOUs (banknotes/currency), hoping and needing to exchange them for coin at the face value stated.

Eventually wealthy speculators, whom must have been protected by government officials, if not working directly in the name of land companies who had collusion, development companies or some sort of real estate contractor (high level banker), go out and offers these individuals 10 to 22 cents in coin on every dollar's worth of notes. By now, the average person had to get something of value in exchange for the worthless notes, and they accepted whatever deal they could find. Later on, Congress put out a report announcing the investment opportunity, but before word spread, shiploads of well-informed speculators head South for the purpose of buying up thousands of IOU banknotes at values even less (pennies) on the dollar.

Congress finally announced that it was going to redeem these notes at full face value to the *speculative investor*, with the amount that was remaining as being owned to the original holder as his purchase price, which as we discussed earlier, equaled 10 to 20 cents in golden coin. In effect what the situation here was, is that all of these ex-Revolutionary War vets (*and citizens whose property had been confiscated to cover their states' tax debt to the federal government*), for all practical purposes, lost the wages owed to them by their own government for their services during the Revolutionary War. In addition to that, many tradesmen and farmers were scammed out of payment for the product that had been confiscated. In many cases, the very speculators who were purchasing these notes by the thousands were members of the national Congress themselves, but what less should we expect?

Is not such a great fraud of the general public, perpetrated through collusion between those with money and power, not what Jefferson warned Congress about and sought to prevent by demanding checks and balances? The influence of centralized British banking elites and their abusive collusion with the heads of Britain's largest corporations had already indirectly asserted its supremacy in American government.[1]

Assumptions and Settlements

As far as this author is concerned, this business of the federal government forcing its debt back onto the states, then confiscating the individual

---

1 Remember that Washington himself was related to the British upper crust; see, for example, https://en.wikipedia.org/wiki/Thomas_Kitson

citizens' personal property when the states defaulted on payment, sounds a sharp cautionary note for the present day.

Most of our 50 states are deeply indebted to the federal government right now, and some[1] are nearing default, if not in default already.[2] We don't hear much about it, oddly enough. But what will this mean for the citizens of defaulting states as time moves forward?[3]

History is the test laboratory for observing how similar scenarios have played out in the past. The ability to see what happened before may very well make the difference between those who survive the coming horror and those whom fate will trample. If the corporate-sponsored tyrant[4] set the rules almost 250 years ago, we can, if we have the courage to face reality, imagine how the results will apply in today's scenario. National leaders do not like to admit incompetence or give up their positions of power. They will go to *any lengths* to avoid doing so, including complete suppression of the plebeians and denying/obscuring the realities of the situation [5]by blaming the inevitable breakdown on something other than reckless over-spending and financial mismanagement.

In order to effectively view how present-day events are unfolding, we *must keep our focus on the money trail* from the very beginning to today. The facts betray the intention lurking behind them. People who know the truth of their past may perceive the suggestion put forth as new details materialize; such people have a chance of removing themselves from harm's way.

Let us be reminded, however, that the rank and file citizens en masse rarely possess this sort of foresight. Unfortunately, the psychological circumstance of complacency nearly always reigns supreme among the masses. To believe in impending chaos is simply too uncomfortable for most. It is the *natural inclination to assume* that life will continue as it always has, in one's own lifetime, and any consideration of the opposite is collectively derided.

But readers who *resist this natural inclination to assume their continued well being,* who make their own observations of history and verifiable facts,[6] can plan and act to remove themselves, their and property from harm's way.

---

1 http://mercatus.org/statefiscalrankings
2 http://www.newsmax.com/Finance/StreetTalk/California-Economic-Collapse-Pension/2015/05/05/id/642699/
3 http://theeconomiccollapseblog.com/archives/tag/detroit
4 Take a look under "The New Dangers" section for some shocking Executive Orders that have been on the books since about 1965, entirely under the radar for most of us.   http://dmc.members.sonic.net/sentinel/gvcon5.html
5 http://www.theguardian.com/commentisfree/2012/dec/29/fbi-coordinated-crackdown-occupy
6 http://www.ipi.org/ipi_issues/detail/barriers-to-entrepreneurship-how-government-undermines-economic-opportunity

The Money Trail

Continuing to follow the money trail, we move forward with the idea of what was labeled as *"assumption,"* the scheme proposed by Alexander Hamilton. *Assumption* meant that the debt of the thirteen states was to be consolidated by the federal government for servicing under a general funding plan. Keep in mind that Hamilton was a Federalist, and that the Federalists worked for the corporate interests. In other words, this plan of *assumption* sounds good on the surface, but it came with a hard and fast catch.

Hamilton's plans were both political and economic, since state securities fluctuated locally in value, and consequently lent themselves to speculative buying and selling. Speculation over the value of the Continental currency spelled ruin for the rank and file Revolutionary War veteran. Unchecked insider speculative buying and selling led to corruption in the national system. In addition, each individual state was responsible for developing its own repayment plan to the federal government, putting it in competition with the federal government for sources of tax revenue. All the burden landed on the backs of the individual citizens, who stood to forfeit everything they owned when they were unable to pay the amounts demanded yearly.

From a political perspective, Hamilton sought to link creditors to a developing centralized government by joining their financial fortunes with the success of his economic nationalism and total domination of the public sector *(up to and including the right of individual citizens to accumulate resources and own property*—rights that are protected by Constitution). This action would eventually remove the fact of individual states/citizens being independent economically, facilitating a deepening control over the states and consequently citizen affairs by the federal government.

Opposition to this idea of *"assumption"* came from James Madison who, as we may recall, was a strong believer in the idea of financial and political progress, but not without checks and balances to curtail the natural inclination toward corruption. We are dealing with two opposing theories of government here; one favoring government ruled by unchecked banking and corporate interests at the expense of individual interests, and the other favoring national progress economically and politically with a system of checks and balances in place to secure the interests of the citizens.

Solvent and Insolvent states

Now let's examine this new scheme of the corporations, banks and their government servants to extort from the areas of the nation that were still outside of their control. Some states had fared better than others, but by distributing collective debts among all of the states, the more solvent states would have to pay a higher share for the more indebted ones. Now *which states* were most indebted and which ones were most solvent? We shall dare the reader to make his own educated guess here, at this point in the information.

Most of the states ruled by those who practiced individual enterprise and owned large tracts of productive land were *solvent/debt free*. Only South Carolina still owed debts from the Revolutionary War. In fact, debt-free Virginia led the fight against *"assumption,"* with Madison arguing that the newly proposed national tax would over-burden planters who already operated on a narrow margin of profit. Forcing those who had managed their debts to support those states who had failed to do so was deemed unjust. The corporate elite were now to be bailed out at the expense of individual productive entrepreneurs, and apparently that set a precedent.[1]

Madison's proposal called for each state to balance its own account, termed *"settlements."* Each state would be able to determine the amount that it would be held responsible for. By surrendering state debt over to the Treasury Department, the states would give the federal government enormous financial authority over state matters and financial affairs, consequently leading to a virtual dictation of individual citizen affairs. Madison and his constituents feared that all power and wealth would be concentrated into just a few hands, as the states would be absorbed more and more into the federal government, a concentration and centralization of wealth and power reminiscent of the royal system they had so recently escaped, leaving a every decision to be made to the advantage of an elitist few.

When the proposal went up for vote, a concession was agreed upon in order to speed its approval. Hamilton's proposal was accepted that Virginia should have closest proximity to the site of the newly proposed capital, and the state would receive back the same amount that it paid in. In other words, Hamilton's plan was adopted and imposed on all the states, and just one out of the states that had managed to remain solvent received special benefits while the other solvent states lost out.

In the end, the urgency of the moment convinced everyone to fall into line and get behind those of the corporatists ruling via government connections. It is hard to conceive that the corporate, banking and government influence were already so well entrenched. Already the only new influence in

---

1 In other words, the corporate aristocracy sought to create a system where they could access an unlimited debt margin, then impose responsibility for paying that debt back upon individual estate owners. Keep in mind here as well, that the primary method for individuals to acquire wealth was, and still is, by owning productive real-estate and selling services back to the population. What the corporations sought was to take over the business activities of the plantation.

government affairs, the notion of favoring the concerns of individual citizens, was melting in the face of corporate, banking and government infringement.

By December 13, 1790, the national debt had reached $80 million and it ate up 80% of annual government expenditures. The interest alone on the debt consumed 40% of national revenue between 1790 and 1800. How was this money going to be paid? Who was destined to pay it? We shall soon see.

Hamilton drew up a report on manufacturing, aimed at encouraging its growth and protection. Let's recall who made up the list of manufacturers in those days, where their main offices were located, and their connections reaching high up in government. The corporate and banking sphere of influence and power was expanding rapidly, but at the expense of whom? And by contrast, what area of the nation most supported the individual's capacity to produce and his Constitutional right to own property/real estate?

Hamilton's success earlier in persuading those who favored individual interests and their concerns to step behind those of corporations, big money and government, caused him to issue another formal report, this time on public credit. The primary intention of this report was to advocate the establishment of a central bank for the purpose of monetizing national debt (as described above) by expanding the flow of legal tender (bills and coins), although monetizing the debt would be accomplished through the issuance of federal banknotes, where the value could be determined by hard metals, supply of notes above value support in metals or via fiscal policy (fiat).

In simple words, the value could be manipulated when and if the decision was made to do so....unless solid checks and balances were put in place demanding that the value be held in true terms. This would be a privately held bank with no one to hold it to the standard of maintaining real value, even though it was supported via public funds *(tax revenue)*.

This was a precursor to today's Federal Reserve Bank which is also *"privately"* held; it's not a "Federal" institution in the usual sense at all; and it is supported by public funds *(federal income tax)*.

A third purpose of the centralized bank would be to process revenue fees and perform fiscal duties for the federal government[1]. This model of a privately-held bank engaging in government work is an interesting aberration. It seems to leave open the suggestion that the federal government was aiming to conceal the patterns of banking/business/government collusion, which could become buried underneath layers of bureaucratic paperwork and miscellaneous donations and appropriations. Identification of the sources could not only back the claims of those advocating checks and balances, but could also invite possible charges of corruption, which had

---

1 Keep in mind that the corporate aristocracy wanted no checks and no debt limits, so anything could be categorized and claimed as legitimate.

already been the case in earlier times, as we have previously demonstrated in this work.

Washington: The People's Hero?

The standing opposition was headed by James Madison. He argued that establishment of a centralized bank gave the federal government powers that rightly belonged at the state level, and it violated the provisions of the Articles of Confederation which had convinced all thirteen colonies to sign on: namely, that "Each state retains its sovereignty, freedom, and independence, and every power, jurisdiction, and right, which is not by this Confederation expressly delegated."

Hamilton and his pro-federal power partners argued, to the contrary, that since the federal government was responsible for taxation and the borrowing of funds, then under the "necessary and proper" clause of the Constitution (in his interpretation), they granted the federal authorities the right to establish reasonable means of carrying out such responsibilities and the bank would be a reasonable part of the picture.

Madison believed in a far stricter, literal Constitutional interpretation. To him, Congress had no broad authority to grant charters of incorporation. Madison claimed that Congress was straying into dangerous territory, an un-ending swamp, in effect.

Hamilton won. At the expense of checks and balances, the amendment to create the First Bank of the United States passed by a vote of 37 to 20, holding a 21-year charter. The 21-year life for the charter is interesting enough to hold for later reflection, as will be revealed in the dramatic events that followed.

Madison's concerns caused George Washington to pause for a moment to reflect, but that did not change what he wound up actually doing. According to the official record, he first consulted with his Cabinet in regard to the legality of the bill. Secretary of state, Thomas Jefferson working with attorney Edmund Rudolph, agreed with Madison that the government was under strictly limited powers to grant these charters of incorporation.

Support for this stance was cited in the Tenth Amendment, advocating the right of states to decide for themselves, outside of the federal government's realm of responsibility. In effect, Madison, Jefferson and attorney Edmund Rudolph simply agreed that having a centralized bank was necessary for future national fiscal and structural development *but not without solid checks and balances* to safeguard individual interests, Constitutional and otherwise!

Washington seems to have reacted pretty quickly, considering the enormity of the implications.. Hamilton argued that the while the authority to create the First Bank of the United States was not granted by the

Constitution, it was never the less inherent to a centralized government and required to fulfill the duties prescribed in the *Doctrine of Implied Powers*.[1]

Barely two days later George Washington signed the bill into law. It all appeared legitimate at first glance and he strategically got it signed before the matter could be further debated. This could all have been planned in advance behind closed doors; Washington's decision, the decision as to *who* would give what justification and *when* he would sign, with an overall strategy. And just as Madison had feared in the end the result was to enhance the power of the financiers and industrialists, an aristocratic few, in the long run.

Where was the compromise demonstrating any concern for preservation of individual interests in the future? Why should any presumption be made that this venture would somehow not be subject to corruption when corruption appears to be a permanent part of human history? Giving free rein to corporate and bank actions enabled via government collusion has dramatically influenced history.

The official history is nothing more than tailor made *propaganda* to hide the facts from the rank and file American citizen. The United States government was and still is dominated by the corporate and banking elite. The centralized bank has unchecked authority to dictate currency values at its own liberty, and their government insiders now constitute the entire US representative body! Altogether, it comes down to a *banking mafia* that will go to any length for the purpose of obtaining its desires, including murdering US presidents and mass murder of the American citizenry, as suggested by historical fact.. This cartel collusion stands with *no check* by the "people's representatives" to oppose or restrain it[2], and has done so ever since conclusion of the American Civil War. In effect what the nation of America has ruling it in our present time is a *collective absolute authority*, ever growing in its efforts to suppress the individual citizen, at times, at the expense of his blood won Constitutional rights.

What was the outcome of this new centralized bank and plans for its establishment? According to historian John Chester Miller, "Revolutionary War debt had been eliminated, the price of government securities had been stabilized, the power of the Federal Government had been exerted over the states, foreign capital began pouring into the United States and the credit of the Federal Government had been established[3]." Or had it? At the expense of whom? What were the ensuing plans which were to come at the expense of individual concerns, Constitutional and otherwise? Let's recall that all of this potentially negative development had occurred by the year 1792. The ink

---

1 https://en.wikipedia.org/wiki/Implied_powers
2 Although both political parties masquerade as doing so, when the lie serves to benefit the cartel collusion
3 Miller, 1960, p. 68-69

on the papers declaring US independence and the anointed Constitution to preserve plebeian liberty had hardly had time to set!

Report of Manufactures

Let's zero in on the *Report of Manufactures*[1] mentioned earlier. This plan was first proposed to Congress in the year 1791, and much of it was adopted. In this massive report, Hamilton outlined a set of policies intended to help build the economic strength of the new republic. He sought to apply tariffs (or taxes) on imported and exported goods to raise money that could not only help domestic manufacturers be price-competitive, but could raise money to help build canals and other infrastructure to support commerce and, most controversially, to provide direct subsidies to manufacturing.

Hamilton said that all this was important in order to ensure that the independence won by the Revolutionary War was secure. Note that the people of the colonies had fought that war as a revolt against a British corporate elite that they felt was imposing laws and fees upon them and against an extended corporate–government collusion that had already been in place for two hundred years (and for nearly another hundred in various isolated locations). The Constitution was intended to provide a barrier to preserve individual interests and concerns from that type of externally imposed burden from the corporate–government conspiracy. But already in just a few short years, the interests of big capital were imposing themselves, bordering on outright Constitutional illegality and infringement. Where lay concern for the average American citizen? Let's examine the opposition to find out.

Thomas Jefferson and the Democratic-Republican Party objected to the idea of subsidy, in particular, for fear of it leading to corruption, on the one hand, and on the other, because it would collect from everyone while obviously giving economic favor to the sections of the nation where the interests of corporations and banks were already entrenched. This would put agrarian regions at a disadvantage. Jefferson agreed that development was absolutely necessary, but he wanted a financial system that could facilitate development under a solidly checked and balanced authority and without essentially taxing one part of the nation to subsidize the development of another.

---

1 https://en.wikipedia.org/wiki/Report_on_Manufactures

The Coinage Act of 1792

The Coinage Act of 1792 [1] fits perfectly into the discussion here. This single Act was the framework upon which all subsequent coinage production was based. The act authorized construction of a mint building, an issue already discussed.

The most immediate result of the coinage act was that depositors simply quit placing money in the bank, since the new silver standard was less than the old Spanish Standard. Depositors had to put in 10% more in silver bullion for every dollar they received. The Act defined set 15 units of pure silver equal to one unit of pure gold. Standard gold was defined as 11 parts pure gold to one part allowed of silver and copper. That makes for an interesting precedent as it applies to future fiscal development.

The Second Bank of the United States

Hamilton's First Bank of the United States ended its charter in 1816. The new bank was supported in those areas of the nation where the prevailing economic system was based on the individual's ownership of productive land and real estate, the Western and Southern states, versus areas controlled almost in the absolute by corporate and banking conglomerates, mainly the Northeastern states. The primary spokespersons for the effort were John C[2]. Calhoun and Henry Clay[3]. The charter was signed into law on April 10, 1816, by Madison.

While it is interesting to note here that the primary persons who advocated reestablishment of the bank came from the areas dominated by individual interest and an area based on the individual's property and economic right to prosper, independent from government or corporate influence to threaten his efforts, it is very interesting to note that the opposition came from those areas just as well. That fact suggests to this author that some sort of change was now afloat in the air around Capitol Hill. For some reason, either the information here has been twisted a bit by the official historical record, to make the bank seem legitimate in the eyes of future citizens and historians, or there has truly been a change of heart due to some sort of irresistible lure. Let's begin by examining Henry Clay.

Henry Clay

Clay was born in Virginia, but he lived in Kentucky where he owned a productive plantation called Ashland, with 60 slaves working his hemp and

1 https://en.wikipedia.org/wiki/Coinage_Act_of_1792
2 https://en.wikipedia.org/wiki/John_C._Calhoun
3 https://en.wikipedia.org/wiki/Henry_Clay

tobacco fields. He was also a lawyer with his own private practice. One of his most notable defense cases, as it applies to this work, was that of *The Kentucky Insurance Company* against the repeal of a monopolistic charter issued by Felix Grundy. He was defending *repeal of a monopolistic charter*, in other words, the advancement of corporate interest intending to dominate solely and exclusively at everyone else expense.

Another interesting situation was Clay's defense of Aaron Burr for planning an expedition into Spanish-held territory west of the Mississippi River, aiming to secure for himself what amounted to a colony—with himself as King—and conspiring in an attempt to overthrow the Spanish government in Mexico simultaneously, which was illegal without explicit clearance from Congress. This was legally equivalent to treason. The charge against Aaron Burr was made by US District Attorney Joseph Hamilton Daveiss. Years later, Jefferson convinced Clay that Daveiss had been right in the charge after all.

But the point here is that Clay had already established, early on, that he *was a champion of big business* and *could be swayed by enough money*, even though he shared the lifestyle of the independent wealthy landed estate owners. Simply speaking, he would sell all of them out for enough money, and had very little in the way of ethical motivation holding him back from doing so. That much we can readily deduce without any farther investigation.

Clay can also be very deceptive. Recall that he nearly passed a bill requiring all members of Congress to wear homespun instead of the finer cloth imported from the British, even though he was of the wealthy class himself (though not strictly speaking "aristocratic"). He wound up fighting a duel over this proposal with Humphrey Marshall. Clay had strongly opposed development of the First Bank of the United States because of his personal ownership of several small localized banks [1] in Lexington, Kentucky. But when he was seeking the office of the presidency, he abruptly changed his position to give strong support for the Second Bank of the United States.

In view of what we have already noted in the history of Henry Clay, we can clearly see that he was quick to seize upon what he thought would be to his own personal advantage, at everyone else's expense. He was what some have labeled a turn-coat lawyer, and when enough money was plunked down before him, he would make an about-face from his original stated position to embrace the opposition. Why would he do that, unless he smelled an opportunity to profit immensely (presumably from an initial payoff as well

---

1 Which were owned by the landed estates, and just one of the services that corporate interests intended to wrest from the individual American endeavoring to "*pull himself up by his own boot straps,*" a propagandist phrase originating from the corporatist presently worn thin on American ears, to conceal the fact that true ability to do so has long been purloined from grasp by the plebeian masses at large.

as nearly guaranteed corporate payoffs for access to financial connections inside the new banking and colluding conglomerates). To judge from his actions, as far as Clay was concerned, individual rights or considerations of the Constitution apparently could be damned. All that he wanted was the money.

John C. Calhoun

Let's closely examine John C. Calhoun from South Carolina. In Calhoun's earlier years, he was a strong proponent of nationalism, modernization and a strong national/centralized government. In other words, he held Federalist views and did not support leaving many powers up to each state. But by 1830, he changed his view and wound up being a champion for the opposing side, the side that supported rule by individuals and states above corporations, banks and government through a system of hard checks and balances.

He seems to have had this change of heart because of the corruption that was already evident, and the blatant disregard for the good of the average citizen. For his past sin against the free-born US citizens in supporting the Second Bank of the United States, we citizens of the future shall forgive him here in this work. At least in later years, he saw the light and understood the results of allowing corporate/government collusion to dig its claws in.

Simply by examining those who opposed the bank, we can quickly detect the propagandist intention to give the impression that opinion leaders in the areas traditionally *against* consolidation of the currency were actually *supporters* of it. The truth is that what was billed as being supportive of the effort to consolidate the currency amounted to being out for one's own self interest, no matter what; although at least one such man, upon seeing the corruption with his own eyes, turned against support of the effort later on in his career.

Let's see what arguments the noted opposition used to justify their position, for it is here that we may find the truth entombed. After all, the opposition never desired anything more than a set of checks and balances to prevent corruption at the expense of individual enterprise people and the productive landed estates generating the supporting wealth.

John Taylor of Caroline

Let's examine the first of two men known as John Taylor of Caroline[1]. JTOC was a politician and writer, whose works would serve as a basis for substantiating the claim for states' rights and libertarian movements. He was a strong believer in natural rights, freedom, and limited government;

---

1 https://en.wikipedia.org/wiki/John_Taylor_of_Caroline

and he was a believer in citizen participation to prevent concentrated power, wealth, political corruption and financial manipulation. Were these exact issues not those that the very Constitution itself sought to neutralize? The Constitution itself was precisely a document of checks and balances to provide a barrier to the ever growing tentacles of government and corporations, limiting their ability to impose laws and regulations that suited their interests to the detriment of the individual person...right?

Taylor justified his pro-liberty stance by declaring that national government was a creation of the states and therefore was subordinate to them. Taylor was against slavery on the grounds that it was morally wrong. We could presume this stance was based in Taylor's avowed libertarian view.

Taylor actually called for Virginia's secession from the United States in 1798. His justification for this was that "enormous politically power invariably accumulates enormous wealth and enormous wealth invariably accumulates enormous political power," and such power no doubt corrupts. Obviously, Taylor was a staunch individualist, the type of American who most assuredly applying supported checks and balances on the collusion of banking and corporate interests.

John Randolph of Roanoke

We have John Randolph of Roanoke, next, in the hard opposition. John Randolph was another Congressman from Virginia and a staunch states'-rights advocate. In other words, he was hardcore on his position of placing checks and balances on the collusion of banks, corporations and their government connections.[1]

He promoted the Principles of '98, which argue that individual states could judge the Constitutionality of laws and decrees of the centralized government and could refuse to enforce laws they deemed unconstitutional. In this author's contention, this claim seems justified enough, especially if the laws violated the Constitution itself. Whatever happened then, since we know that events failed to go that way in the future? Obviously the banks, corporations and their contacts inside government won out. We, the American people, are most guilty for allowing it to be so, are we not?

John Randolph of Roanoke was a descendant of Pocahontas. He must have personally been very proud of his ancestry, that ancestry giving him great insight on just how terrible the effects of corruption between big money and government could be on the people of the land.

The official history degrades the stance of these two individuals, as well as any opposition to the efforts of big money, corporation and government imposing itself against the individual. Obviously the official history was

1 https://en.wikipedia.org/wiki/Principles_of_%2798

written by individuals who indeed were a part of the great problem, catering outright to the corruption and not part of the solution to neutralize it.

Eventually this corrupt collusion moved to outright *exterminate* their opposition who sought only to safeguard the interests of the individual citizens at large. They moved to force their will on citizens who lived outside the corporate, banking and government sphere of influence. This was, in a sense, a repeat of what we already witnessed as the federal government and corporate dealings intruded on the free, independent Native Americans. The intent to force their self serving will on the independent people of the land has never waned, and very soon in our own future, it appears, this will manifest itself in a manner that will astound and *terrify* even the most fearless among us.

To put these opinion and matters into more direct, simple wording, the SBOUS (Second Bank) was viewed as being unconstitutional and a point blank threat to the individual's freedom, a threat to state sovereignty, and an effort to overturn an individual's Constitution-backed right to own slaves if he so chose. There were slave-owning families in the North and the South, cities and countryside, including among the freemen or ex-slaves (whom we never hear about in the officially-endorsed history). Even so, popular history tends to exaggerate the view of how widespread slave holding was. Only about 25% of Southern whites owned slaves; and most families had fewer than 20, if they had slaves at all.

Now, some individuals who exercised their liberty by owning community banks had almost dismantled The Bank of the United States in 1811, by resisting the unchecked centralization of US currency. With the coming of the Jacksonian administration, the power and liberty extended to the individually-owned banks gave the gift of strength in Jackson's war on the SBOUS.

Under the management of the first bank president, William Jones, the bank *intentionally* failed to control the money issued from its branch banks in the West and South, allowing those who were in collusion to profit from speculation in land. Excessive issue of money caused massive inflation, driving property values down. When the centralized bank then withheld issue of its metallic currency, upon being presented the same banknotes issued by the centralized bank, from the state chartered banks, the state chartered banks had no choice but to foreclose on heavily mortgaged farms and business properties that they owned. In addition, investigations revealed that branch directors from the Baltimore office had engaged in rampant fraud and larceny. Keep in mind that Baltimore is just slightly north of Washington D.C., which may suggest some connection between Capitol Hill and the corruption in the Baltimore bank branch.

Bank President Jones resigned in 1819 and was replaced by Langdon Cheves, who continued to withhold the metallic currency. This caused a deepening turn in the financial collapse, leading to more massive unemployment and crashing property values that persisted until 1822. Afterward the currency would pick up in value until 1833, right on into the Presidency of Andrew Jackson. This expansion happened under the management of Nicholas Biddle. There is more here, however, than the official history record allows us to see.

Government During the Jacksonian Era

Andrew Jackson took office in 1829 and the bank was doing very well, according to the official history. Jackson immediately attacked the bank on the grounds that it had failed to produce a stabilized national currency, and that it was unconstitutional to establish a national bank to centralize currency without solid checks and balances to prevent corruption. Both Houses responded by investigating and generating reports to verify a historical precedent for the bank's Constitutionality, in the absence of checks on the currency, and its pivotal role as such in producing a uniform currency!

The problem, however, was not the bank's existence and that of a centralized currency. The true problem was that there were no provisions for preventing the corruption that was sure to come and that even by 1829 had already been manifest. Most assuredly, there had been rampant corruption witnessed by Jackson already, prompting him to take such a hard stand against unchecked banking and centralized currency. After all, the forces of wealth combined and placed into the hands of an elitist few would surely serve their interests at the expense of all others concerned. Those who bore the main burden were individuals owning and managing agrarian estates, as well as individual business enterprise in general.[1]

One can anticipate that with the recovery in value and stabilization of the currency, the corporate/banking/government collusion and even government officials themselves had already purchased millions of dollars worth of foreclosed real estate and government lands. The recovery witnessed and mentioned by the official history was simply due to a manipulated rise in currency value, once the properties had been secured by "the right people." Since powerful elements known by Jackson to be a part of that corrupt conspiracy had carried out the investigation to determine the legitimacy of the SBOUS, Jackson simply stood by his own convictions, publicly declaring

---

1 This author highly suspects that government files revealing negative intentions and their consuming depths are still sealed on this matter of corruption in absence of checks and balances to this very day.

that the bank was a corrupt institution and most dangerous to individual American liberties. True history has no doubt, proven him very right in that conviction.

Both William Jones and Langdon Cheves were from South Carolina, and the forces opposing their stance for checks and balances in the system crashed it out from underneath them.

The truly successful bank manger was Nicholas Biddle. Let's take a look at his background so see how he became so successful in management of the bank, as well as any hints of possible corrupt collusion.

Nicholas Biddle

Biddle was from Philadelphia, an area of the nation already heavily under the control of the corporations and banks. Upon emigration from England, the Biddle family had acquired extensive rights over 43,000 acres of lands in New Jersey. They were part of the British gentry, not average folks. (The Biddle family has connections through which they have continued to influence big government, even to this very day.) He graduated from Princeton University. One of his cousins became an exchange broker in Philadelphia. Biddle served as secretary to James Monroe. Monroe appointed him as federal government director and representative of the bank in 1816. Biddle became president of the bank in 1822.

In 1803 the Louisiana Purchase was made and in 1818, an interest payment in the amount of $4 million was due on bonds used to purchase the land. The bank was required to make payment, in either gold or silver, to European investors on behalf of the United States government. The bank, therefore, required that private commercial banks that had been lent money in the form of *fiat* paper or paper, where the value was determined by regulation, had to pay in toward the debt with gold or silver coin.

Here lies the corruption that Jackson so violently warned against. Essentially the centralized bank forced the privately owned banks to hand over its gold and silver to pay for federal government debts, even though they had had no say in taking on that debt.

This caused the privately held banks to default on loans and made property values crash. This effectively shut them down, making way for the imposition of a centralization of banking and currency, while using the gold and silver reserves to serve the interest of an elite few.[1]

At the same time, the LP was simply an attempt of the elite in federal government to acquire more raw land to be traded out among their corporate

---

1 Large plantation owners also invested in local banks, notating here a stab at the economy supporting those who called for checks on the corrupted collusion.

backing constituents with manipulated currency looted from the American people.

Jackson, being an advocate of individual enterprise, as differentiated from the elitist minority, had to borrow money from the same bank that fraudulently manipulated the currency. Of course with the value of notes fluctuating wildly, since the gold and silver were being withdrawn, then reinserted, he had trouble paying back his debts as the value of the currency jumped and dropped. Wages, after all, only consist of negotiated dollar amounts over a predetermined passage of time, rather than current value of the individual banknote.

During this time period, Biddle helped establish Girard College, a private school for poor orphaned boys in Philadelphia. The college was named after Stephan Girard, one of the wealthiest men in America. Girard had been the original promoter of the SBOUS and the reorganization of the second bank and its largest investor. Biddle had colluded with big money and an obvious corporate elite; naturally, he fully intended to serve their interests, regardless that it came at the expense of the ordinary citizen.

Girard, by the way, made his fortune in international shipping and merchant activities. He was one of the wealthiest individuals in America at the time, as well as being considered by historians today as being among the wealthiest who ever lived in America. His descendants are still very active on the top end of the political spectrum and more than likely, very active in the top end corporate business scene as well.

It should be very safe to assume that Biddle wanted access to unregulated funds to accomplish his own investment objectives, as well as having laws tailor made to accompany that unfettered access to bank funds and specific state representatives, supreme court judges, and other people who were elected to both represent and protect the citizen interests, who had voted them into office. In other words, among those in high government and banking circles who held to the same self-serving convictions, it was understood that Biddle was the man to faithfully serve those convictions. This strongly suggests that his "revered" success as president of the SBOUS was a result of manipulation in the system at large, as were the failures of those before him.

Via these suggestions, the truth is revealed that the corporate/banking/ government collusion coveted privately owned real estate, primarily raw productive land, and were in the process of devising a plan to wrest control of those possessions from the individuals who owned them; especially in view of the propaganda[1] devised to create a diversion in the form of a divisive

---

1 https://en.wikipedia.org/wiki/Elijah_Parish

appeal to emotion.[1] As a result of the astounding success of this program of emotional manipulation, it was destined to serve as a primary tactic of deception against the people and was utilized by the United States federal government for many decades to come, even up to the time of this writing.[2]

The collusion also had other desires, including taking over the provision of services to communities surrounding the large estates. Don't forget that many of these large produce-based estates also owned and operated local private banks. The plantation general store and the services offered on the grounds will be discussed in detail later on. The individual American citizen, by the time of Jackson, was viewed by the corrupt collusion as a servant, someone who scarcely had a right to own anything, certainly not to profit from any individual efforts. There is some question as to whether this[3] attitude has changed even today.

As alluded to earlier, Jackson was a witness to the height of corruption in the federal banking system and government at large. That is why he launched his "war" on the bank, as the situation has been historically labeled. What the official historical record has neglected to mention is the clear and specific justifications for this hard stance in demanding checks and balances.

Before we get into discussing the bank war, first consider that both the FBOUS and the SBOUS had already demonstrated a history of issuing *fiat* notes or "banknotes" in the form of an IOU, essentially, not backed by gold or silver. This fact allowed for an excessive issuance of these notes to facilitate inflation, or a retraction of the gold or silver (known as specie) to deflate the value of the notes. In other words, it was obvious that the value of the currency could be intentionally manipulated, hence the claim that the institution was open to corruption and had already demonstrated instances of corruption.

The reason for manipulating the value of the currency, again, is that those "in the know" can profit—on the way up and on the way down, as we have described. When land values plummeted, those in the "know" could lay back vast sums of notes or acquire them through unquestioned loans, purchasing real estate property at vastly reduced (crashed) value. Then once these holdings had been bought up by the conspiring few, the value was raised by re-issuing specie, gradually, and then there would be a sell-off made at a high

1 https://en.wikipedia.org/wiki/Elijah_Parish_Lovejoy
2 http://www.huffingtonpost.com/entry/terry-mcauliffe-gun-control-virginia-shooting_55ddd4fbe4b0a40aa3acea2f
3 Yearly taxes on property rob the individual of his Constitutional right to own property. It essentially means that the government actually owns all property, even after you "bought" it. If you've already paid for it and "own" it, how can it be taken away for failure to continue paying? Aren't we then, in fact, only renting it? Furthermore, income tax in any amount exceeding 12% in total (6% *state*, 6% *Federal*) amounts to extortion and robs the individual of his Constitutional right to prosperity.

profit. The land companies could then carve up undeveloped land that had been purchased from the federal government (recall how government had acquired this land) into tracts, reselling them to poor settlers who would get more or less inflated loans from the same bank involved in the manipulation.

Even if the banks were part of a private charter, still they had no option but to borrow notes from the primary bank of the US. Private banks were almost forced to lend at high rates of interest just to make a profit, since selling the tainted property back to the people was the last traitorous step in this infected scheme of theft. When the SBOUS was noted as performing well under the Biddle presidency, now we know why.

Another note to make here is that all of this *war on the banks* occurred at the same time Jackson had removed the protection of property owned by Native Americas east of the Mississippi.[1] Obviously some sort of a deal between corporate and banking interests and the Jackson administration had been concluded. Evidence of that conclusion shows in the later stages of the war on banking, when Jackson appears to have made concessions to those whom he had previously so bitterly opposed. The connections in these circumstances are astounding to observe and very tough to ignore. In a court of law, the verdict would certainly be guilty, based on a continuous line of strong circumstantial evidence.

Another interesting point is that while the focus in the official history is primarily on native people residing within boundaries of areas that produced representatives heavily supportive of checks and balances on banking and corporate interests, "Indian" removal also applied to natives residing in states such as Illinois, Ohio and others.

Take a glance at this direct quote and the footnote that follows:

> In 1807, the Wyandot joined three other tribes, the Odawa, Potawatomi, and Ojibwe people, in signing the Treaty of Detroit. The agreement, between the tribes and William Hull, representing the Michigan Territory, gave the United States a part of today's Southeastern Michigan and a section of Ohio near the Maumee River. The tribes were able to keep only isolated small pockets of land in the territory.[2]

Now consider this, and the footnote:

> In the 1840s, most of the surviving Wyandot people were displaced to Kansas through the US federal policy of forced Indian removal.[3]

1 https://en.wikipedia.org/wiki/Indian_Removal_Act
2 "Treaty Between the Ottawa, Chippewa, Wyandot, and Potawatomi Indians". *World Digital Library*. 1807-11-17. Retrieved 2013-08-03
3 Weslager, C.A. (1972). *The Delaware Indians: A History*. Rutgers University Press pp. 399–400. ISBN 0-8135-0702-2.

Indian Removal was not only directed toward Natives who resided in a certain specific region of the nation, other than east of the Mississippi River; that sole region specified being the one producing representatives demanding checks and balances to neutralize corruption, protecting individual interests; but such is what the twisted official historical record would have children and college students believe, obviously an attempt by the propagandists to vilify an entire culture of people. There were other tribes not mentioned here, but this author felt mentioning this particular tribe of Wyandot would be sufficient to make the point here.

In other words, our official history has been twisted to conceal the powerful influence of banks and corporations via their government collusion. Another most interesting point is the manner in which guilt for the crimes of big money has been displaced onto the shoulders of those who called for checks and balances on the system, and dared to make the ultimate stand in challenge to the authority of those conspiring interests.

The guilt for those crimes of what amounts to outright treason is routinely displaced onto those who dare to challenge authority by calling for checks and balances. This trend can be followed on throughout US history.

The Bank War

There were clear and valid reasons for Jackson to initiate an effort to halt the resurrection of the SBOUS. Corruption was rife throughout the system; Jackson had been witness to it. He well knew that the secret to pulling the currency value back into line would be to enforce a rule that each banknote produced be backed by a value of a stated amount in gold or silver, preferably gold.

In using this tactic, excess notes that amounted to IOUs could not be produced for the purpose of inflating the value, nor could the gold and silver be withheld so that the market would become flooded with non-backed notes, another way to see the value deflated. To put a check on this end of the system, the receiving institution would demand that the depositor trade the amount of the notes' worth in gold or silver coin. As a matter of fact, the same call is being made even today in regard to monetary issue and currency values, no doubt for the purpose of putting a stop to corruption (known to some but as yet veiled from the rest of us) involving the Federal Reserve, the corporate elite and their government insiders, just like in Jackson's day; but without a strong viable, self supporting body inside the halls of Congress to demand checks on the system to safeguard individual interests, how can the people demand them?

From a personal perspective, Jackson's loyalty was to the time-honored ideals of individualism, the same individualism that motivated the rank and file colonist that defeated the British and their corporate collusion, and forged the Constitution to shield individuals from any corporation and government imposing their greedy provisions upon us all. This ideal is now determined to reassert itself. Such loyalties were, in essence, inviolate vows made to the necessary virtues of limited government, checks on judicial determination regarding the written constitutional document, the states acting independently of the federal government and the rights of individuals reigning superior over banks, corporate interests and any government collusion in general.

Though the bank was not made an issue during Jackson's presidential campaign or election, in private he was known to refer to it as "a hydra of corruption, dangerous to our liberties, with demoralizing effects on our citizenry." What we already know of the bank's past certainly supports Jackson and his confidential statements.

Jackson made an annual address to Congress on December 7, 1830, stating that the new bank/reformed bank would be entirely public, with no private stock holders, nor would it engage in lending or land purchasing and would retain only its role in processing custom duties for the US Treasury.

Eventually a compromise was reached, in 1831, where Jackson would accommodate a recharter as long as modifications were made that produced a centralized national institution, and Biddle pledged to refrain from petitioning Congress for renewal until the general election of 1832. In the end, Jackson's own appointed secretary explicitly called for a post 1832 rechartering that reconfigured the government bank.

Earlier on it was mentioned that one could deduce that Jackson and the corporate, big money and government interests conspired in some sort of secret deal in which he agreed to remove the block on native lands east of the Mississippi. In other words, his part of the bargain was to simply sell out the indigenous people to banking/corporate interests, in return for their temporary relinquishing of the hard line stance on an unchecked centralized bank. This back room trade-off must have taken place between the years 1829 and 1831, since it appears that a compromise was finalized in 1831.

Even Jackson's anti-bank associates were shocked and outraged by this abrupt change on the issue[1],[2]. No doubt something went down that facilitated this change of heart, something that Jackson agreed with; although in truth, he had no other choice but concede on some level, if he ever hoped to make progress on other aspects of his vision of reform. Keep in mind that the Indian Removal Act was passed on May 28, 1830, just between the years

1 Hammond, 1957, p. 384
2 Wilentz, 2008, p. 367

1829 and 1831, when the compromise was reached. You steal the golden egg for us and we'll let you have the goose—for a while.

Nicholas Biddle did not feel that Jackson would pursue reform for a compromise on the bank, but his informants closest to the Jackson administration assured him that Jackson would not veto re-authorization measures,[1] a most interesting detail to note.[2] In spite of that, Jackson's anti-bank constituents, pro checks and balances in the name of individual interests won out. In the end, Jackson wound up vetoing the recharter on July 10, 1832.

What we must presume here is that banking and corporate interests must have failed to come through on their end of the deal. Jackson had already turned his end of the deal over by signing the IRA. Jackson justified his actions with a speech that linked decisions made of citizen concerns with those of the executive powers of government, calling it "a leveling of opportunity under the protection of the executive branch."

To further explain how this new link between the executive branch extending beyond Supreme Court judicial powers was used to justify the veto, the next few sentences are helpful. According to Jackson, the powers of the executive branch were not limited to decisions of the Supreme Court, nor to compliance with Congressional legislation, when the issues involved were in the interests of the citizenry. In other words, executive power could be asserted on social, political or economic grounds; a somewhat new approach, but not that much different from that of Hamilton in his justification for the FBOUS.

Evidently when the IRA was passed as one side of the tainted bargain being fulfilled, Jackson had very wisely anticipated that the other side would fail to uphold their end of the bargain to the end that it had been agreed upon, so he had presumptively deduced the method by which he would neutralize all concessions made supporting the reestablished bank charter, and yet still veto the effort to recharter the bank. On July 13, 1832, the veto was sustained, but all was still too bad for the Native Americans who already had their lands traded out from underneath them to their disadvantage, resulting from the obvious secret deal.

The goal of Jackson was to eliminate the centralized bank before its 20-year term ended in 1836. To facilitate the quashing of a proposed recharter, Jackson's cabinet members Kendall[3] and Blair[4] had convinced Jackson that to transfer 20% of bank funds into private holdings would be prudent. The

---

1 Remini, 1981, p. 343
2 Jackson had already made the deal with the "devil."
3 https://en.wikipedia.org/wiki/Amos_Kendall
4 https://en.wikipedia.org/wiki/Francis_Preston_Blair

justification for this move was that Biddle had used the bank's resources to fund Jackson's campaign opponents in the 1824 and 1828 elections.

The fear prevailing among Jackson's constituents was that Biddle might induce a financial crisis in retaliation for Jackson's veto and reelection.[1] In other words, it was acknowledged between high government officials that Biddle, the president of the SBOUS, possessed the power to induce a financial crisis—and would do so, if a collapse would benefit his political and business constituency.

This alone verifies the position that manipulated financial crises had occurred in the past, and they would certainly do so in the future.

Jackson continued to point at Biddle's program of economic warfare, justifying his claim that the SBOUS was unfit to receive deposits of the public's hard earned funds. The forces of Biddle versus Jackson intellectually dueled over the questions of banks, corporations and government; and on February 1836, the bank became a private corporation under Pennsylvania Commonwealth law.[2] In 1839, payments were suspended and the bank was officially dissolved in 1841.[3]

Here we are standing at the point where the forces demanding checks and balances on the corruptible collusion of banks, corporations and government appear to have won. Did the opposition simply cower down and resolve to change, to begin acting in ways that were best in the name of individual interests, the people who had elected a majority of them into office? If the bank war was so bitterly fought, then most certainly those who fought were not going to simply concede. Biddle and his allies were not ready to give in.

To fully comprehend the growing enormity found in the unchecked power of the corporate/banking/government collusion, one must first comprehend Jackson's position and his dedicated resistance to it. Jackson represents the first impassioned hardcore stand, since the days of Jefferson, in the face of this powerful force seeking to impose its own rules on the nation. Even so, Jackson himself was forced to forgo on what was, no doubt, his moral composure when he agreed to remove the obstacles preventing takeover of Native lands in exchange for a victory over the forces of the great corrupt collusion. While those negative forces had been abated for the time being, even Jackson understood this was only a temporary maneuver. These forces were certain to return, if not during his administration, then most certainly immediately afterward, and with a renewed vengeance.

Judging from the subsequent history, Jackson was not finished in his attack on the big money–government conspiracy to take over the nation. Once more he fired back at them, in an incident known as the *Species Circular*

---

1 Wilentz, 2008, pp. 392-393
2 Hammond, 1947, p. 155
3 Hammond, 1947, p. 157

[1]*of 1836.* The SC demanded that payment for government lands be made in gold or silver, preferably gold. This order effectively neutralized the ability of the banks to issue loads of notes, superseding the amount backed by gold to deflate the currency (or simply pulling back on gold and silver to facilitate the same results).

Values of currency could also be raised by reinstating the note to extend to a smaller quantity of gold. This well worn tactic would crash the economy, inducing real estate values to plummet. Corporate insiders could stock up on the notes, purchase devalued land and other holdings for fractions on the dollar; then once they had loaded up, the currency values could be increased to facilitate a sell-off. Such is the manner in which fortunes could be reaped while bringing ruin to those too small to defend themselves. Thus, any plebeian Constitutional right to own property was simply flushed down the drain by those holding power.

Preventing such schemes was certainly not going to generate a very kind response from the well-funded opposition. The order for the SC was given just as Jackson was about to end his tenure of service as president. More than likely, in this author's opinion, this was a tactical move on his part, limiting any vindictive response that would negatively affect his own time of service and throwing the effects onto the next candidate; and he silently hoped that candidate would be from the opposition. Jackson was already aware that the president of the treasury *most definitely* held the power to crash the economy and his ability to do so was a lingering fear.

In spite of his adversity, Jackson managed to pay off the national debt in total, which not only made him appear very competent in his ideology, but sent the message to his anti-check opponents that neither the workings of government nor the average American citizen needed their so called "services."

The level of vindictiveness must have been intensifying and a negative response from Biddle was not long in coming.

The Panic of 1837

On May 10, 1837, the banks in New York City suspended specie payment. In other words, they no longer redeemed commercial paper at full face value, only a meager fraction. In other words, the banks in NYC pulled their gold and silver supplies for the purpose of crashing the economy. That is a splendid method of ruining a president's tenure in office, especially one who was a good president in the eyes of the plebeian masses. For the next seven years the economy was in a state of raw depression.

---

1 https://en.wikipedia.org/wiki/Specie_Circular

The banking systems of Europe and the United States were now growing increasingly more interconnected. When New York banks held back on the specie and intentionally raised the interest rates, the prices of American securities dramatically dropped. As a result, in Great Britain the demand for cotton plummeted. That was a big part of the calculated program for revenge. The price of cotton fell by 25%, devastating the economy of the South (the area that, along with the West, was not fully under the control of the banking/corporate/government collusion).

Many planters went totally bankrupt. Many plantations were completely withdrawn from cultivation except just on a subsistence level, as they were getting almost nothing for their products. Here, in this early precedent, we can already see what amounts to an attempt to totally destroy the economic base that supported elected representatives on one side of an issue. In fact, it might be said that the only people left inside the system at this point, who seemed to care any at all about individual concerns on the ground, were the Jacksonian Democrats.

Retraction of the specie and its after effects sent such a shock through the system of state banks that they never fully recovered. Even the publishing industry was seriously hurt by the crash. (This might account for at least some of Edgar Allan Poe's failures as an author,[1] in particular his efforts at getting a literary journal publication called *The Stylus* off the ground.) The United States economy did not completely recover until 1850.

As can be noted here, when the corporate/banking/government collusion feel threatened, they can play their self-serving games ruthlessly. This is a suggestion in itself of the calculating games that pervade Congressional boards and back room meetings all over Capitol Hill even to this very day.

These people will stop at nothing to get whatever they want. They have less of a code of ethics than the Mafia, and they rule as an absolute authority, all on their own account. This ruthlessness was carried to the extent of outright murder, rape and the merciless plundering of an entire section of the United States in the same identical manner that had already been done to the Native Americans; all for the objective of knocking out the economic base that fiercely supported the opposition demanding checks on big money and their corporate collusion, securing basic economic rights of the individual American citizen.

Following the veto of the second national bank, the situation of the United States banks and currency remained intact along Jacksonian lines. The presidents who followed held to the policy of checks to prevent corruption by insider collusion. The West had begun to open up, however,

---

1 Journal subscriptions dropped dramatically, so fewer author names were being published, especially those who were relatively unknown.

and land was plentiful, with towns that needed to grow and lots of business interests, people and enterprise that desired easy access to the money flow.

During this same time period we had the rise of the railroad and the huge industry that facilitated it, such as the Union Pacific Railroad Corporation, known then as the Transcontinental Railroad. These corporations were given millions of acres of land (public land) in the West in the form of land grants that they were free to sell or pledge to bond holders, who were also part of the wealthy inside collusion. Over 51 million acres of land were given by the federal government for corporate benefit!

Here the collusion of government and industry magnified the profit shared as the value of the land grants was increasing. The land was considered "raw," and if there were any people dwelling there, they had no hope of resistance[1]. The same pattern of appropriation had already been seen in nearly all of the Northeastern states. Investors and developers had run land prices there sky high. The West fit the bill: profit to be gained in disregard for any people of the land, with no word of dissension to be heard.

The years from 1850 until 1857 were prosperous times. Beginning in 1841 the nation was picking itself up out of the depression that was started during the last two years that Jackson was in office, obviously brought on by the president of the centralized bank in order to stain Jackson's tenure of office. The presidents who followed Jackson continued to support checks and balances on the banking and corporate cartel and the actions of their government collusion.

But when James Buchanan came to office in 1857 and supported the idea that these merging forces of big money should be submitted to some limitations in order to protect the interests of the average people, these forces had exhausted their tolerance. The time was now perfect to really put the scare in the leader of the nation, forcing him to drop all his opposition to the collusive forces.

The message had to go out that the next leader would support the malignant collusion in every aspect—or the entire nation would suffer destruction. When Buchanan baulked, a crash in the currency and the economy came immediately.

Buchanan was from Pennsylvania. To illustrate his stance and his belief that the corporate/banking/government collusion should be held in check, read this statement.

> Although in Pennsylvania we are all opposed to slavery in the abstract, we can never violate the constitutional compact we have

1 http://railroads.unl.edu/blog/?p=125

with our sister states. Their rights will be held sacred by us. Under the constitution it is their own question; and there let it remain[1].

Buchanan was firm in his beliefs, having made his career as a lawyer. The Constitution was the law of the land and that law was not to be compromised under any circumstance, and there would be no exceptions for any person, regardless of his status.

Some incident had to occur that would force the president to concede and submit to the will of the devil in the centralizing efforts of the bank and its conspirators on Capitol Hill. Once such force was applied in the weak areas, they could shatter for eternity the foundation of individual freedom of choice and free enterprise that supported the economic system behind precisely those elected representatives who stood proud in such strong opposition. This would compel the entire nation and its leadership to bow before the will of the corporate powers, sacrificing liberty of will and endeavor on the altar of what was euphemistically labeled as progress by the propaganda of the day and the intentionally twisted official historical record. (The word "progress" suggests a positive benefit, but analytical thinkers must always ask, "for whom?" If we plebeians do not really benefit, then who does? Does the word "progress" mean that individuals must give up their Constitutional liberty to the forces of some[2],[3] brokers hiding behind corporations?

The Panic of 1857

In the Panic of 1857, the international corporate/banking/government collusion conspired together not only for the purpose of shaping events inside individual nations, but to achieve their goals in more than once country at once—of course, in complete disregard for the interests of their own citizens. Where international business is being conducted, changes in currency value affect all parties. Wars and the end of wars, crop failures or discoveries of gold, all change the price and value of land, commodities, and even railroad companies.

There was a short, sharp downturn in 1857, but it affected the various sections of the US in different ways. When a major New York financial institution failed, British investors pulled funds out of US banks. Failures of banks and railroads meant that land speculation projects were falling apart, bankrupting more people. In the meantime, for other reasons, grain prices dropped, hurting agrarian areas.

---

1 Klein 1962, p. 150
2 http://money.cnn.com/2012/07/10/real_estate/tax-liens/
3   http://www.forbes.com/sites/instituteforjustice/2014/08/26/philadelphia-civil-forfeiture-class-action-lawsuit/

Perhaps much quickly than the conspirators anticipated, the financial situation started to pick up again in Great Britain[1]; but in the United States another strange occurrence made this into a "double dip" collapse that really destroyed public confidence.

A dispassionate, rational review of historical events makes it hard to ignore the ongoing war between the forces of banking and corporations on one side, against the interests of individual property owners and individual enterprise people on the other. There is a strong smell to such history that reeks of engineered booms and busts, risings and sinkings, and intentional sabotage. The next pivotal event was the sinking of the SS *Central America*.

The Sinking of the SS Central America

The SS *Central America* was one in a line of ships contracted out to haul mail for the federal government. The SSCA had also been contracted to haul gold from the fields of California since 1849, stopping in a number of Northern ports, primarily New York, to drop the gold off for shipment to the banks that used it as specie to back the banknotes, as we shall recall.

Her Captain was well respected, highly decorated, and accomplished. He hailed from Fredericksburg, Virginia, just 50 miles from Washington D.C. His name was William Lewis Herndon, and he was one of the Navy's outstanding seamen. In 1851 he led a US expedition to the Amazon River Valley. During the Mexican–American War he had commanded the brig *Iris* with distinction. In other words, this man was highly skilled and talented.

Navy captains were assigned to command mail steamers on the Atlantic and Pacific runs back in that day, and these shipping lines were under contract to the federal government. Not only did the government know what ship was hauling what specific material, and how much of it, they also knew who was the captain of the ship and where it was leaving from, as well as going to. The SS *Central America* was loaded with gold, fifteen tons of it at that, all destined for the ports of New York City and then to be transported to the banks.

The ship paused first in Colon, Panama, to load general supplies. It proceeded to the port of Havana for general security checks and more supplies. After leaving Havana on September 7, 1857, the Captain and crew moved forward into eternity. By September 12 the ship was in the midst of a three-day hurricane; had they not seen signs of impending "weather" just

---

1 In this author's opinion, the British could not allow their own economy to collapse long term, so presumably they redeposited the gold specie back into their own central bank. Evidently either the president of the British central bank could not get more benefit in a proposal from the American side, or the Americans intentionally failed to come through as they had promised. That is this author's view.

five days before?[1] The ship was taking on water in the fierce winds and there were much more serious problems. Let's closely examine the details of the primary leak[2] that sent the ship to the bottom of the sea off the North Carolina Hatteras coast.

The main detail recorded in relation to the ship going down was a leak in the seal between the paddle wheel support and the main boiler. This leak shut the boiler down by putting out the coal fire that powered the ship. Water began to fill the ship's hold, according to the official record. Was it just a maintenance failure? It would have been fairly simple for someone to have punched the rubber seal. Perhaps there is more to the story than will ever be revealed, since more than likely all specifics have deteriorated at the bottom of the sea since 1857.

If we indulge in a little speculation we can imagine the possibility that some sort of subtle, potentially life threatening event had occurred to someone in the Herndon family. Maybe a late evening confrontation while in town, or an unexplainable property fire that could have destroyed the household when there should have never been one; or a buggy wheel that mysteriously slipped from its fixture, shaking up the family one warm spring Sunday afternoon coming home from church. Herndon could have read about the situation in a letter sent from home or it may very well have happened during his seasonal furlough time, while he was at home himself.

Herndon was assigned the position of Captain of the SSCA in 1855, [3] from service on another ship that had sailed and docked in the Caribbean and in Hong Kong. He must have had at least a six-month furlough, beginning well before Christmas. That would have been a perfect time for some astounding "message" to be conveyed—when he and the entire family were all gathered around to quietly enjoy the pleasant company of one another and their tranquil surroundings.

While the ship was in port at Havana, Cuba, the tropical storm was already brewing southeast of the Bahamas. The storm clouds were gathering. Is it conceivable that the Captain was accosted along the dockside by men who claimed to represent the federal government office who in reality were agents from the primary Bank of New York, with a message that the ship had

---

1 When Katrina was over the Caribbean Sea in 2005, dark clouds were seen on shore back in the States to precede it for more than a week.

2 which we discussed earlier in detail..

3 Some sources cite that he assumed command on June 10, 1857. This suggests that he came off of furlough on that date and resumed his assigned command; which would be a reasonable assumption being that he had been assigned command for the past two years approximately. Other works mention that he and his family had relocated to New York City in 1856, one more suggestion of a furlough period and possibility of a threatening "experience."

better go down in the coming storm? That he and his entire family would die if the ship got close to New York?

The details don't matter much. Given the ruthlessness of the participants in such events, it is easy to imagine a scenario in which the captain would have been forced to go ahead.

Preserving his honor as best he could, then, the Captain gave priority to rescuing his passengers and crew. One ship appeared in the distance, and Captain Herndon supervised the transfer of all the women and children on board; there wasn't room for the men. He carefully gave his pocket watch to a lady, asking her to please deliver it to his dear wife and tell her that he loved her; how much more must he have wanted to say? Most of his men were still aboard, though some had broken loose pieces of wood in hopes of staying afloat until rescue. Of course, the captain had to go down with his ship. He was last seen hat in hand, head bowed in prayer.

Herndon had assisted with his best efforts to aid the innocent into safety. He had no other option himself but to go down in the stormy sea, if he was to save face and preserve his spotless name and career, with the respect of his family name in proud recall of his service. Especially if, indeed, there was a hidden hand behind the event, an ice cold Mafioso-style hand. Visualize a merciless *cartel* with the careless violence and ruthless disregard for human life that these people have, in a modern sense of the image.

Results

The calculated economic result was most devastating to behold in the United States. The large corporations took a hit, the railroads specifically. Four of the largest railroad companies were forced to shut down: The Illinois Central, Erie–Pittsburgh, Fort Wayne and Chicago, and the Reading Rail Road. Merchants and farmers also suffered who had taken business chances before the crash and return prices were higher.

A number of other railroads were compelled to file bankruptcy. The most noted of these companies are: The Delaware, The Lackawanna and Western Railway, The Fond Du Lac Railroad. The Boston and Worchester suffered too, and was forced to reduce employee pay by 10%. The huge drop in value of railroad securities caused farmers to default on their mortgage payments, especially in the West, thereby pressuring the private banks even more, who now held notes not backed by specie due to the central bank withholding the gold and silver coin.

Another noted incident that corroborates the general theme of corrupt corporate collusion with government is the failure of the Ohio Life Insurance and Trust Company at the beginning of the crash. The OLITC failed due to fraudulent activities by the company management. The OLI had a branch in New York City, suggesting possible collusion with the central bank, indirectly implicating government insiders who knew what was going on. The failure created a run on the banks and panic selling of stocks, and threatened to spread even farther. More than $7 million were unaccounted for,[1].

The full power of the corporations would most certainly be turned against Buchanan now; it must have been anticipated that he would balk under the pressure and come to the dark side in this clash between corrupt wealth and individual concerns. Strangely enough, but obviously well calculated, the states that were based on production and individual property ownership rebounded quickly and held their own; again no doubt to the greater ire of the banking/corporate collusion and due to their offshore product exchange with the British, who had rebounded quickly from the original crash, as we may recall[2]. Merciless predatory action designed to destroy was sure to be forthcoming.

Buchanan wanted the state banking system to establish a separate account exclusively for state government business, just as the National Treasury had done for the Federal Government. This action would reduce the flood of paper notes, allowing the amount of specie to catch up with the saturation of notes, and the notes would increase in value as a result. Under the Buchanan administration, it was publicly stated that while government sympathized with the individual's suffering, it could do nothing to assist. He asked state banks to keep one dollar in specie for every three issued in paper notes, hoping to quell inflation until the specie value could be raised to meet the face value of the banknote.

The Morrill Tariff of 1861 and Secession

In 1857, the tariffs had been reduced to about 20% in an effort to stimulate an economic recovery. Representatives from sections of the country outside the domination of the big corporations and banks had won, but not for long. These tariffs were always seen as highly prejudicial, as they repeatedly protected (Northern) manufacturers by raising the prices on manufactured goods, which created a hardship for those sections of the country that were not built on industrial manufacturing.

In February 1861, the Morrill Tariff [3] was passed, which dramatically raised the importation fees, again to protect the big corporate industrialists.

---

1 This author highly suspects theft by the management, who were colluded with government insiders
2 The American banking system failed to come through on their end of the secret bargain.
3 https://en.wikipedia.org/wiki/Morrill_Tariff

Individual producers specialized in single cash crops and products, and consequently needed imports to sustain other developmental concerns.

But the voice of opposition in the Senate and Congress was already beginning to melt away, as evidenced by the calls for secession by South Carolina (at the end of 1860, following Lincoln's election) and Mississippi (early 1861), whose senators resigned. Seven more states followed suit by January 1861.

Buchanan had no choice but to gradually shift his support to the banking/corporate partnership seeking to run the nation at the expense of its citizens' Constitutional right to prosper and live life in liberty. Without the opposition, any tax rate on imported goods or any financial move made to discourage the individual's freedom of liberty could be implemented with impunity.

By February 1861, more and more Southern states were choosing to exercise their Constitutional right to secede from the Union, and then the war to destroy their economic base was on. The financial independence of the only true representative force standing to oppose corporate over-reach and government corruption was destined to be removed from the halls of US Congress forever.

The extortionist Morrill Tariff sought only to benefit the corporations at the expense of individual interests, so its materialization only served to further alienate the states who were already uncomfortable. All of the divorcing states had already been speaking of secession when the issue of tariffs was first brought up, going back to the presidency of Andrew Jackson, so their decision now could not have been a surprise in Washington.

With the call for secession by South Carolina in December of 1860, Buchanan's stance in favor of those demanding checks and balances had somewhat began to shift, since he did not want to go against his home state of Pennsylvania, according to the official history. When the representatives from those states in secession began resigning from Congress, the Morrill Tariff was easily passed, with few still around to contest it. The power base had shifted against the President. Regardless of his personal convictions, he now had no choice but to do the banking cartel's will: simply resign out of office...or else.

As has been noted before in this work, slavery was not ruled out by the Constitution but the consensus of public debate had been to leave that decision as a matter of choice. It was seen as an economic matter, and it was used in all sections of the country to varying degrees, even by ex-slaves themselves, although this is rarely mentioned in popular histories. In order to profitably work the huge landed estates, the use of slavery was scarcely a matter of choice; there was very little in the way of mechanized farm equipment at the time. Slaves could also be traded in the market exchanges as well as rented out, so the profit margin and potential rewards could be considerable. The problem for the average subsistence farmer was that slaves were really expensive.

An untrained male was $1,000 in 1860 currency values; that is around $20,000 in today's money. A skilled slave was valued on average at $5,000. In today's values, that price is on par with a cab enclosed, duel-wheeled White or a John Deere tractor, about $100,000. Less than 10% of the population could afford one, about the same number as could afford a fully loaded ultra-modern tractor.

The issue was intentionally distorted, however, and made into a primarily moral question, that is, an emotional distraction. This divisive appeal to emotion had been well crafted, as many people are more swayed by the heat of emotion than by cool, rational logic—as you can see at election time again and again, when the electorate literally votes against its own interests.

The so called "abolitionist" literature had done its job well. Soon the war would be on to destroy the economic base that supported all opposition and individual freedom of choice justified by Constitutional law. The very Constitution itself was to wind up being infringed upon with the conclusion of the conflict.

Just prior to Buchanan leaving the office of the President in 1861, the ship *Star of the West*, transporting federal military goods to Fort Sumter was fired upon. Well ahead of time, the Captain, Major Robert Anderson, had been warned by the governor of South Carolina—as had the Buchanan administration[1,2]—not to seize any military installation or territory inside of what amounted to foreign soil with the birth of the Confederacy. The federal government intended to force the hand of the Confederacy, believing that the war would be a quick affair, allowing the forces of the banking/corporate/government collusion to infringe upon the cherished Constitution and intending to eventually steal all precious liberty from the citizens of America. For this reason the fight was on, and the determination to resist was very powerful.

Immediately prior to the ship being fired upon, Buchanan stated that those elements supporting corporation and government collusion had been swayed by the power of divisive appeal to emotion, and had continually infringed upon the Constitutional rights of states who embraced their own

[1] The official history claims that he did not know of a deal between Buchanan and Pickens, the governor of SC, but the circumstantial evidence strongly suggests a back door deal between opposing agents (*if not coerced*) and Major Anderson, for him

[2] Charles Edward Cauthen, *South Carolina Goes to War, 1860-1865*, pp. 95-97

individual freedom of choice—the freedom to engage in the slave trade being just one of them. He observed that if the Northern states refused to

> ...repeal their unconstitutional and obnoxious enactments... the injured states, after having first used all peaceful and constitutional means to obtain redress, would be justified in revolutionary resistance to the Government of the Union[1].

Now, since it was clearly the belief of the federal government that the battle would be a short one, what were the bankers doing that would suggest what the true goals were, betraying exactly who the real enemy was that those most perceptive citizens of America were now doing battle with?

A nationwide call for centralized currency labeled as *Demand Notes* was issued between August 1861 and April 1862. The Southern states rejected this call for centralized currency in the name of Andrew Jackson and the corruption that they already observed.

These notes were based on the federal government's ability to trade land in equal value for the note in a promised amount, strongly suggesting that the Federal Government suddenly anticipated having great access to new land holdings! We may only wonder as to just whose land they anticipated acquiring, all of a sudden. The species order was also suspended before the onset of 1862.

The Legal Tender Act moved to replace the Demand Notes as the first true centralized currency, calling it the United States Notes on February 25, 1862. These notes bore the US Treasury seal of approval, which was a major change from the Demand Notes. But keep in mind here that the new currency was still only a promise to pay later, with virtually no backing in gold. Over 150 million of these notes were printed up.

Since the gold to back this currency did not exist, the notes were printed with no backing. There was an intent to initiate some sort of act in the future to reclaim the value presumed, however. Demand notes could be used to pay import duties and Legal Tender Notes could not. Since import duties were a major source of income for the Federal Government, the value of Demand Notes soared against the LTN. By June 1863, only 3,300,000 were outstanding, compared to 400,000,000 of the LTN.

The National Banking Acts of 1863 and 1864

This act represented the final conclusion for imposed centralized currency. In addition, this act represents a streamlining, a clear defining and broad endorsement of the great baneful collusion's final conquest of finances in American life, and its ability to function in absence of any check with

1 https://en.wikipedia.org/wiki/James_Buchanan#Buchanan1860

real influential power. The NBA pushed all private banks with state issued currency out of the market, thus effectively killing any sort of check on the ability of states and individual people to avoid impact from any manipulated rise or sudden fall in value by the Fed, where no representatives now stood to question any sort of collusive move.

The NBA of 1864 established federally-issued bank charters, which officially took banking away from the hands of state governments.

By this time it was pretty well presumed that the Confederacy would lose the conflict, since the battle of Gettysburg had already been fought. The federal call for total warfare had already commenced as well. Thus, from the dark mist of deception, now the true enemy of the individual American citizen and his co-conspirators was revealing himself.

The National Banking Acts of 1865 and 1866

The NBA of 1865 demanded that every state bank pay a 10% tax on any notes paid out to them. The NBA of 1866 went beyond that and carried the demand to include every individual person, state bank and state banking association to pay the tax! So now we see who benefited from the chaos, destruction and death.

An interesting court case arose during this time period, related to the National Banking Act of 1865 and 1866. The conclusion was that the tax was to be paid out upon demand by the Commissioner of Internal Revenue. The case *Veasy Bank v Fenno* was made between a Maine state-chartered bank and the collector of internal revenue. The bank refused to pay the 10% tax, declaring that it was unconstitutional. Of course, the chief justices sided with Congress, effectively quashing the last vestige of any call for checks to balance their collusive extortionist endeavors. This case proved that the financial control was moving against all American citizens, and not just those in the South; but then who was there left to stand on the victim's side of the Congressional court room?

So now the great fight pitting individual interests and freedom of choice against the will of the banking/corporate/government collusion was finished. There was no one left to fight in all the states; it all was up for grabs by corporate interests at the expense of the people who owned the land.

A state's right to produce its own currency had already been annulled, imposing on each state the corrupt collusion between government, corporations and centralized banking. In actuality, the Constitution did and still does allow states the right to produce their own currency. As has been stated before, the federal government forcing its way upon the states was an illegal act.

Here is what the original Tenth Amendment stated, before the Civil War, in 1860:

> The powers not delegated to the United States by the Constitution, nor prohibited by it to the states, are reserved to the states or to the people.[1]

What this means is simply that the Constitution alone delegates authority to the United States. If that authority is not specifically delegated by the Constitution, and is not prohibited to the states by the Constitution, then the states or the individual people hold the authority. Is there a specific prohibition against slavery or a secession of states in the 1860 Constitution? No. The authority to initiate that action of secession or to embrace the use of slavery is left with the states and the individual people who reside therein. Was there a moralistic opinion against slavery? Sure, there was, and on both sides of the fence, but the choice was a Constitutional matter.

Consider the fact that the individual's use of slavery was an economic pillar that allowed the large landed estates to perform. The liberty to trade the produce generated, to retain the profit therefrom free of any extortion or repressive regulation, and to render services to the surrounding communities, was what enabled individual plebeian citizens to [2]make a comfortable living and in some cases become wealthy.

The largest plantation estates did provide a large variety of services to the citizens in their surrounding areas; services that corporate interests desired to wrest from individual control. These services include: banking, grocery sales (in fresh or processed vegetables and meat), finished tobacco products, sales of spirits, tool and buggy repair service, blacksmith tool orders and sales, clothing orders and sales in the plantation general store, real-estate development and contracting services, and the list goes on. The plantation also included money lending services.

The landed estates could be sources of immense wealth on par with that of aristocracy. In a majority of these cases, the owners were descended from self-made individuals who had worked and invested their way up through their production based estates:

> Industrious merchantmen, craftsmen, bankers, and farmers. Together these hardworking and enterprising men created an elite merchant-planter society in Charles Town.

> In the early days of the Carolina Colony little distinction was made between the planter class and the merchant class—this was a later antebellum phenomenon. Marriage between members of successful

1 http://legal-dictionary.thefreedictionary.com/Tenth+Amendment
2 https://en.wikipedia.org/wiki/Drayton_Hall

planter and merchant families was common. In early Charleston the distinctions were not between merchant and planter, but between black and white and rich and poor. These enormously wealthy planters and merchants were eager consumers, happy to show off their wealth and social superiority through their plantations, townhouses, and lifestyle. Drayton Hall, Crowfield, Mulberry House, Magnolia Plantation, Middleton Place, Heyward-Washington House, and the Miles Brewton House were all constructed during this affluent time.

In their desire to emulate upper class English society, Charlestonians bought European furniture, silver, and linens. They ordered porcelain from China and architectural and garden design books from England. They created musical societies, built theaters, and established private social clubs such as the St. Cecilia Society and the Agricultural Society. They adopted British manners and sent their children to England to be educated. The years between 1720 and 1760 were a Golden Age in Charleston.

It was this body of well landed self-made American gentry that sought to have a system of checks and balances to preclude corruption and collusion between government, corporations and national banks. From the moment when the First Bank of the United States was born, a war was fought between individual interests and that of big money and government

But the freedom for individuals to choose to employ slavery had now illegally been eradicated, destroying the economic base that supported government representatives who would vote into law any form of check on the currency or otherwise in government.

Soon the large landed estates would be taxed into oblivion, even though it went against the Constitution to do so. Massive tracts of land were then confiscated by federal officials and the productive capacity of the land eliminated in ways from whence the individual property owner had once profited.

Were the individuals who battled with so much fortitude for their Constitutional rights, including the right to separate and form their own nation, appropriate in their convictions? Where was the Constitutional justification for that? Take a look at Jefferson's own words in the preamble to the *Declaration of Independence*:

> We hold these truths to be self-evident; that all men are created equal; that they are endowed by their creator with certain unalienable rights; that among these are life, liberty, and the pursuit of happiness; that to secure these rights, governments are instituted among men, deriving their just powers from the consent of the governed; that whenever any form of government becomes destructive to these ends,

it is the right of the people to alter or to abolish it, and to institute new government, laying its foundation on such principles, and organizing its powers in such form, as to them shall seem most likely to effect their safety and happiness.

Take note of the section above which states that *governments derive just powers from consent of the governed*[1]. Whenever any form of government becomes destructive to these ends, as is the case with government supporting a centralized bank and the corporation's ability to manipulate currency values in absence of any checks and balances, and at the expense of the people, then it is the right of the people to alter or abolish it. The people also have a right to institute a new government, to set the principles of Constitution and organization as its base and further organizing its powers with checks and balances to secure their safety and happiness; which includes the individual's right to attain prosperity via unsuppressed property ownership rights. Not only was secession legally valid for the Southern states in the past and others in that day and age, it is also valid for the states of Texas and Alaska now, in this present day and age, and for many of the same reasons!

The forces of big money, the banking/corporate/government collusion, fought an all out war in Congress from the time of Washington, for absolute control over the nations financial institutions, so that this infected cartel collusion could literally *dictate* the value of the nations currency, even at the expense of the average American citizen. In the end, the cartel collusion won that right when the battle on Capitol Hill manifested into outright war among the citizenry, the might utilized in divisive appeal to emotion to instigate what transformed into a bloody four year battle for and against an economically liberated citizenry, individual freedom of choice and enterprise via personal property acquisition. Obviously the forces instigating this fight had no concern for the average citizen on the ground, who was certain to suffer to an extreme, just like those same forces acting in disregard of any concern for the innocent passengers on the *SS Central America*. All that this corrupt collusion cared about was generating wealth at all cost; and just like any cartel, concerns of the people were and still are simply barriers to be swept away and cast aside, even if they must engage in mass murder to accomplish their ends.

Now, if this intent to absolutely dominate the resource base of average citizens was present before the Civil War, where is it today? We have shown how these forces held the Constitution in disregard, violating it to disregard the freedom of choice granted by it to the individual people, but what about

---

1 Note that government assumes an uncontested authority, then forces those governed to submit.

the slavery issue? Was not slavery outlawed? What does the Constitution have to say about this matter even today?

According to the official history, slavery was outlawed in the United States by the thirteenth amendment. But a close examination of the thirteenth amendment bears some astonishing revelations otherwise. Contrary to the official history, slavery was not abolished! Examine the amendment here:

> n Neither slavery nor involuntary servitude, except as a punishment for crime whereof the party shall have been duly convicted, shall exist within the United States, or any place subject to their jurisdiction.

That's a surprise. So slavery is NOT rendered illegal![1] The false check is the exclusion that slavery is still legal, as determined by court of law. During times of tyranny, the first element that is thrown out is legitimate rule of law, virtually always being replaced by inquisition, which comes about in two forms: political or religious. Unless some future development arrives on the scene in the United States suggesting otherwise, the inquisition imposed inside US borders will always be political.

Now the federal government may impose its will upon the people, force them into debt via an imposed centralized currency, then property foreclosure by crashing the currency; and when they protest about it, round them up into concentration camps for the purpose of compelling them into conscripted service.

Who is it that holds slaves in concentration camps now, labeled inmates? The corporations, for the last 100 years, have profited immensely from the business of modern day slavery,[2]. The legal right to own slaves simply exchanged hands, from the individual over to the corporation and government! And as prisons are being privatized, turned into money-making enterprises for corporations, any last hindrance against abuse from the corporations has surely been removed. And don't forget, President Obama has actually signed Executive Orders essentially putting us under a suspended state of martial law, that would include even the allocation of food and other necessities at the government's discretion.[3]

In the history of America, the first great illustration of the principle was the Indian Removal Act. Without a doubt, it was the power of corporate and banking collusion that facilitated this act.

---

1 http://www.globalresearch.ca/the-prison-industry-in-the-united-states-big-business-or-a-new-form-of-slavery/8289
2 http://www.vice.com/read/whos-getting-rich-off-the-prison-industrial-complex
3http://www.disclose.tv/news/president_obama_signs_martial_law_order_in_usa/118055; see also http://en.wikipedia.org/wiki/National_Defense_Authorization_Act

And do the banks and our government not force a situation of involuntary servitude onto the people, simply when they purchase a home? Try multiplying house payments by thirty years and observe that the cost of the home multiplies three times, in most cases! The people do not even own the land underneath their homes, in many cases, and in an increasing trend, so in this manner the governments, state and local, may dictate what people do on that property! These acts, as have been shown, violate the Thirteenth Amendment of the Constitution. Where are the protesters, the angry masses demanding their liberty, as every freeborn citizen should before all liberty has been purloined for an eternity?

Look at real estate taxes and obligatory utility hook ups and fees. If a home could be purchased and a ten percent tax paid at the time of purchase, there would not be much room for complaint since the home would be free and clear once paid for, but such is not the case. Every year an ever growing amount is extorted from the property owner simply for him exercising his Constitutional right to continue to own his property, with only two months to pay up in most localities or foreclosure proceedings shall commence on the third month.

In this manner, the local tax office works both for the local government officials as well as the bank with absolutely no regulation in place to take into account the personal situation of property owners. In effect, what has happened is that the basic Constitutional right to own property altogether has been stolen. In many areas, the property tax on a basic 1400 square foot home equals nearly 10% of the wages for 90% of workers (especially in view of the extortionist post-tax figures on wages).

Disregard official figures, where the top 10% of the wage opportunities stand far beyond the reach of the average person. For officials to throw in those top figures is only part of a deception plan, designed for concealing the pervasive reduction in overall wages resulting from exploitation of the citizen masses by corporate and government interests.

As demonstrated above, the huge corrupt collusion that exists at the expense of the citizen, even in this day and time, was what Jefferson and those powerful individuals aligned with him sought to neutralize. Indeed when the forces advocating checks and balances lost the fight to secure them, all of the nation's citizenry lost, no matter which state they called home. The force that won was for the corporations and the centralized bank, at the expense of the plebeian citizen on the ground. Does being compelled to live under an extortionist system contribute to the benefit of the property owner's life, allowing him the liberty to pursue and grow in his own wealth? Indeed, this author thinks not!

What are the plans then, of big money, corporations and government in the future? Has their insatiable greed been sated? Are the officials in the process of crashing the nation's currency even as we read along, as a prelude to provoking violence among the masses and seizing individually-owned resources? The news in recent times points to a potentially tragic story that is bound to shape the destiny of America and its citizens in years to come.

CHAPTER 6. THOSE WHO RESISTED, HOW AND WHY

It all started with Jefferson

The first move to impose rule via centralized currency came with the development of the First Bank of the United States. The individual who held as much clout as George Washington, if not more, was the intellectual Thomas Jefferson. Jefferson and his reasoning help us truly understand the resistance and see the reality that unfolded from it. As the passage of time shall most assuredly reveal, the enormous travesty for future generations will result because the great corrupt conspiring collusion came out victorious five generations ago, over the interests of individual people.

Wikipedia has this to say about the First Bank of the United States:

Secretary of state Thomas Jefferson and James Madison led the opposition, which claimed that the bank was unconstitutional, and that it benefited merchants and investors at the expense of the majority of the population.

Jefferson among others, also were against establishing an official government mint without measures of checks and balances. Take a quick glance here at the reasons why gathered from the same source:

They believed this centralization of power away from local banks was dangerous to a sound monetary system and was mostly to the benefit of business interests in the commercial areas of the nation, not landed property owner's interests, arguing that the right to own property would be infringed by these proposals. Furthermore, they contended that the creation of such a bank violated the Constitution, which specifically stated that Congress was to regulate weights and measures and issue coined money (rather than mint and bills of credit).

It must be clear and evident by now that what this group truly desired was simply to impose the security of a set of checks and balances on the nation's currency and in the prevailing system, so that the value could not be manipulated to the advantage of an elitist few, whom it was known were in collusion with corporate interests. One of the primary demands was simply that the face-value stamped on the bank-issued notes (dollar bills) be backed with an equal value in gold.

Otherwise, currency manipulation could favor a collusion by crashing the system[1], causing widespread property foreclosure, while inside operators could hoard banknotes, knowing that the values would be later be raised[2]. These inside operators, who in many cases were members of Congress themselves, could then race out and buy up all of the valuable foreclosed property on the cheap. As prices recovered, the purchased properties could then be resold to corporate representatives, netting the new owners profits beyond belief.

As the value of the notes was still in an upward climb, the corporate representatives could work through the local banks, making loans easily available to the plebeian masses, then dump all of their property holdings off for even a greater profit. Does any of this sound familiar?

Even the banks themselves would stand to profit from this collusion via a doubled or even tripling of values through deceptive interest charges, not to mention the government tax office. If the person failed to make a payment at some future point, the bank simply foreclosed again and resold it, keeping the money already paid out by the former owner. The only real losers in the deal would be the average individual, who lost the real estate to foreclosure, as well as the new purchaser, who now had to pay the tax and the interest from the leveraged loan.

The primary limitation on this type of scheme would come in *value to value* backing in gold or silver. This way the gold or silver value noted on the note could not simply be changed with a new printing of bills. An example might be if the note bore the stated value of .50 mg gold to the $1.00 note. The bill itself would bear the written value of $1.00 and the fine print might state the exchange value in real gold value. A later printing of the notes might bear the exchange value of .10 in gold, while salaries and business had been conducted in a prior assumed, written dollar value.

Such is the reason that people defaulted on their mortgages, since the property held its value and demanded more banknotes since the value of the

1 By removing any gold backing or by over producing worthless notes
2 By reinserting the gold

banknotes had been dropped. Wages, however, were paid only in a stated amount of banknotes within a period of time, be it by the month, day, or hour, and never were increased or lowered due to a reduction in gold or silver value. As a matter of fact, as the notation indicated, the Constitution was even *against* the issuance of notes or bills, favoring a medium of exchange in solid gold or silver coin.

What is revealed is the methodology that a corrupt cartel collusion system could use, if no one is looking over their shoulders. On these grounds Jefferson, Madison and the others, stood to demand that solid balances be issued, preferring to hold Congress to the Constitution. With the signature of Washington effectively giving birth to the FBOUS, the conspiring collusion won out.

Andrew Jackson: The Plebeian's Knight In Shining Armor

While there were many who stood for the interests of individual and the Constitution, as a matter of fact a majority, none made a more solid stand for the interest of the common man than did Andrew Jackson

In the end, even he himself was forced to concede on his basic principles[1,2,3] to the power of the banking/corporate/government collusion. The bank came under attack at the outset of Jackson's presidency in 1829. Jackson's justification for this attack was that *the centralized bank had failed to produce a stable currency, and that it was unconstitutional*. Both Houses launched an investigation, determining that the centralized bank did have Constitutional backing and that it held a pivotal role in providing for a stable currency, even though it possessed no hard solid measure to ensure that currency values could not be manipulated to the advantage of an elitist few.

Jackson rejected the findings, observing the record of corruption mentioned beforehand, that had already occurred at the expense of the American citizens. He labeled the centralized bank as a corrupt institution that threatened individual liberties of the citizens at large, the same label as Jefferson had used earlier.

Biddle, President of the SBOUS, made an appeal to Jackson for reconsideration of the recharter. Jackson held his ground. Henry Clay's political ultimatum to Jackson sparked the Bank War[4], the ultimatum being that if Jackson did not recharter the bank, then those in power with the bank would see to it that Jackson would not be re-elected.

1 Jackson raised two orphaned Indian boys (no evidence of hatred for Indians)
2 Brands, H.W. (2005). *Andrew Jackson: His Life and Times*. Random House. p. 198.
3 Remini 1:194
4 As we shall recall, there appears to have been a backroom deal and the cartel neglected to completely fulfill their end of it, a possibility that we must deduce that Jackson rightfully anticipated and acted immediately in lieu of.

Jackson withdrew the federal deposits, diverting them into private bank holdings, ending the SBOUS's ability to dictate fiscal value. In response to this, Biddle induced a financial crisis [1] that was blamed on Jackson's executive action. Congress saw through it, however, and in a backlash against Biddle's currency crash all efforts at rechartering the bank were brought to an end. In 1836 the bank became a private charter under Pennsylvania Commonwealth Law—and the grand effort to centralize America's currency in absence of all checks to regulate a guaranteed face value equivalent in gold appeared to have died on the limb.

However, in response to Jackson's efforts to force the bank to accept limitations on its ability to manipulate currency value, the bank simply withdrew the gold and silver to be redeemed on the face value of the banknotes. Such action rendered the notes virtually worthless, when depositors attempted to reclaim the value of banknotes in gold or silver. Prices skyrocketed as the notes lost value, leading to a seven-year depression known as the Panic of 1837.

The Panic was particularly hard on individuals who owned large landed estates not under the authority of the banks, and it undermined the prices of produce derived therefrom. Once we digest all that, we may observe what was the true intent of the crash all along; to destroy the economy supporting those who persist in demanding checks and balances on banking, corporations and their representative base in government.

Only when money once again was backed by gold, as gold became more plentiful with the California Gold Rush that began in 1848, did the situation improve, completely reviving the economy by 1850.

In addition to gold being discovered in California, gold that was used to pay down the national debt and stabilize the currency, the newly appointed national treasury president, James Guthery (1853) bore skills on par with Alexander Hamilton.

Due to his observations of corruption in the national bank, Treasury and among managing officials, Guthery did not believe in centralized banking without hard checks and balances, such as a requirement that notes have backing in gold equal to the face value. Guthery also moved to purge the Treasury of corrupt employees, managers, officials and tariff collectors, who were withholding funds from the government to their own enrichment. All of these positive developments allow the economic boom to continue for the next seven years.

This fiscal improvement reinforced the wisdom of backing banknotes with species, or redeemable gold and silver. The benefit of it, and the

---

1 Verification that currency manipulation is used to effect presidential decisions rendered.

objection to it, was that it wrested the ability to manipulate currency values away from the self serving banking/corporate/government collusion, who meant to rob the citizen of all that he had labored to have. A strong push back was inevitable.

When Buchanan was elected president, the hope and feeling among centralized banking constituents was that he would allow big money to continue on as they pleased, without having to respond to any call for checks on that ability in any way. When the situation was observed that Buchanan would continue on in the Jeffersonian tradition, then the proponents of centralized banking and non-specie backed currency determined that some sort of trigger event must be used to convince him of the wisdom in doing otherwise. After all, he hailed from Pennsylvania, an area dominated by the centralized banks and their corporate collusion.

In an obvious effort to destroy the presidency of Buchanan, the currency values again were manipulated by withholding the gold and silver coin backing the banking notes, causing the Panic of 1857. Since the interests of banking had now expanded offshore, a tainted association had developed between the US central bank and the bank of England, as well as the centralized banks of other European nations. In the areas of the nation outside the sphere of centralized bank domination, primarily in the South, Mid-West and the raw lands of the West, trade that benefited the large landed estates was conducted between those areas and the ports of England.

This time when the currency was crashed, not only would the pain be felt on the home front at large, but there would be no means of escape by simply shipping product offshore. In spite of the negative strike at those liberated areas by the forces of centralized banking, the economy dipped sharply, then rebounded just as quickly, more than likely due to British central banking officials not getting satisfaction in their end of the back room bargain from high end American banking officials. Only the sinking of the SS *Central America* would reinstate the collapse on the American end and hold it for an extended time. Even then, however, the Southern economy proved to be astonishingly resilient in a relatively short span of time.

In the end, when the Democratic national convention of 1860 met in Charleston, South Carolina, and the Southern wing walked out, confirming their intention of secession, Buchanan had no alternative but to gradually shift sides to those forces remaining in national office. He had attempted to negotiate a settlement between the opposing sides, but the banks, corporations and their government connections were simply too powerful.

Matter of fact, the power of the cartel was so great at this point that with the ship *Star of the West*[1] being stationed near Charleston Harbor, the Captain, Major Robert Anderson, was induced[2] to force the South's hand by shipping supplies for military reinforcement of Fort Sumter. Buchanan had been previously warned that South Carolina now considered the fort theirs and would open fire should any attempt at federal reinforcement occur.[3] This announcement paved the way for the banking cartel to take the initiative that would make manifest their true intentions all along, which were to destroy the economic base of the region; thereby they aimed to impose their absolute authority, dictating to the United States Government and to the population at large.

With the election of Lincoln, there was only a single side to contend with in office. Lincoln knew his duty and the only choice that he had was to execute it; although in this author's view, this choice was far from a simple compliant attitude on Lincoln's part. His duty was to preside over the conflict that was intentionally designed to destroy the only economy that produced any elected representatives opposing the corrupt collusion running the US government, to force a consolidation of the currency in the absence of that opposition, and then behind the backs of the citizens, to adulterate the Constitution to embrace the new corporate and banking absolute authority which presently is running the nation and dictating the very intimate lives of everyday citizens.

Since conscripted labor was valuable then, as it is now[4], the legal right to own conscripts was first transferred from the individual to the corporation and the centralized government. Then the individual's Constitutional right to cast aside an extortionist government by popular vote was eliminated.

By 1867 the federal government could impose its will against the Constitution or the people and manipulate the currency to force them into deep debt, since all other currency except the centralized national currency had been outlawed in 1863. When the people protested their extortion, the forces of government- and corporation-backed military could freely move against them to purloin all privately held resources and to compel them into maintaining the infrastructure, and/or force those who continued to stand outside of the imposed system into existing as an expendable resource for corporate profits, in complete absence of any incentive whatsoever.

---

1 It was on the same Panama–New York run at the same specific time as the SS Central America. Its cargo is not known, but this author surmises that at least a portion of it may have been gold and mail.
2 Possibly by force or at least threat of his command relief.
3 See bibliography
4 http://siteresources.worldbank.org/SOCIALPROTECTION/Resources/SP-Discussion-papers/Labor-Market-DP/0911.pdf

All that was now needed was to remove the checks preventing any president from imposing himself as an absolute authority, and the land of America would effectively have a corporate-backed mono-authority who owned all privately held resources, while the people are reduced to an expendable commodity. This change would come about much later, but would all be executed in accordance with a pre-ordained plan that had originated in the administration of George Washington, with Washington's signed charter for establishment of the First Bank of the United States establishing the glowing precursor.

The Productive Landed Estates

A majority of the productive landed estates were started by men who began with a land purchase[1] from a distant property owner, who had purchased huge tracts of land from one of the Lord's Proprietors [2] or who possessed a charter directly from the Crown itself, very rarely being the case. The vast majority of those who possessed the original charters were the ones cutting up the land tracts and selling them to the planters who would one day construct the big house and build up the estate enterprise.

Some individuals who owned such estates were businessmen, ships' captains who were also ship owners, who desired to make landed purchase for the purpose of constructing rice plantations, for example, or tobacco plantations. People who made these types of purchases in time tended to possess the largest and most valuable plantations, such as Drayton Hall[3], in Charleston, South Carolina.

Many of these plantations also yielded produce other than cotton, rice and tobacco, which provided for additional business ventures. Most produced spirits for private purchase, export and consumption. There were food crops of nearly every variety and type, both freshly gathered and prepared in the estate bakery, for private purchase and consumption. There was also an estate blacksmith, who in fact might be a skilled tradesman just as aptly as a conscripted servant, who would produce wares for use by the surrounding community at large. An itinerant silver smith might also drop by for a while, to craft a few items of quality for the estate display and to facilitate customer-financed sales thereof. All of these products were made for sale in the estate general store[4], as well as for export.

Regulation and taxes on profits or products were non-existent for the most part back in this day and time, in the area of the nation where the

---

1 https://en.wikipedia.org/wiki/William_Drayton,_Sr.
2 https://en.wikipedia.org/wiki/Lords_Proprietor
3 https://en.wikipedia.org/wiki/Drayton_Hall
4 With financing in many cases

estates were most numerous. In that area estates were the sole economic base and they were for the most part highly functional and efficient. The income generally went back into improving the estate grounds, caring for the needs of workers who were so vital to the survival of the estate,[1] and to the general well being of the family in charge.

The estate,[2] also typically built the local church. An individual could purchase all of his daily living needs from the estate general store—his food, imported coffee or locally grown yaupon tea; tools, saddles, clothing, general hardware, arms and the like. Some estates even crafted buggies for sale, but few locals could afford them. The local estates also lent money out for larger purchases, taking land, golden leaf cured tobacco, quality livestock or other valuables as collateral when feasible. In other words, this uninhibited liberty to produce and engage in free enterprise was how men built their way up.

Lumber production was also important, second only to tobacco and cotton, where it could be widely grown. Commonly, if not universally, one estate would allow another to gather timber and process lumber into boards for construction projects of various types or sale inside the estate general lumber store. Payment for processing it could be made in retaining processed lumber, obviously at high percentages, distilled whiskey if high quality run was known to be produced on the exchanging estate, or its value in gold coin leveraged from the bank or even another estate. The value given, more than likely, amounted to two thirds of the value in timber, since the estate being employed exerted the effort and resources as well as labor gathering in and processed the timber. The accumulated gold or product could then be traded for other products, or the gold could be lent out at one third value to the two thirds in collateral.

The larger and more productive the landed estate, the more influence it had inside the surrounding community. The majority of estate owners were fair and honest people and there were very few local complaints; so in the overall scheme of things, the banks at large were seen as imposing obstacles, rather than assets, inside a number of local communities. These realities were why simply handing absolute control over to a centralized bank, owned and operated by a centralized government, heavily backed by huge impersonal corporations and without checks and balances, was simply out of the question.

As time passed, and local privately-owned banks arose across the land, these huge landed estates invested in them, either under a single family owner or multiple co-operational family owners from the surrounding estates. The value in the coin was stable, being valued at what the stamped amount on

---

1 https://en.wikipedia.org/wiki/Andrew_Jackson, see section under African American men.
2 http://uncpress.unc.edu/books/T-8697.html

the banknote was in weight of the gold. A dollar was a dollar, whether the amount was one fifth an ounce or one sixteenth an ounce in gold. When notes were beginning to be issued, the value of the gold dictated the amount stated on the dollar note and it seldom fluctuated. When it did move, then the note could be redeemed for the declining amount at liberty of the holder.

The addition of what amounted to IOU notes not backed by gold in weight, imposed by a corporate-backed centralized bank, allowed the values to be manipulated by retracting the gold and silver backing the notes and printing more notes, intending to saturate the market with notes or ceasing production of notes and adding in more gold and silver coin. When the market crashed, foreclosed real estate holdings would suddenly drop in value to attract possible buyers, who would then take the property off the market.

Insiders who knew that the intentional crash was imminent would begin collecting all of the devaluing notes that they could possibly get their hands on.[1] When the property values hit rock bottom, these notes could then be utilized to purchase property for nearly nothing in anticipation of a climb in value that insiders already knew would occur. In this manner, the rank and file on the ground were beguiled out of the property that they had legally acquired via diligent labor and Spartan lifestyles, if they owed money on it or if any sort of tax were imposed.

A Well-Run Plantation

One weekend trip into Charleston or Beaufort, South Carolina, or Savannah, Georgia, or Natchez Mississippi, will show the success that was possible with a well-run plantation.,[2] By well-run, let me emphasize, I mean one that provided adequately for all its workers, slave or otherwise.[3] If one compares historical representations of the cabins of both the slave and those subsistence farmers of the back country in 19th-century America, the slaves fared relatively well in terms of living space and basic conditions. There were instances of abuse, of that there can be no question, but widespread abuse would run counter to the purpose of having slaves in the first place—and that purpose was to extract production from the land. The intensity of labor needed to accomplish this required healthy, strong, well fed bodies, and able, willing minds. Those who did not, or could not, provide adequately for the workforce certainly gained less from their work.[4],[5] Owning and operating a

---

1 Recall the government speculators defrauding the Revolutionary War Veterans
2   http://www.theroot.com/articles/history/2015/01/black_confederates_not_a_myth_here_s_why.html
3 https://en.wikipedia.org/wiki/Free_people_of_color
4 http://www.cnn.com/2015/07/15/us/confederate-flag-whats-next/
5 https://en.wikipedia.org/wiki/William_Thomas_Beckford

huge landed estate was hard, labor-intensive work in the fields as well as in the office, all week long. A visit to the area around Charleston, for example, will reveal that a number of plantation owners invested heavily in tenements much closer to town, selling the plantation and getting out of the business altogether; primarily because[1] it was very hard work to run an efficient agricultural operation. Managing rental properties was then, and is now, a far less labor intensive occupation. Most landed estate owners enjoyed the city life and more sophisticated entertainments anyway, when they could find the time to indulge in them. Otherwise, they might hold an occasional house party; but for the most part, their neighbors were far off and free time was scarce.

Official history also suggests that the owners of plantations had little regard for formal education. Again, this is an economic question that is used in a moralistic way to denigrate the population of a region. Practical, real world education was a premium necessity in order to run plantation enterprises. Few had the leisure to engage in philosophy and literature. The type of education needed to own and operate the estate were the three basics; reading, writing and arithmetic. One learned by observation and engaging in hands on activities, as one does in virtually any self directed enterprise engagement or farm-based region, with no alternative from replacing the hands on experience. Remaining education came in the form of practical day to day, hands-on experience learned from the father that can never be replicated or replaced, who endeavored to pass on the business to his son, usually the eldest. Etiquette and manners in general were important, as were the conventions of professional business negotiation and interaction. Throughout this work we have discussed a number of well known landed estates, many of which may still be visited and some very few are still operational but nowhere near to their former glory. What makes these examples outstanding is the fact that they successfully integrated a multitude of highly organized enterprises occurring at the same time. All of this undertaking was managed by the owner, who stood at the top, and the family, who organized and managed as his subordinates, with the owner's eldest son standing as the next in command beside him. The mother and the son's wife were chief over the household and its inside duties, with some of the older children standing over the general store, the blacksmith shop, the kitchen and other household fixtures.

The general store made produce available to the public, with the exception of specialized cash crops (a small area of tobacco might be processed into finished products for sale). The majority of the cash crops were traded at the dock side market in town to be shipped out for export, if the plantation

---

1 Dorset And Weaver, 1991

owner did not have his personal transport ship, negotiating between foreign corporate importation enterprises and that of his own standing.

Examples of produce sold in the general store into the surrounding community are: fresh unprocessed vegetables, canned and pickled vegetables after 1790, meats that had been cured to order—smoked with apple, peach or hickory wood; salted meats, especially salt pork; clothes made to order; beer, wine and liquor of nearly every sort; leather, leather goods; hand rolled and flavored cigars made according to a secret house recipe; lumber in the estate lumber yard; and hardware purchased via shipping order. Loans were made and finalized inside the general store, if not the estate-owned local town bank.

Services to the public were offered in repairs made at the estate blacksmith shop on tools, worn out buggies, clothes and the like. Orders for products and purchases were also taken. Livestock was traded and sold on the estate grounds. At times also, product might have been displayed on-site for others in exchange for a twelve percent profit.

All of these businesses have by now been taken over by corporations, by and large, and are subject to so much government control that few small operators are able to survive (think of tobacco and alcohol, cheese, pickled and canned goods.) Another justification for micromanaging an individual's business life is for the purpose of income taxation, with the federal government imposing its extortion onto the individual states regardless[1]. Thus, Americans as individuals have lost their right to engage themselves productively via their own enterprise, which would ultimately allow an individual who began with nothing but the clothes on his back and a clear idea to attain a better life. That was what we used to call *"the American dream."* That dream is now so far out of reach for most people that we would have to call it *"the original American dream lost."*

Additional justification for the federal, state and local government taxing citizens at such extortionist rates may be found in the intent to prevent citizens from ever financing the return of a representative base who would demand that checks and balances be imposed on the currency and back into the system at large, protecting citizen interests from corruption imposing itself at their own expense. This fear of the general public protecting its own interest is why a true third party candidate is discouraged and denounced heavily by the establishment from all angles. Such a party would exert tremendous power in every systemic avenue, and would give an original meaning to the definition of what Constitution and liberated individuality really means.

---

1 https://www.law.cornell.edu/wex/income_tax

Some business enterprises, with landed estates standing as the superior all-inclusive example, being forced to adapt, did so, and allowed federal, state and local officials to dictate business plans, though granted via well thought out negotiations that offer a certain amount of flexibility and profit incentive back to the owner/property managers. These are the estates that survive and still maintain a measure of continuing prosperity, their presently owning families maintaining all of their former respect and that of the estate as well. While the agricultural aspects are retained, the institution that once catered to the lending needs of the public, among most other service functions discussed, have long since vanished in the wake of centralized banks and huge corporations imposing themselves to perform those services.

In other words, the few surviving examples exist simply because the owners were willing to accommodate the demands of the banking/corporate/government collusion at the local, federal and state levels, choosing simply to bear their loss in exchange for the option of retaining the theoretical right to own and manage the time-honored family property.

Boone Hall Plantation

Boone Hall Plantation and farms stands at the top of my list simply because the owners have consciously struggled to maintain the original plantation's air and splendor while still managing to make a living, in spite of the adverse situations into which the estate has been thrown over the last 155 years. Just for the record, the Civil War with its negative after effects were only the beginning of troubles for this estate, but they didn't have any difficulties before the Civil War.

Boone Hall Plantation was established in 1681, when English Major John Boone sailed to Charleston and established a very productive plantation including the mansion home, on the banks of the Wampacheone Creek. The family of Major Boone became very influential in South Carolina and national politics in due course of time.

The McRea family purchased the estate in 1955. Mrs. McRea opened the estate to the public and began giving tours. The McRea family still owns the property and they continue to improve upon it, making it available for public tours. The estate has been continually growing and producing crops for over three centuries.

Boone Hall Estate originated from a 470-acre land grant given to Major John Boone. It was granted by Theophilus Patey as a wedding present to his daughter, Elizabeth. The original two-story wooden house, with a one-story front porch, was constructed in 1790.

The present day structure was built by Thomas Stone, who wanted a colonial revival style mansion home. The house of today sits on 738-acres consisting of a nature preserve, wetlands and productive property. The property stands as one of America's oldest still-working plantations. The crops of today include strawberries, tomatoes, squash, cucumbers and watermelons, as well as other food crops. Boone Hall Farms market opened its doors in 2006. In addition to food crops it also hosts a café, market, fresh local seafood and a gift shop.

Many of the past products, such as distilled liquor and the estate-crafted tobacco products once found in nearly every plantation general store, are now absent. Government licensing and other burdens just may have something to do with that. The estate lumber production yard is no longer present; nearly all timber production has been taken over by the corporation, rendering any individual effort virtually worthless. Processed vegetables are largely absent as is the general store itself, carrying the lines of products that it once did, even though nearly all of them would still be held in very high demand, if only they were crafted to the estate's own unique standard.

Gamble Plantation

Gamble Plantation is located in Ellenton, Florida. The mansion was developed by Robert Gamble in 1845 who received a 160-acre grant for serving in the Seminole War. By his own industrious labor and innovation, he eventually expanded to well over 3,000 acres. The plantation once contained 3,500 acres and a 45,000 gallon cistern for household water. The estate today includes at least 16 acres of the original sugarcane fields.

In 1925, The Daughters of the Confederacy purchased the estate and donated it to the state as a memorial to Judah P Benjamin, memorialized for serving three cabinet positions under Confederate President Jefferson Davis during the Civil War. In 2002, the state of Florida purchased the property and the ruins of the estate sugar mill, one of the largest in the broad area.

The estate stands more as a memorial to the liberty lost that allowed individuals to work their way up from a void. The plantation specialized in products developed from the juice of the sugarcane. The products include sugar, molasses, rum, bakery goods derived from the molasses and sugar, food crops and livestock. No doubt, salt, sugar and smoke cured hams were sold in the estate general store, among many other products. A range of services were once more than likely provided to the surrounding residents for profit from there on the mansion estate as well.

Burnside Plantation

This estate is a historic complex in Burnside, Louisiana. The plantation was established in the late 1700s and was completed in 1840. It was originally named for the Hamoa people, who originally inhabited the estate lands. Today the complex consists of ten acres, eight buildings and one structure.

The history begins when Alexander Latil and Mares Conwan obtained all of the Hamoa people's land on the east side of the Mississippi in 1774. It is not known *how* he obtained the land, but there are no battle records to suggest anything but some form of purchase. Latil built a French-colonial style mansion on the site the following year. By 1803 the estate was a working sugar plantation.

The estate must have not been too productive, since it was sold the following year to Daniel Clark, who continued to develop the property and built one of the first sugar mills along this stretch of the river. In 1811, General Wade Hampton purchased the property. Hampton was one of the wealthiest land owners and had more slaves than anyone of the time period, according to the available information.

In 1825 management of the property was taken over by Hampton's son-in-law John Smith Preston. The Prestons built a new, more elegant main house in front of the old one. In time the estate grew to 10,000 acres, and was sold to John Burnside in 1857, probably as a result of changing fortunes during the [1] economic Panics described in Chapter 4.

Burnside increased the estate to include 12,000 acres and four sugar mills. The estate also included 750 slaves. The house and estate finally were purchased by Dr. George B. Crozat in 1940. He restored the mansion house and the gardens. The house remained with the Crozat family until 2003, when it passed to a new owner, Kevin Kelly.

Today the home appears to function as a set for various movies and commercials, as well as a residential home. Quite a glamorous situation in contrast to its rough and tumble agricultural past, which was far more labor intensive, including the tremendous duty of keeping the books up to date. Nevertheless, this estate home, as all the other examples here presented, stands as a monument to a different economic model, one in which an enterprising family could engage in as many forms of productive activity as they could imagine, while submitting to the controlling realm and it's specified regulatory demands .

Evergreen Plantation

Evergreen plantation is an estate established in 1790, near Wallace, Louisiana. The primary historical crop was sugarcane. The products

---

1 We also have the Panic of 1857, which affected product sales stateside and exported. When the Civil War erupted, the tariffs designed to destroy the estate productive capacity and the economic collapse following, the author can visualize a number of reasons why it might have been tough to render a profit from the land.

exported were those derived from sugar, being crystallized sugar, molasses, rum, along with a variety of food crops sold locally and exported. This estate was a working plantation until 1930, when the banks took it over due to another financial collapse[1], the Great Depression. The plantation was then reestablished and is still a working sugar plantation to this very day. The house is the most complete standing plantation estate complex in the United States today. The estate still keeps afloat though exported sugar products, tours, and renting out the property for film setting backdrops.

The plantation estate has been privately owned for most of its history. German immigrants claimed the land originally in 1760. Cristopher Heidle, who married into a local French family, constructed the big farm house in 1790. What a splendid old farm house it was!

Christopher's great grandson, Pierre Clidament Becnel, renovated the mansion and expanded upon it. The Becnel family owned the estate until 1894, when it was sold to Alfred Songy. A flood in 1927, a disease of the sugarcane and the Great Depression, drove him into insolvency, causing the bank to foreclose on the property. The official account states that the Songys were forced to depart. This author takes that word to mean *evicted*, presumably by the police.

The property was vacant for 14 years afterward, with the mansion itself used as a stable for farm animals! Soon the property grew derelict. With demand reduced by the Depression and the derelict condition of the property in general, it was ripe for some corporate CEO to scoop up at rock bottom price, with the owning family basically rendered homeless.

An oil heiress, Matilda Geddings Gray, who had historical architectural interests and was head of her highly successful family oil enterprise, [2]was the next individual to lay claim to the estate in 1944. By the time her niece, Matilda Gray Stream, inherited the property in 1971, the property had begun to fall in disrepair.

Today the estate has been restored once again and is self supporting. Four hundred acres of sugarcane is still productive. The farming families on the estate are descendants of the original owners, the Songys and others. The riverbank docks are rented out to maritime companies and others, for parking and storage. Huge tracts of land are rented out for hunting leases as well. Since 2002, the property has been leased for film production to go along with the other forms of enterprise. One of the largest ventures is tourism, beginning in 1998, with tours going all up and down through the mansion house and estate grounds. Mrs. Matilda Geddings Gray still resides on the grounds in one of the smaller cottages.

---

1 There is substantial evidence that the depression of the 1930s was intentionally caused by banking worldwide.
2 no doubt, had close contacts on the bank board

A Conclusion

What I have worked to describe is the fact that the cartel forces of centralized currency and banks, working hand-in-hand for mutual benefit with the corporations via their government insiders, has engaged in a tug of war since this nation was founded, opposing those who stood to defend the rights of the individual American citizen to engage in free enterprise without undue burdens imposed by an authoritarian government with its regulations, taxes and engineered financial upheavals.

A majority of US presidents stood for citizens' rights; yet still, the power of big money won out, all the while intending to seize control of the resources owned and operated by citizens. Even the toughest US presidents were forced to concede on one end or the other, as this rising rapacious force of wealth continued to dominate the powers that dictate regulations and mandates against the average American citizen in nearly every arena of life.

In a future volume, I plan to present further alarming evidence of how this process continues today, and the removal of freedoms we take for granted.[1,2,3]

In the end, the demands of centralized banking, corporations and their \ government collusion threatened even the Constitution itself. A great war was instigated on American soil and it killed more American men than both World Wars and all the wars the US ever fought right up until Vietnam; over 600,000

---

1 https://en.wikipedia.org/wiki/Individual_mandate
2 http://www.washingtonsblog.com/2015/05/why-the-powers-that-be-are-pushing-a-cashless-society.html
3 http://townhall.com/tipsheet/leahbarkoukis/2015/09/22/some-states-will-soon-require-a-passport-to-fly-domestically-n2055416

---

men[1] died in the fighting, in captivity, and from the rampant diseases in the field. By some estimates at least that many more perished later on due to disease and injuries, and more continued on as surviving amputees and disturbed, psychological casualties.

And the purpose was to destroy the economy of those who consistently voted to rebuff attempts by the corporate/banking elite to impose their own rules on America. We have witnessed again and again as our fellow Americans have suffered dearly since then, at the blood drenched hands of the same voracious cartel[2],[3]; we must never forget that the same ruthless tyranny still seeks to extend their reach into the lives and pockets of Americans.[4],[5],[6],

---

1 http://www.history.com/news/civil-war-deadlier-than-previously-thought
2 https://en.wikipedia.org/wiki/History_of_union_busting_in_the_United_States, police and military force
3 https://en.wikipedia.org/wiki/Battle_of_Blair_Mountain
4 http://www.truthandaction.org/4th-high-level-banker-dies-2015-36-died-last-year/
5 http://beforeitsnews.com/alternative/2013/12/the-debtors-prison-system-resurrected-from-the-grave-2858204.html
6 http://www.nytimes.com/2015/11/08/nyregion/real-estate-shell-companies-scheme-to-defraud-owners-out-of-their-homes.html?_r=0

BIBLIOGRAPHY

Sterling, Keir Brooks (ed.) *Biographical Dictionary of American and Canadian Naturalists and Environmentalists.* Greenwood Press, Westport, CT : 1997

http://911research.wtc7.net/sept11/trillions.html

http://abcnews.go.com/US/jade-helm-15-facts-training-exercise-causing-jitters/story?id=30915367

http://batr.org/forbidden/032415.html

http://beforeitsnews.com/economy/2014/06/forbes-predicts-stock-market-crash-worse-than-the-1930s-another-great-depression-is-coming-and-where-not-to-be-when-it-hits-2629256.html

http://dailycaller.com/2015/09/15/president-obama-orders-behavioral-experiments-on-american-public/

http://dissidentvoice.org/2014/09/why-the-deep-state-always-wins/

http://ellabakercenter.org/blog/2013/06/prison-labor-is-the-new-slave-labor

http://heavy.com/news/2014/01/nsa-contractors-money-dianne-feinstein-mike-rogers/

http://hiddensecretsandlies.blogspot.com/2014/11/unicor-slave-labor-in-us-prisons.html

http://journals.plos.org/plosone/article?id=10.1371/journal.pone.0025995

http://personalliberty.com/study-illegal-legal-immigrants-use-social-welfare-more-than-native-citizens/

http://reality-bytes.hubpages.com/hub/Americans-Who-Supported-European-Fascism

http://redicecreations.com/article.php?id=29711

http://seekingalpha.com/article/3707656-negative-interest-rates-coming-to-the-u-s

http://superstore.wnd.com/books/Current-Affairs/HOW-EVIL-WORKS-AutographedPaperback

http://www.amazon.com/American-Lion-Andrew-Jackson-White/dp/0812973461/ref=sr_1_3?s=books&ie=UTF8&qid=1449256670&sr=1-3&keywords=andrew+jackson

http://www.amazon.com/Exploration-Valley-Amazon-Direction-Department-ebook/dp/B00MLP0V9M/ref=sr_1_1?s=books&ie=UTF8&qid=1449256913&sr=1-1&keywords=william+lewis+herndon

http://www.amazon.com/Federal-Reserve-Private-Concern-ebook/dp/B00C3QAIDI/ref=sr_1_6?s=books&ie=UTF8&qid=1449256027&sr=1-6&keywords=the+banking+cartel

http://www.amazon.com/History-Money-Banking-United-States/dp/1479325546/ref=sr_1_4?s=books&ie=UTF8&qid=1449256027&sr=1-4&keywords=the+banking+cartel

http://www.amazon.com/Thomas-Jefferson-Power-Jon-Meacham/dp/0812979486/ref=sr_1_1?s=books&ie=UTF8&qid=1449256759&sr=1-1&keywords=thomas+jefferson

http://www.amazon.com/Unions-Employers-Central-Banks-Macroeconomic/dp/0521788846/ref=sr_1_11?s=books&ie=UTF8&qid=1449255694&sr=1-11&keywords=rise+of+the+central+banks

http://www.baltimoresun.com/news/opinion/oped/bs-ed-immigrant-war-20150630-story.html

http://www.bibliotecapleyades.net/biggestsecret/bigsec/biggestsecret06.htm#Bank of England

http://www.bibliotecapleyades.net/sociopolitica/sociopol_globalbanking92.htm

http://www.breitbart.com/big-government/2015/09/01/san-bernardino-dumps-calpers-as-pension-death-spiral-looms/

http://www.engadget.com/2013/11/21/lg-admits-smart-tv-data-collection/

http://www.globalresearch.ca/rich-get-more-in-tax-breaks-than-the-poor-get-from-welfare/25933

http://www.huffingtonpost.com/james-peron/why-one-hiv-drug-costs-5000-percent-more-

http://www.infowars.com/charleston-shooter-was-on-drug-linked-to-violent-outbursts/

http://www.ips-dc.org/the-poor-get-prison-the-alarming-spread-of-the-criminalization-of-poverty/

http://www.lovethetruth.com/books/pawns/05.htm

http://www.mmisi.org/ir/45_1-2/westley.pdf

http://www.newyorker.com/news/john-cassidy/is-america-an-oligarchy

http://www.peakprosperity.com/blog/93050/war-cash-officially-sanctioned-theft

http://www.profit-over-life.org/pdf/books/report_on_the_investigation.pdf

http://www.rationalrevolution.net/war/american_supporters_of_the_europ.htm

http://www.safehaven.com/article/4617/transnational-corporations-the-new-world-order

http://www.secretsofthefed.com/china-poised-demand-u-s-land-payment-u-s-debt/

http://www.theguardian.com/commentisfree/2014/jul/11/the-ultimate-goal-of-the-nsa-is-total-population-control

http://www.thenewamerican.com/usnews/constitution/item/7674-nsa-supercenters-to-store-americans-private-data-permanently

http://www.tulane.edu/-sumter/Dilemmas/DDec26Comm.html

http://www.wnd.com/2015/06/big-list-of-drug-induced-killers/#71dLgiTmuSUZfls6.99

http://www.workers.org/2011/us/pentagon_0609/

http://www.zerohedge.com/news/2015-05-19/someone-finally-read-obamas-secret-trade-deal-and-admits-tpp-will-damage-nation

http://www.zerohedge.com/news/2015-09-16/record-467-million-
   americans-live-poverty-median-houshold-income-back-1989-levels
http://www4.dr-rath-foundation.org/features/drug_industry_earning_1_
   trillion_a_year_still_not_curing_chronic_diseases.html
http://www4.dr-rath-foundation.org/pharmaceutical_business/history_of_
   the_pharmaceutical_industry.htm?do=print
https://en.wikipedia.org/wiki/China_Lobby
https://en.wikipedia.org/wiki/Currency_Act
https://en.wikipedia.org/wiki/Extermination_through_labor
https://en.wikipedia.org/wiki/Immigration_and_Nationality_Act_of_1965
https://en.wikipedia.org/wiki/Indian_massacre_of_1622
https://en.wikipedia.org/wiki/Irish_Americans_in_the_American_Civil_War
https://info.publicintelligence.net/USArmy-InternmentResettlement.pdf
https://www.bis.org/cpmi/publ/d137.pdf
https://www.ffiec.gov/bsa_aml_infobase/pages_manual/OLM_015.htm
https://www.lewrockwell.com/lrc-blog/today-congress-votes-to-take-
   your-passport/
https://www.moneymetals.com/news/2015/06/03/better-than-cash-
   alliance-000716
https://www.monticello.org/site/plantation-and-slavery/thomas-jefferson-
   and-sally-hemings-brief-account
https://www.nraila.org/articles/20150911/virginia-senator-kaine-
   introduces-bill-to-turn-innocent-mistakes-into-felonies
https://www.washingtonpost.com/blogs/in-the-loop/wp/2014/05/14/
   which-foreign-countries-spent-the-most-to-influence-u-s-politics/
https://www.youtube.com/watch?v=O34Oeg6GUIk

INDEX

U

"Unbearable" acts, 49
US Revolutionary War, 34, 55, 59, 62, 64,
  72, 112, 115, 116, 118, 119, 121, 122, 125, 126,
  151, 167
Utopian society, 32, 33

V

Van Buren, Martin, 86, 88, 89
Veasy Bank v. Fenno, 152
Venus fly-trap reference, 57

W

War of 1812, 75
Washington, George, 65, 68, 72, 73, 87,
  94, 112, 113, 119, 124, 125, 131, 145, 149,
  155, 159, 161, 165
Whiskey Rebellion, 64, 68
witch trials, 45

Y

Yankee Doodle, 63
Yorktown (VA), 56, 57
yuopon tea (cassina), 43, 50

Printed in the United States
By Bookmasters